Teachers and Politics in Japan

Studies of the
EAST ASIAN INSTITUTE
COLUMBIA UNIVERSITY

Teachers and Politics in Japan

BY DONALD R. THURSTON

PRINCETON UNIVERSITY PRESS
Princeton, New Jersey

TO MY PARENTS
Robert and Pauline Thurston

Acknowledgments

I OWE my deepest thanks to Professor James W. Morley, Director of the East Asian Institute, Columbia University, who throughout my years at Columbia and thereafter has never failed to give generously of his time, guidance, and encouragement. At an early stage in the writing he read the manuscript meticulously and offered numerous constructive criticisms. I wish to thank also Herschel F. Webb, Professor of Japanese History at Columbia University, who made my early years of exposure to Japanese history a delight and who more recently guided this study through its final stages. Whatever merits this book may possess are theirs, its shortcomings mine.

To Mr. Frank Yorichika, Japanese Reference Librarian at the East Asian Library, Columbia, I wish to express my gratitude for cheerfully assisting me in locating materials. I am also particularly grateful to Mr. George Potter of the Harvard-Yenching Institute Library and his staff for providing me with office space in the summer of 1971 and for responding to my numerous pleas for help.

Many people in Japan have made this study possible. First, I would like to thank the dozens of elementary and lower secondary school teachers who took many hours out of their busy schedules to talk with me and to fill out a questionnaire. Among leaders of the Japan Teachers' Union I would particularly like to thank Mr. Miyanohara Sadamitsu, former Chairman, and Mr. Makieda Motofumi, former Secretary-General, for providing time for interviews and for requesting their staff to assist me in every way possible. In the Ministry of Education, I am most deeply indebted to Mr. Sawada Michiya and Mr. Beppu Tetsu of the Local Affairs Section for giving unstintingly of their time and their thoughts and for making available to me reports compiled in their office.

The research and the writing of this study were made possible by timely and vital financial assistance from the Ford Foundation under a Foreign Area Fellowship; by the Japan Studies Committee of the East Asian Institute, Columbia University; and by Union College. I would like to express my appreciation to all three institutions for their financial support.

Finally, I wish to express my deep gratitude to three friends: Dr. Lois More, Professor of History at Montclair State College, who started me on my teaching and academic career and who has been a source of encouragement every step of the way; Mr. Saeki Kaoru, who helped me through the maze of Japanese materials in the Diet Library and who arranged contacts with principals and teachers; and Mr. Everett Taylor, whose deep concern and irrepressible optimism eased the path towards completion of this study.

Union College
August 1973   DONALD R. THURSTON

Contents

Tables

Teachers and Politics in Japan

CHAPTER I

Introduction

SCHOOLS BLANKET JAPAN. Perhaps no other people in the world are as well served by their elementary and lower secondary schools as are the Japanese. The attendance rate at this compulsory level is more than 99 percent and the nationwide literacy rate more than 98 percent. Only the Japan Teachers' Union (Nikkyōso, hereafter JTU) can seriously claim to represent the more than 500,000 teachers in these elementary and lower secondary schools. In sheer size the JTU dwarfs all other teachers' organizations, whether they be independent unions or associations backed by the Ministry of Education, and it is the only visible giant that can meaningfully claim to represent the teaching profession. As such it is a striking example of the many interest groups that sprang up in Japanese political life immediately after the war. The JTU is a product of the new concept introduced into postwar Japanese political values that an individual possesses legitimate private interests that he has the right to protect by joining unions and associations of his choice. The new liberal attitude, encouraged by the American Occupation authorities and upheld by the new 1945 Trade Union Law and the new 1947 Constitution, made possible the postwar proliferation of interest groups across the political spectrum. Perhaps the most significant aspect of this phenomenon has been the spectacular rise in the strength and number of interest groups that constitute the left-wing labor movement and the bulk of the support for the renovationist left-wing Marxist-oriented political parties. Such groups have come to dominate the class-conscious left wing since 1945. Within this labor movement, the most

3

powerful interest group in the field of education has been the JTU.

The leaders of the JTU, by taking the fundamental position that "teachers are laborers" and by viewing "people's education" as a means of reforming Japan's existing capitalistic society, have aligned themselves throughout the postwar period with the left-wing renovationist camp in Japanese politics. The heart of the renovationist camp, which seeks to establish a Socialist state and is therefore polarized from the conservative camp led by the ruling Liberal-Democratic Party (LDP), centers on the Japan Socialist Party (JSP) and its chief instrument of support, the huge labor federation called the General Council of Japanese Trade Unions (Sōhyō). Smaller parties within the renovationist or "progressive" camp include the Democratic-Socialist Party (DSP), with its supporting labor group, the Japanese Confederation of Labor (Dōmei), and the Japan Communist Party (JCP). Recently the Clean Government Party (Komeitō) has also entered the renovationist camp on specific occasions by forming temporary joint opposition fronts with the JSP and the DSP, such as in the election to the House of Councillors in June 1971. The JTU, as a JSP-supporting union and an affiliate of Sōhyō, all of which have cooperated from time to time with the JCP on a case-by-case basis, is squarely within the renovationist camp, a position that places it in direct conflict with the "permanent" conservative government not only over educational policies, the area of concern here, but also over a wide range of governmental policies, both domestic and foreign.

Firmly entrenched within the left-wing "permanent" opposition, the JTU has waged fierce struggles against a whole series of major governmental policies concerning education and teachers. The dispute between the two sides, in which for a long while each wished to destroy the other, has been violent at times and has constituted one of Japan's most serious domestic problems. Throughout this period neither side has been unaffected by the other, neither the unqualified

victor nor loser. Instead, the on-going bitter antagonism between the opposing forces has reflected a process by which
the government, with apparent success, has step by step attempted to reduce the strength of the JTU and to revise a
number of the liberal reforms in education inspired by the
Occupation and supported by the JTU. In its struggle
against these government-proposed revisions, the JTU has
served as the leader of the opposition around which dissatisfied teachers, parents, and intellectuals have gathered
for the purpose of preserving the fundamental principles of
the new postwar liberal education that they see as being
threatened. The JTU's constant efforts to resist these revisions, even though not entirely successful, have nevertheless
acted as a moderating influence and a brake upon the government's reactionary tendencies in education.

The purpose of this broad cross-sectional case study is to
evaluate the influence the JTU has had as a renovationist
interest group on its own members and on the formulation
and implementation of educational policies. At a higher
level the purpose is to evaluate the significance of the JTU
in postwar Japanese politics and society. Essentially, the
concern here is with the question of influence, not merely
on a single governmental educational policy at a particular
point in time, although a number of such policies and the
JTU's influence on them are analyzed in some detail, but
rather on a whole range of policies dealing with teachers
and education throughout the twenty-five year postwar period. This attempt to analyze the influence of the JTU has
been stimulated by the observation of a number of Japanese
and American political scientists that interest groups are increasingly coming to play an important role in the formulation and execution of public policy in Japan,[1] but that left-

[1] Robert E. Ward in "Japan: The Continuity of Modernization,"
in Lucian W. Pye and Sidney Verba (eds.), *Political Culture and
Political Development* (Princeton: Princeton University Press, 1965)
has written that after 1945, "the way was prepared for a major
involvement of such groups in politics," that a "whole new dimension

wing opposition-attached groups, such as the JTU, have been largely ineffective.[2]

Analyses of interest group behavior in Japanese politics have so far been based on a dearth of extensive case studies.

---

of informal participation and competence" was opened up and that in the 1960's the Japanese people were continuing to move in the direction of "greater acceptance of and participation in associational interest groups." Frank Langdon in *Politics in Japan* (Boston: Little, Brown and Company, 1965), pp. 97-101, has observed that the growing influence of associations in Japan represents a major trend "and that their greater role in present-day Japanese politics evidences the greater development occurring in this area." In "Notes by the Editor," *Journal of Social and Political Ideas in Japan* (hereafter *JSPIJ*), Vol. 2, No. 3 (December 1964), p. 98, Sannosuke Matsumoto has asserted that "by 1956, the activities of pressure groups in the field of practical politics had become very prominent and were being widely discussed in newspapers, journals, and magazines." Kyogoku Jun-ichi, in the same issue of *JSPIJ* in an article entitled "Changes in Political Image and Behavior," p. 124, has recognized the increasingly important role he believes interest groups are playing in contemporary Japanese politics; he declares that "The gradual, postwar maturation of parliamentary politics under mass-society conditions made it possible for pressure politics to flourish in Japan." Finally, Japan's leading authority on the behavior of interest groups, Ishida Takeshi, has concurred in this general view, stating that "the Japanese political system is being reorganized in an entirely new direction. . . . (Postwar) events paved the way for the full operation of party politics, the establishment of a 'two-party' system, and an increase in the importance of pressure groups in the overall political process." ("The Direction of Japanese Political Reorganization," *ibid.*, pp. 24-25.) The list of political scientists who share this view could be extended considerably. See particularly, however, the volume entitled *Nihon no Atsuryoku Dantai* (Pressure Groups in Japan) of *The Annuals of the Japanese Political Science Association* (Tokyo: Iwanami Publishing Company, 1960).

[2] Richard Willey in "Pressure Group Politics: The Case of Sohyo," *Western Political Quarterly* (December 1964), p. 715, makes the point that ". . . organized labor and Sohyo have been quite ineffective." Theodore McNelly in *Contemporary Government of Japan* (Boston: Houghton Mifflin Company, 1963), p. 146, states that "the political influence of labor in Japan is weak except when it engages in extra-parliamentary tactics."

An important exception and perhaps the best to date is the study of the Japan Medical Association by William Steslicke.[3] Steslicke's study reinforces the view that interest groups are increasingly coming to play an important role in Japanese public policy-making, even though, within the confines of his study, the JMA did not get what it wanted. One of the great differences between the JMA and the JTU, however, which challenges this generalization as far as the JTU is concerned, is that the former, as an interest group that has given the bulk of its support to the LDP, has been successful at times "in penetrating the LDP's policy-making mechanism,"[4] while the latter, as a renovationist interest group outside the power structure, has had almost no direct contact with the "LDP's policy-making mechanism" at all. In spite of such obvious and important differences between the JMA and the JTU, the analysis presented in this study of the JTU supports the same general conclusion.

While recognizing that interest groups such as the JTU have been outside the ruling power structure of contemporary Japanese politics with little *direct* access to the key policy-making groups in the nation at the *highest* level, this study nevertheless strongly questions the assumption that such groups have had no influence on the formulation and implementation of public policy. The question asked is to what extent an interest group may overcome its unfavorable strategic position in society and exercise effective influence. In wrestling with this question as applied to the JTU's behavior and degree of influence on governmental educational policies, this book suggests the importance of analyzing ways of exerting influence other than that of direct access at the highest level before an evaluation of any such unfavorably placed interest group in Japan or in any political system is made.

[3] William E. Steslicke, *Doctors in Politics: The Political Life of the Japan Medical Association* (New York: Praeger, 1973).

[4] William E. Steslicke, "The Japan Medical Association and the Liberal Democratic Party: A Case Study of Interest Group Politics in Japan," *Studies on Asia*, 1965, p. 160.

7

Three ways of exerting influence on the formulation and execution of public policies other than through direct access at the highest level suggest themselves: first, *indirect* influence, or influence stemming from such actions as demonstrations and strikes or fear in the minds of the public policy makers of a group's possible negative reaction to or non-compliance with a contemplated policy; second, *united* influence, or influence resulting from the united action of like-minded groups, thereby augmenting the force of a single group; third, *implementation* influence, or influence at the level of implementation that actually changes policies formulated at the top to correspond more favorably to the interest of the group at lower levels. As analyzed here, the JTU has had considerable success in exercising all three kinds of influence. On several occasions, the potency of the JTU's indirect influence on policy makers at the highest level has been evident. Similarly, the united influence of the entire left wing, including labor unions and the JSP, along with that of the International Labor Organization, has led to numerous modifications in governmental educational policies, despite the minority political position represented by the united influence. Finally, the potency of the JTU's *implementation* influence at the prefectural and lower levels, where relations with the government-side have been less strained and where policies formulated at the top have been changed by JTU influence in the process of their implementation, may be witnessed in almost every area of educational policy. In fact, one of the major conclusions to emerge from this book is that the JTU has been much more influential than may seem apparent at first glance, precisely because it is capable of being so much more influential at the prefectural and local levels, where educational policies are implemented—and changed in the process of implementation—than at the national level, where these policies are formulated. Born of necessity, the JTU has devised tactics that have mitigated its difficulty with the problem of direct access and that have, in fact, given it considerable influence

8

over educational policies. In regard to this point, this study illustrates the general proposition that extreme difficulty of direct access to key points in the decision-making process does not necessarily deprive an interest group of considerable influence in achieving its policy objectives.

While it is true that such left-wing interest groups as the JTU have not succeeded in achieving their ultimate aim— seizing the reins of government and transforming Japan into a Socialist state—the analysis here stresses achievements short of this goal. That is, the JTU, as an alienated interest group, is seen in its dual nature. Although it is a "radical pressure group," to borrow Willey's phrase,[5] which advocates the most fundamental and sweeping changes in government and society and frequently acts "radically," it nevertheless is also a "regular" pressure group that acts "regularly" in the sense that it continues to play the political game within the existing structure. It has a dual nature that advocates revolutionary change in the existing political system while at the same time demanding rewards from that existing system. It is, in other words, out to get what it can from the existing system until the "ideal" system it is striving to create becomes reality.

This study is descriptive and analytical. It describes and analyzes how and why the JTU was established, what its ideology and objectives have been, the methods it has used to achieve those objectives, and the degree of its success through 1971. Given the prewar and postwar history of the antagonistic relationship between the government and all *independent* teachers' organizations, as well as the postwar polarization of Japanese politics in which the government and the union have been at opposite poles, the major determinant of the JTU's behavior at the national level has been attitude. The underlying attitudes of both JTU leaders on the one hand and conservative party leaders and bureaucrats on the other have determined the JTU's behavior

[5] Richard Willey, "Pressure Group Politics: The Case of Sohyo," p. 723.

9

and degree of influence at the national level. The overriding ideology or attitude of the JTU leaders toward the existing society, government, and educational system has made its ideological base more significant than its structural base as a behavioral determinant at the national level. So, too, the hostile attitude of conservative party leaders and bureaucrats toward the independent JTU has been more important than the structure and function of the government in determining the JTU's behavior. As one proceeds down the organizational structure of the JTU, however, structure and function tend to become more important as behavioral determinants than ideology or attitude. At the prefectural and local levels the structures of the government and the union come into closer and closer proximity until at the bottom they co-exist in the same individual: the teacher, who is both a governmental employee and a union member. Similarly, regarding function, at the prefectural and local levels, schools must operate and teachers must teach. The function of the teacher to teach and to be responsible to his students tends to determine his behavior as a union member to a greater extent than ideology or attitude.

Since attitude is nevertheless so important, the study relies heavily on numerous interviews with national and prefectural leaders of the JTU, with teachers in the schools, and with Ministry of Education and prefectural boards of education officials. Analyses of the union-consciousness of teacher members and of their attitudes concerning a host of educational and political problems are also based upon the results of two questionnaires, one drawn up and administered by the writer to teachers in 1965 and the other administered by the JTU itself in 1968.

In an effort to build up a comprehensive picture of the JTU in the context of Japanese political culture for the purpose of evaluating its influence on educational policies and teachers, the study first looks at the members of the union: the elementary and lower secondary teachers themselves, their social role in prewar modern Japan and their reasons for unionizing immediately after the war. Recognizing the importance of the internal characteristics of an interest group in determining its ability to influence favorably public policy-making, the study then proceeds to describe and analyze a number of the most important internal characteristics of the JTU, such as its ideology, objectives, organizational structure, membership, style of leadership, and the degree of union-consciousness of its members. Having discussed the most significant internal characteristics, the study then turns to the JTU's external relations and describes and analyzes the relations between the JTU and three key groups in the society with which it interacts in an effort to influence public policy-making: first, the JTU and the educational bureaucracy, including relations between the JTU and the Ministry of Education at the national level, between the prefectural unions and the boards of education at the prefectural level, and between the school union leaders and the principals at the school level; second, the JTU and the political parties, particularly the JSP; and third, the JTU and the Diet. In other words, after describing and analyzing the union's internal characteristics, an analysis is first made of several important claims and demands the JTU has made on the educational bureaucracy, of the means used in an effort to transform these claims and demands into public policy, and of the degree of success achieved. In a succeeding chapter, the JTU's ability to elect its own ex-officers to the Diet, in which it acts largely as its own political party, is analyzed, as is the JTU's ability to exert pressure in the Diet. Finally, conclusions are drawn concerning the influence of the JTU on its own members and on the formulation and implementation of educational policies, and an evaluation is made of the significance of the JTU to Japanese politics and society.

CHAPTER II

Prewar Origins

VIEWING the history of Japanese society through a class-conscious Marxist lens, the Japan Teachers' Union since its founding in 1947 has time and again proclaimed its strong disapproval of the role the ruling class forced the prewar elementary teachers to play.[1] The JTU has taken the fundamental view that, in the prewar period, "the teachers of Japan, under the pressures of a half-feudalistic ultra-nationalistic system, were forced into a logic of subservience."[2] To the JTU, prewar Japanese education was bourgeois education that served only the interests of the ruling class and not the interests of the "people." Since the ruling class held a tight grip on the content and administration of education, elementary teachers as members of the "people" were oppressed by the ruling class and locked into the position of having to teach all the children of Japan precepts that supported the feudalistic Emperor system and the ultra-nationalistic militarists. Thus the JTU has denounced the prewar Emperor-centered ideology of the Japanese state and the authoritarian educational system that served to sustain that ideology and to produce the "subservient" teacher. The explicit fear that the prewar-type subservient teacher might be re-created has lain at the root of the JTU's hypersensitive and negative reaction to almost

[1] For a discussion of the JTU's beliefs about prewar Japanese education, see Chapter II of *Kokumin Kyōiku* (People's Education) edited by the Propaganda Section of the JTU, published by Gōdō Shinsho, October 1958.

[2] Japan Teachers' Union, *A Code of Ethics for Teachers*, quoted in *Education in Japan: 1945-1963*, JSPIJ, Vol. I, No. 3 (December 1963), Appendix IV. See Appendix B.

12

all postwar governmental educational policies. The JTU has been prepared to prevent the re-creation of the prewar teacher with all the strength at its disposal. Its postwar role in Japanese education and politics must, therefore, be seen in the light of its profound fear of this possibility. In a search for an understanding of this fear, an examination of the JTU leadership's perception of the role of the elementary teacher in prewar Japan is undertaken. What follows is not necessarily reality but the JTU leadership's perception of reality.

PERCEPTION OF THE ROLE OF THE ELEMENTARY TEACHER

Five perceived characteristics of the elementary teacher's prewar role bear brief discussion. First and perhaps most important, leaders of the JTU are convinced that the primary role of the elementary teacher from 1890 to 1945 intensified increasingly to that of transmitting to pupils a state doctrine of reverence for the Emperor, patriotism, and filial piety. This principle was stated early in the *Explanation of School Matters*, issued by Education Minister Ōki Takatō in 1891: "In the elementary schools, the first objective—namely, the spirit of reverence for the Emperor and patriotism—will be achieved by cultivating morality and practicing the Way of Humanity. Children must be . . . developed into good and loyal subjects."[3]

JTU literature criticizes the excesses that occurred in practice, particularly in the 1930's, of this prewar Japanese educational principle. It objects strongly to the fact that teachers were "forced" to teach "morals" or moral education, the content of which was determined by the government and contained in government-approved textbooks, allowing the teachers no freedom to question or to deviate from the pre-packaged doctrine. According to the JTU's in-

[3] Quoted in Herbert Passin, *Society and Education in Japan* (New York: Teachers College, Columbia University, 1965), Document 22, p. 234.

13

terpretation, such an approach constituted a travesty of education because it focused too much attention on the fundamentally misguided concept that education ought to be for the good of the state rather than on the concept that education ought to be for the good of the individual. Given such an emphasis, the JTU argues, the state was too easily able to foster ultra-nationalistic sentiment, which eventually led Japan into the disaster of World War II. In fostering ultra-nationalism, the government employed a variety of means: authoritarian control over the content and administration of education, the teaching of courses in morals by elementary teachers, and the pageantry of school ceremonies that elevated nationalistic symbols, such as the national flag, the national anthem, and the Imperial portrait, to sacred objects. The ceremony described below, designed in the view of the JTU to foster "feudalistic" (unquestioning loyalty to the Emperor) and ultra-nationalistic attitudes, helps one to understand why the JTU has fought vigorously against the reintroduction of nationalistic symbols of any kind into the postwar educational process: "When the entire school filed into the hall and were seated on the benches, the organ began to play, signaling the assembly to get up and bow. Then we sang the national anthem, at the end of which the dean of the school quietly advanced toward the shrine in the upper end of the hall where the Imperial images were installed, and in the most respectful manner opened the doors of the shrine on both sides. . . . Then the organ began to play again, and the school master respectfully advanced first to the sacred image of the Emperor Meiji and with the signal of the organ he bowed deep before it, followed by the entire school. . . . The atmosphere became more than ever solemn. Now the principal stood on the platform before a table covered with purple brocade. On it was a wooden case fastened with purple silk strings which he now untied and took out of the case a scroll. He held it high with both hands and unwound it. When the scroll was completely unrolled, he held it higher still and with this signal the entire assembly bowed low and kept this position for some ten minutes. In his clear voice the master read the Imperial Rescript on Education out of the scroll."[4]

The fundamental view of the JTU leaders on this first point is that teachers ought not to be mere agents of the state propagating a single doctrine determined by the bourgeois ruling class. Instead, they should be encouraged to be creative and be allowed to exercise their own initiative and judgment.

A second characteristic of the role of the prewar teacher to which the JTU strongly objects was the concept that teachers were participating in a "heavenly calling" (*tenshoku*). JTU literature more often uses the term *seishokusha* (a person engaged in a sacred occupation) to refer to this concept.[5] Both the prewar teacher himself and society in general viewed the teacher's role as that of a "heavenly calling." JTU leaders argue that this characteristic was extremely influential in fashioning weak, powerless teachers. Embalmed in such an attitude, the teacher was expected to live a life of noble poverty and not be concerned with improving his livelihood. Noble and poor, he was also expected to be a living model of the Confucian virtues, refraining from acting in ways unbecoming to a teacher, such as participating in demonstrations or strikes. JTU leaders believe that this attitude was of crucial significance in keeping teachers impotent in the face of undesirable administrative policies and practices. Saddled with this attitude and almost wholly unorganized in groups created to protect their interests (the weakness of prewar teachers' unions will be discussed below), teachers had almost no influence on policy decisions affecting education or their own welfare. Although the connotations surrounding the term *tenshoku* suggest an elevation of the status of teachers above that of the common people and were used to make teachers

[4] Sumie Seo Mishima, *My Narrow Isle* (New York: John Day Company, 1941), p. 28.

[5] JTU, *Kokumin Kyōiku*, p. 106.

15

themselves and the general public feel that they were participating in a special calling and in possession of superior ethical qualities, the connotations surrounding the JTU's term, *seishokusha*, suggest the sanctimonious nature of the prewar elementary teachers and are used to convey the idea that they were wrongly separated from the "people" when they should have been "of the people," a fact that resulted, from the JTU's point of view, in their powerless position vis-à-vis the government.

Thirdly, because the prewar elementary teacher did not have the right to create his own courses or choose his own textbooks, JTU leaders view the role he played as passive and non-creative. As education was subject-matter centered rather than pupil-centered, teachers relied almost exclusively on the government-approved textbooks and did not have the opportunity to determine what they would teach or how they would teach. JTU leaders take the view that this prevented teachers from developing their own creative and critical faculties, and that this led not only to inferior education but also to their lack of resistance to the government's increasing militarization of the schools in the 1930's. Fearing a recurrence of the prewar pattern of control over curricula and textbooks, the JTU has fought fiercely throughout the postwar period against the government's persistent tendency to move in that direction.

A fourth characteristic that in the eyes of the JTU "forced teachers into a logic of subservience" was the paternalistic relationship that existed in every school between the principal and teachers. True to the familiar *oyabun-kobun* pattern of group relationships in every aspect of Japanese life, the principal played the role of "parent" to the teachers' role of "children":

"The schoolmaster's idea of the school as a family ruled by his paternal authority came from his faith that our country was a great family most blessed under the gracious rule of the great national father, the Emperor. . . . We had our great Emperor whose divine love enlightened the entire nation and whose absolute authority each family head and head of each institution administered as his vicar."[6]

Teachers were expected to obey their principal's dictates unquestioningly, just as the principal himself was expected to obey his superior administrators. Although discussions between principals and teachers took place in faculty meetings, it was the rare teacher who would openly disagree with policies of the educational bureaucracy as presented by the principal. Faculty meetings, far from being used to air teachers' views or solve teachers' problems in cooperation with the principal, were instead normally used for the issuance of instructions to the teachers and for the discussion—that is, clarification—of how best they could be carried out. With the ever-present possibility of suffering isolation from one's fellow teachers for having created a disharmonious atmosphere as well as the possibility of disciplinary action without adequate judicial review, few teachers dared to disagree with administrative or educational policies to any significant degree. JTU leaders take the position that the relationship between principals and teachers should be on a more equal basis, allowing teachers to participate more freely and creatively in the solving of educational problems.

A fifth characteristic of the role of the prewar teacher that has contributed to the JTU leadership's postwar stance concerns the way in which teachers were trained in the prewar ordinary normal schools. In the JTU's view, these schools, which prepared students for teaching at the elementary level, were little more than indoctrinating institutions. The normal schools operated on the assumption that the loyalty and patriotism of the elementary teachers, responsible for training the character of all the Japanese people, had to be insured. As expressed in the 1892 Regulations for the Lower Normal School, the training of elementary teachers placed primary stress on loyalty, filial piety, and obedience:

[6] Sumie Seo Mishima, *My Narrow Isle*, p. 40.

"It is of utmost importance for the teacher to possess an exuberant spirit of reverence for the Emperor and love of his Fatherland. Accordingly, the pupil shall be fully inculcated (in the virtues of) loyalty and filial piety. . . . It is of prime importance for the teacher to have dignity worthy of the respect of others by observing the rules and social order. Therefore, it is of absolute necessity for the pupil to obey his superiors and listen to their advice, and behave straight in his daily life."[7]

Proper indoctrination of future elementary teachers in these nationalistic virtues required that they be trained in government-operated schools. These state normal schools became the only institutions qualified to certify elementary teachers. Students were recruited from among higher elementary school graduates and given four years of professional training. All aspects of the training were tightly controlled by a centralized administrative system headed by the Ministry of Education. It was this authoritarian governmental control of the training of elementary teachers that insured that they would fulfill their assigned role as guardians of the state's official morality.

Three features of this bureaucratic control are worth noting, particularly in the light of the JTU's great fear of their revival. First, students were accepted only on the recommendation of the prefectural governor, the county head, or the ward mayor, and they were subjected to a probationary period of three months. In addition, all students received state scholarships covering their tuition and living expenses and, in return for this assistance, were required to teach after graduation up to ten years in a public elementary school. This afforded the government not only the opportunity of watching over their daily conduct while they were in normal school, but also the right of determining the locality where graduates would teach. "Difficult" students could

[7] Japanese National Commission for UNESCO, *The Development of Modern Education and Teachers' Training in Japan* (Tokyo: 1961), Art. 324, p. 36.

18

be threatened with assignment to remote posts or, if necessary, expelled. Students were normally sensitive to these undesirable possibilities since most of them were higher elementary school graduates who had failed the entrance examinations to middle schools leading to a university education, and consequently they looked upon their normal school education as their only road to advancement. Commoners and especially students from farm areas, whose families counted on them to honor the family by becoming *sensei* and perhaps eventually principals, were particularly sensitive to these threats and therefore readily acquiesced in playing the quiescent roles required of them.

A second feature of bureaucratic control over normal school education was the fact that principals of normal schools were government officials appointed or approved by the Emperor, and subject to the dictates of the special section of the Ministry of Education devoted to normal school education. Although enjoined by law to make no regulation without the approval of the Ministry, they had the authority to dismiss students whose character and conduct were undesirable. Since they were also empowered to inspect elementary schools in their prefecture and to report their findings to the Ministry, the central administrative authority of the government was exercised over elementary as well as normal school education. The third feature of bureaucratic control over ordinary normal school education—the Ministry's total authority over the content, so thorough as to dictate the teacher's course of study down to its merest details—undoubtedly had the greatest influence in creating "subservient" elementary teachers. One significant factor in molding the personalities of the prospective teachers was that of military gymnastics (*heishiki taisō*), introduced into the curriculum by Mori Arinori, Minister of Education from 1885 until 1889, who firmly believed that those qualities of character necessary for teachers to possess if Japan were to achieve its national aims could not be cultivated without military training. As Mori put it:

19

"The things we hope to achieve by means of this training are three: first, to instill—with the sense of urgency possessed by actual soldiers—those *habits of obedience* which are appropriate in the classroom; secondly, as you know, soldiers are always formed into squads, each squad possessing its own leader who devotes himself heart and soul to the welfare of his group, and thirdly, every company has its commanding officer who controls and supervises it, and who must comport himself with dignity. By the same token our students, by trading off the roles of common soldier, squad leader, and commanding officer, will build up the traits of character appropriate to each of these roles."[8] (Italics mine.)

The "traits of character" referred to in the above passage, and that Mori's 1886 Normal School Ordinance stipulated teachers ought to cultivate, were *junryō* (obedience), *shin'ai* (friendliness), and *ichō* (dignity). Six hours a week of military gymnastics were to inculcate these virtues into the students. Perhaps these three virtues were the most significant factors in assuring that elementary teachers would acquire a submissive attitude and properly fulfill their role as the nation's teachers of the national doctrine, even though Mori did not entirely foresee that these virtues would have such an effect. Since even Mori, as can be seen in the above passage, felt that strict obedience was a necessary quality for teachers to possess, however, it is difficult to disagree with the JTU's assertion that these three virtues actually sustained a hierarchically structured authoritarian educational system. Since obedience was expected to be the guiding principle of the teacher's relationship towards those in authority above him and friendliness towards those at his own level (his fellow teachers) and dignity towards those below him (his pupils), these virtues provided the cement that held the hierarchically structured system in balance. In

8 From Saitama address, quoted in Ivan P. Hall, "Mori Arinori and the Reshaping of Japanese Education, 1886," unpublished paper for the Seminar on Japanese Society, Harvard University, 1965, p. 46.

terms of Maruyama's "transfer of oppression" theory, the teachers, oppressed by the administrative authorities above, who were closer to the ultimate authority (the Emperor) than themselves, transferred, in the guise of dignity, their sense of oppression to the students below, who were further from the ultimate authority than themselves.[9] Friendliness was the virtue that would maintain harmony among the teachers at the middle level. In this way, the teachers freed themselves of their sense of oppression and, by so doing, remained docile rather than antagonistic towards the authorities, thereby preserving the balance of the educational structure as a whole. The effect of this syndrome of obedience, friendliness, and dignity, which was to guide the conduct of teachers until the end of World War II, was to keep teachers subservient in the face of authority.

With the assignment of officers or noncoms on both the active and retired lists to the staffs of the prefectural normal schools to conduct military drill, the atmosphere of these institutions began to resemble that of army camps. Life became regimented and detailed instructions were published regulating every activity of the daily schedule. Boarding at schools was made compulsory and, with the placing in each dormitory room of prefects chosen among older students to discipline the younger ones, the atmosphere became barracks-like. The change was symbolized by the replacement of the *geta* and *kimono* with combat shoes and cotton uniforms. Although early classes focused on such traditional military arts as *kendō, judō,* and *naginata* (halberd practice), it was not long before Western-style military drills were introduced. Two- or three-day marches became part of the curriculum and by the 1930's the teacher trainees were throwing hand grenades instead of the shotput and practicing swimming carrying packs and

[9] For Maruyama's statement of his "transfer of oppression" theory, see Maruyama Masao, *Thought and Behaviour in Modern Japanese Politics*, trans. Ivan Morris (London: Oxford University Press, 1963), pp. 17-18.

21

rifles. The effect of this "militarization" of the normal schools was to train the minds of teachers to obey unquestioningly the orders of a superior. Because of this militarization of the prewar elementary teachers the JTU has referred to them as *sebiro no gunjin* (military men in business suits).

For all of the above reasons, the postwar JTU leaders view the prewar normal school system as an evil that contributed mightily to the creation of subservient, obedient teachers. Consequently, the JTU has fought against all policies of the government in the postwar period that have even remotely hinted at the possibility of re-creating the prewar normal school system.

The sixth and final characteristic of the role of the prewar elementary teacher that JTU leaders deplore was his political impotence vis-à-vis the government. Numerous factors robbed teachers of any independent basis of power. From 1881, with the issuance of the government's Instructions for Elementary School Teachers, until 1945 teachers in Japan were politically neutralized. They were prohibited from attending political meetings, from making speeches on politics, and from belonging to political parties. Restrictions on their freedom of speech and assembly were further curtailed by numerous regulations and laws, such as the Peace Preservation Regulations of 1887, the Order Restricting the Liberty of Speech in 1894, the Peace Preservation Police Law of 1901, and the Peace Preservation Law of 1925. In short, under the rubric of "political neutrality," teachers were forced to remain politically impotent and thus had no influence on the making of educational policy. The JTU has deplored this prewar political neutralization of teachers as one of the many devices employed by the ruling class to force teachers into a "logic of subservience."

To sum up, the JTU leadership views the prewar elementary teacher as an agent of the state. As a graduate of a normal school whose curriculum was tightly controlled by the government, he was a product of state training and indoctrination, with the duty of transmitting to his pupils those facts and values prescribed by the government. He was a public servant who played a passive role as a "transmission belt" between the government and his pupils. Although personal relationships with his pupils were usually close, he was neither taught nor encouraged to use his own creative energy and imagination. The emphasis had been elsewhere —on being told what to teach and how to teach it. Schooled to be a model of virtue in his community, he was expected to obey his superiors, be politically neutral, and display unwavering loyalty to his Emperor and country. His activities were carefully circumscribed by custom and by law to insure the fulfillment of this role.

Given the above perception of the prewar role of the elementary teacher, the JTU leaders' strong disapproval of that role and their fierce struggle in the postwar period against any policies which might tend to re-create that role become understandable. Individuals who emerged as leaders of the JTU after the war held this view of the role of the elementary teacher in the 1920's and 1930's, a fact that helps us to understand the prewar origins of the JTU. A few dissatisfied teachers went so far as to attempt to establish teachers' unions, in spite of—and because of—the strictures placed on teachers. The prewar period, therefore, witnessed the faint beginnings of a teachers' union movement. Although periodically suppressed and never strong enough to capture the allegiance or imagination of more than a handful of teachers, the movement nevertheless provided the kernel of personnel and the core of ideas for the explosive postwar teachers' union movement. It must, therefore, be examined briefly before an analysis of the JTU as an interest group can be undertaken.

VULNERABILITY OF PREWAR TEACHERS' UNIONS

The prewar Japanese political climate was not conducive to the emergence of strong, independent, left-wing interest groups. The natural inclination of Japan's modernizing elite, whether one considers the initial Meiji oligarchy, the party cabinets of the 1920's, or the military-dominated oligarchy of the 1930's, was not to encourage the development of independent employees' organizations. Traditional cultural emphasis on harmony, coupled with the need for national unity in order to build as rapidly as possible a strong and wealthy Japan, tended to inhibit the growth of labor unions. In harmony with this attitude, extreme left-wing groups that called for changes in the *kokutai*, or Japan's national polity, were periodically suppressed.

Suppression was possible because the 1889 Meiji Constitution permitted Japanese subjects "liberty in regard to . . . association" only "within the limits of the law" (Article 29). The qualifying clause allowed for the passage of numerous restrictive laws, mentioned above, which enabled the government legally to disband groups regarded as public peace problems. In addition, no trade union law guaranteeing the basic rights of trade unions, such as the rights to bargain collectively and to strike, was ever passed in prewar Japan.[10] Unions were thus in an extremely vulnerable and precarious position. Fundamentally, the absence of a trade union law in the industrially advanced Japan of the 1920's and 1930's may be attributed to the monolithic, rather than pluralistic, concept that underlay prewar Japanese society and that stressed unanimity and harmony rather than diversity, leaving little room for the coexistence of dissimilar-thinking groups.

If prewar unions were weakened as interest groups by the absence of a trade union law, they were also weakened by the fact that "political power was predominantly in the hands of the military and of bureaucrats, and that the status

[10] Japanese trade unions reached their highest peak of the prewar period in 1936, with a total of 420,589 members. For a discussion of the status of the prewar trade unions and for the activities of the ILO in Japan, see Iwao F. Ayusawa, *A History of Labor in Modern Japan* (Honolulu: East-West Center Press, 1966), pp. 219-31.

24

of parliament and political parties was very low."[11] In other words, in prewar Japan public policy was not made by the Diet or the political parties, but by bureaucratic, military, and business elites. Therefore the target area of trade unions desiring to influence public policy-making had to be these elites, not the parties or the Diet. But trade unions had little or no access to the decision-making process as it was carried out among those elites. Consequently, they were extremely weak and were continually faced with policy decisions formulated on high and handed down from above.

This was especially true of groups concerned with matters that were regulated exclusively by Imperial ordinances, and not by parliamentary law, as was education. The centralization of authority over educational matters within the Ministry of Education and the practice of establishing basic policy through the issuance of Imperial ordinances lent to educational policies as well as to Education Ministry bureaucrats an ethically superior weight gained from their proximity to the focus of state authority. It was normal, therefore, for teachers to regard educational policies as "right" or "correct" and, in any case, as "absolute, impartial, and non-political."

With this attitude it was almost unthinkable for elementary teachers to join groups opposed to the Ministry. They viewed themselves as rightfully belonging under the shelter and protection of the Ministerial umbrella. At the same time, Education Ministry bureaucrats, who also viewed the Ministerial policies as "correct," and who felt they knew more about educational problems than any other group in the society, saw no reason for the existence of independent teachers' organizations and especially no need for teachers' unions. Consequently, the teachers' organizations that did exist in the prewar period were of two types: those which

[11] Kiyoski Tsuji, "Pressure Groups in Japan," *Interest Groups on Four Continents*, ed. Henry W. Ehrmann (Pittsburgh: Pittsburgh University Press, 1958), p. 146.

25

were officially sanctioned by the Ministry and those which attempted to exist without the blessing of the Ministry. The Ministry-sponsored organizations, while more numerous and larger in membership, were nevertheless merely extensions of the Ministry and subordinate to it. Their relationship to the Ministry was governed by the values of paternalism. On the other hand, the relationship between the independent organizations and the Ministry was characterized by non-cooperation and antagonism. In fact, these independent teachers' organizations were never encouraged by the Ministry and were, instead, subject to periodic suppression. The highly significant result of this situation, which bears heavily on the postwar relationship between the Ministry of Education and the JTU, is that neither type of prewar teachers' organization was able to develop a relationship on the basis of equality with the Ministry. No slow painful evolution of the concept of independent teachers' organizations as equal partners with the Ministry, both vitally concerned with educational problems, took place. Consequently, no institutionalized channels for communicating the views of *independent* teachers' organizations to the Ministry of Education for the purpose of influencing policy-making were established.

The Prewar Imperial Education Association

The most important Ministry-sponsored teachers' organization was the Imperial Education Association (Teikoku Kyōikukai), renamed the Great Japan Education Association (Dai Nihon Kyōikukai) in 1944, to which all teachers were required to belong. Founded in 1883, the IEA developed into the sole teachers' organization of national significance, since it became the practice for all educational societies to coalesce with the IEA. It was not an organization, however, that was either formed by the teachers themselves or reflected their views, since it was originally created by the Ministry and continued to be authoritatively controlled

26

until it was re-formed after the war. Control was achieved by Ministerial appointment of its president and vice-president, who, in turn, appointed its directors and councillors. Given this control, the IEA appears to have been little more than an extension of the Ministerial arm used to keep teachers in line and to disseminate educational policy. According to the testimony in 1947 of Tanaka Kōtarō shortly after he stepped down as Education Minister in the first Yoshida Cabinet, the IEA was "obviously nationalistic and functioned as virtual agent of the Ministry of Education."[12]

In spite of its stated aims to promote "the educational ideal of the Japanese people on the fundamental principle of our national policy," to render "loyal service to national education by uniting all educators and those who have an understanding of national education," to secure "the stabilization of teachers' livelihood" and to give "assistance for the encouragement of research," this did not prevent an overwhelming reaction on the part of the teachers against the Association immediately after the war. The reaction indicates the negative, if not repressive, role the Association actually played in its relation to teachers.[13] In 1946 the IEA was charged with using its teachers' dues of half a million yen to provide "handsome salaries for its officers and staff without contributing anything for the protection of teachers."[14] Union organizers, such as Hani Gorō (see page 52, n. 17, below), charged that the aim of the Association was to crush the initiative of the teachers, to prohibit their intellectual freedom, and to imbue them with obsequious attitudes towards authority. Although these charges may be excessive, it is nevertheless undeniable that the Association was not popular among either the moderate or

[12] SCAP, GHQ, CIE, *A History of Teachers' Unions in Japan*, Tokyo, 1948, pp. 1-2, quoting Tanaka Kotarō, "Reply to a Questionnaire," July 16, 1947, n. 4.

[13] *Ibid.*, p. 2, quoting "Dissolution of Dai Nihon Kyōikukai Decided," Kyōiku Rōdō, July 24, 1946.

[14] *Ibid.*, p. 3.

radical wings of the postwar teachers' movement. Both berated the Ministry for maintaining in the immediate postwar years that the IEA was striving for the "spiritual improvement" of teachers and that its strong cooperation with the government was essential for raising the cultural level of Japan. The teachers' attitude toward the government-dominated IEA was indicated by the "silent revolt" of the young teachers of Kagoshima prefecture in February 1946 when they withdrew and formed an independent organization of their own.[15] In March the teachers' hostility forced the dissolution of the IEA in Aomori prefecture.[16] These were not isolated instances, and even though great efforts were made by the Occupation to democratize the IEA by terminating the annual subsidies from the government and by having the councillors elect the president, most of the prefectural chapters of the Association were dissolved and their office space taken over by newly created, independent, prefectural unions,[17] a phenomenon discussed in the following chapter.

The strong postwar demands of the new unions that the Ministry of Education either dissolve the IEA or drastically modify and democratize it suggest a measure of discontent among some prewar teachers with the dependent status of the Association to which they belonged. A few teachers attempted to express this discontent by breaking out of the all-embracing Ministry-controlled IEA and establishing truly independent unions. To this prewar teachers' union movement we must now turn.

The Prewar Teachers' Union Movement

Given the fact that most prewar elementary teachers, as a corollary to their subservient roles, were inclined to accept the policies of the Ministry of Education as "correct," and the fact that teachers' unions that placed themselves in

15 *Ibid.*, p. 2.   16 *Ibid.*, p. 3.
17 *Ibid.*, pp. 4-6.

opposition to the Ministry were periodically suppressed, it is not surprising that the prewar teachers' union movement did not attract large numbers of teachers. Nevertheless, in the "liberal" decade after World War I, several teachers' unions sprang up and continued until the mid-1930's to persist in their efforts to organize teachers and to establish "democratic, independent education." An examination, first, of the general trend of Japanese politics in the interwar period and, second, of the creation, demands, and activities of teachers' unions during these two decades will help to place the prewar teachers' union movement in perspective, even though its relative lack of influence on the government and on teachers themselves is clearly recognized.

In the decade after World War I a new liberal mood swept Japan. The Western democracies had emerged victorious from the war, a fact that stimulated in Japan a vogue for democratic ideas. Although in retrospect it is clear that Japan's ruling elite was not seriously challenged, it is nevertheless true that the political atmosphere during the decade of the 1920's was charged with the cry for parliamentarianism and that some changes took place within the political system that appeared to be leading Japan towards a greater degree of democracy. Thus, the 1920's may rightly be viewed as the high tide of prewar Japanese liberalism. At the same time, the emergence of Bolshevism in the Soviet Union stimulated the Socialist movement in Japan and greatly influenced the labor movement. For Japanese liberals, however, democracy represented the trend of the world and the theories and proposals of liberal thinkers like Minobe Tatsukichi and Yoshino Sakuzō, who argued for a less authoritarian and more responsive political system by advocating the "Emperor-as-an-organ" theory of government and the creation of party cabinets respectively, enjoyed considerable support. The notion of subordinating Japan's various elites to a party cabinet resulted in the establishment of the first party cabinet in 1918. From that year until 1932 most of Japan's cabinets were party cabinets, although several were "transcendental" and did not contain party members. The mood of the times was in the direction of more effective parliamentary government as well as greater concern and participation on the part of the people. The latter was reflected by the passage in May 1925 of the Universal Manhood Suffrage Act by the first Katō party cabinet. As a result the electorate rose from three to over twelve million. Perhaps the high-water mark of parliamentary government was reached during the two Katō party cabinets from June 11, 1924 to January 30, 1926, even though the Katō government coupled the passage of the suffrage bill with a Peace Preservation Law that prohibited the formation of groups advocating a change in the Japanese "national polity."

Nevertheless, the liberalism that was reflected in the formation of party cabinets also had its influence in the budding labor movement. Many organized labor groups supported the liberal idea of evolving towards a more effective parliamentary government, although some called for revolution in the hope of achieving a responsive government immediately. In the new liberal atmosphere labor unions, although they never achieved large membership, blossomed. They were, of course, also stimulated by the doubling in size of the industrial labor force that occurred as a result of industrial expansion concomitant with World War I. Inflation and the inability of salaries to keep up with galloping prices contributed to the growth of labor unions. Although much of the labor movement by the early 1920's —as symbolized by the transformation of the Friendly Society (Yūaikai), founded in 1912 by the moderate Christian leader, Suzuki Bunji, from a society "based on the principle of harmony between capital and labor" to a "trade union federation dedicated to the fight against capital in the interests of labor"[18]—had come under the influence of Bolshevism and may therefore be regarded as part of the Socialist

[18] George O. Totten, III, *The Social Democratic Movement in Prewar Japan* (New Haven: Yale University Press), 1966, p. 32.

30

movement, the teachers' union movement until 1931 may be more accurately viewed as part of the liberal movement. The aims of the leaders of the earliest teachers' unions' association, The Japan Teachers' Unions' Association for Enlightenment (Nihon Kyōin Kumiai Keimeikai, commonly referred to as the Keimeikai), were the aims of liberals, even though by their opposition to state orthodoxy and their support for more effective parliamentary government they sometimes found themselves in the company of leaders of the Socialist movement. Not until the end of the decade did the teachers' union movement clearly take on the coloration of a Marxist-Leninist Socialist movement.

THE JAPAN TEACHERS' UNIONS' ASSOCIATION FOR ENLIGHTENMENT (KEIMEIKAI)

Meeting in Tokyo on August 4, 1919, under the leadership of Shimonaka Yasaburō,[19] then a teacher at the Saitama Prefectural Normal School, the members of the Keimeikai referred to it as a nationwide organization, even though the overwhelming majority of its members seem to have come from Saitama prefecture.[20] All but three of the fourteen

[19] Shimonaka Yasaburō, born in Hyōgo prefecture in 1878, not only founded the Keimeikai, but was a vigorous leader of the general prewar labor movement. In 1923 he founded the Heibon Publishing Company and became the leading publisher of encyclopedias in Japan. After World War II he published *The World Encyclopedia* and became an advocate of the World Government movement, which he envisioned would lead to establishing world peace by civilians. *Japan Biographical Encyclopedia and Who's Who*, 1958.

[20] This discussion of the prewar teachers' union movement relies heavily on the first two volumes of *Nihon Kyōiku Undō-shi* (History of the Japanese Education Movement), (Tokyo: San-ichi Shobō, 1960), in three volumes: Volume I, edited by Inogawa Kiyoshi and Kawai Akira, entitled *Meiji-Taishō-ki no Kyōiku Undō* (The Education Movement During the Meiji and Taishō Periods), and Volume II, edited by Kurotaki Chikara and Itō Tadahiko, entitled *Shōwa Shoki no Kyōiku Undō* (The Education Movement During the Shōwa Period), which brings the movement up to the beginning of World War II.

31

members of the first board of directors were graduates of the Saitama Normal School and were probably Shimonaka's colleagues or students. By 1920 there were a hundred members of the Keimeikai, almost all of them elementary school teachers;[21] Shimonaka himself, in an essay written in 1925 to commemorate the sixth anniversary of the Keimeikai, placed the membership at that time at about one thousand.

In spite of its small membership, the Keimeikai, as the forerunner of teachers' unions in Japan, was to have considerable influence on the movement as a whole. This influence grew partially from its demands for higher salaries, but to a greater extent from its demands for the reform of Japanese education. One of the characteristics of the teachers' union movement in Japan has been its unwillingness to limit itself to improving the welfare of teachers. Instead, both before and after the war, the movement has always been vitally concerned with the reform of educational policy and administration, which by definition is a political issue. This is a major reason why Japanese teachers' unions have been more than mere trade unions interested only in the economic betterment of the teachers. The activists, if not always the rank and file, have seen the vital questions surrounding Japanese education as political rather than economic. Thus, even though the immediate impetus for the founding of particular unions at specific points in time has tended to be the economic hardship of teachers, the long-range impetus has been the demand for educational and societal reforms, although activists have tended to believe that the economic deprivation of teachers was actually a situation that could be solved only by social reform, carried out by either parliamentary or revolutionary means. Of the two, educational reform, so much more directly related to social revolution, was the aspect of the teachers' union movement that galvanized the activists. Thus, it was the Keimeikai's proposals, as the leader of an "enlightenment

[21] Munakata Seiya and Kokubu Ichitarō, *Nihon no Kyōiku* (Japanese Education), (Tokyo: Iwanami Shinsho, 1962), p. 25.

movement," for the reform of education that had the greatest influence over the long run. Its "Program for Educational Reform," issued in 1920, for example, contained a number of ideas that were to be taken up by later teachers' unions and included in their education demands. In fact, the four main points of the program are still the key issues for which the JTU raises its flag today.

Without resorting to such Marxist-Leninist terminology as "the ruling class," "capitalism," or "teachers as laborers," the Keimeikai's 1920 "Program for Educational Reform" nevertheless focused on the democratization of Japanese education and stressed four main points:

1. The democratization of educational ideals, or the creation of an educational system that would foster the democratic spirit and exist for the good of the individual rather than for the good of the state.

2. The establishment of equal opportunity of education, or the creation of an educational system that would permit all qualified students to receive an education at public expense up to the university level.

3. The realization of independent education, or the abolition of bureaucratic control over educators. One of the most important proposals for implementing "independent education" was the popular election of elementary school principals.

4. The establishment of a dynamic, flexible educational system, or the abolition of uniformity and standardization of education and the fostering of freedom in the educational system: for example, the freedom of educators to select textbooks.[22]

In order to popularize the above ideas, the Keimeikai sponsored meetings of elementary teachers in which these ideas and other important educational problems were discussed. It also published an organ, *Keimei*, as well as the

[22] Kido Wakao, "Kyōshi no Jikakuto Danketsu" (The Consciousness and Unity of Teachers), in Inogawa and Kawai, *Meiji-Taishō-ki no Kyōiku Undō-shi*, pp. 172-75.

magazine *Bunka Undō* (The Cultural Movement), and from July 1925 to September 1926 issued a series of pamphlets. These activities, and especially the Keimeikai's demand for the popular election of elementary school principals, did not escape the watchful eye of the government. Throughout its existence its members were subjected to numerous interrogations by the authorities and in a variety of ways, such as the periodic suspension of its publications and the transfer of some of its members, it was suppressed. In 1928 it dissolved itself as an association and ceased to exist, although a number of its leaders, such as Shimonaka Yasaburō, Ueda Tadao,[23] and Ikeda Tsuneo,[24] appeared soon after as leaders of subsequent teachers' unions. Ueda and Ikeda, for example, founded in the same year as the Keimeikai's demise the Young Educators' League (Seinen Kyōikuka Remmei), which one year later became the League of Elementary School Teachers (Shōgakkō Kyōin Remmei, or Shōkyōren).

The Shōkyōren was established in October 1929 in Tokyo partly because the Keimeikai had been suppressed, partly

[23] Ueda Tadao, born in 1902 in Ishikawa prefecture, graduated from the Department of Philosophy at Kyoto in 1928 and has had a long career in education. He taught at the Ibaraki Prefectural Normal School and the Tennōji Normal School before becoming the principal of the Attached Elementary School to the Nagano Prefectural Normal School. Moving up the ladder, he became Education Commissioner of Shiga prefecture and later of Saitama prefecture before becoming in 1950 President of the Kanazawa Women's Junior College. He has also acted as the director of the Kanazawa UNESCO Cooperative Association. In prewar days, he founded in 1928 the Young Educators' League (Seinen Kyōikuka Renmei), which one year later changed its name to the League of Elementary School Teachers (Shōgakkō Kyōin Renmei, or Shōkyōren). *Japan Biographical Encyclopedia and Who's Who*, 1958.

[24] Ikeda Tsuneo, born in 1909 in Miyagi prefecture, served first as a clerk and later as the Chief of the Organization Division of the National Farmers' Union (Zenkoku Nōmin Kumiai, or Zennō), founded in 1928. He also helped Ueda Tadao in establishing the Young Educators' League mentioned in the preceding footnote. After the war, he was elected to the House of Councillors from Ibaraki prefecture in April 1947. *The Japan's Who's Who*, 1950-1951.

because of the financial crisis of 1927 and the subsequent depression of 1929 that had caused delays in the payment of teachers' salaries, and partly because of the increased militarization of the elementary schools.[25] Most of its approximately sixty members were from Tokyo, with a few from Saitama, Kanagawa, and Yamanashi. The Shōkyōren's program included the four main points for the reform of education espoused by the Keimeikai, but picked out several subordinate points for particular stress. For example, it protested against the arbitrary power of principals to appoint and dismiss elementary teachers, called for abolishing the influence of the military in elementary schools by removing militaristic training and thinking from the curriculum and textbooks, demanded the founding of special schools for the children of workers, and requested a guarantee from the national government that teachers' salaries would be paid in full.[26]

The Shōkyōren, however, was short-lived. After participating in a struggle against the government's suspension of an increase in salary and a cut of 20 percent in the 1929 year-end bonus, the heretofore legal Shōkyōren was suppressed in January 1930 under the provisions of the 1925 Peace Preservation Law. Forty-five members were arrested in Tokyo, of whom twelve were fired from their teaching positions, one suspended, and thirteen reprimanded. Its leading members, however, some of whom had been members of the Keimeikai as well, surfaced once again in still another teachers' union, the Japan Educational Workers' Union (Nihon Kyōiku Rōdōsha Kumiai), founded in May 1931.

Unlike the previous teachers' unions, the Educational Workers' Union had intentionally formed as an illegal organization and for the first time the teachers' union move-

[25] Moriya Kiyoshi, "Shinkō Kyōiku Kenkyūsho no Hossoku" (Establishment of the New Education Institute), in Kurotaki and Itō, *Shōwa Shoki no Kyōiku Undō*, pp. 42-50.

[26] *Ibid.*, pp. 56-60.

ment openly took on a Marxist-Leninist flavor and became a part of the Socialist movement. Governmental restrictions on the previous teachers' unions contributed to driving the teachers' union movement to the left. Recognizing the restrictions placed on the activities and the program of a legally registered organization, the leaders felt they could develop the teachers' union movement more effectively if the new union made no effort to operate within the bounds of the law. It therefore proceeded in open defiance of the law, although a legal organization, the New Education Institute (Shinkō Kyōiku Kenkyūsho), was set up at the same time to raise money and fight the legal battles the leaders knew would befall the members of the Educational Workers' Union. Again consisting of elementary and ex-elementary teachers, the union drew its membership primarily from the Kantō area, although chapters were formed in Kyoto and Akita as well. Similar reasons to those given for the establishment of the Keimeikai and the Shōkyōren were given for the founding of the new union, although with the cloaks worn by these other unions thrown off, it revealed itself far to the left. It frankly declared its intention of establishing a truly class-conscious teachers' union and of creating proletarian education, and it did not hesitate to use Marxist-Leninist terminology. Stating that teachers were laborers who belonged to the proletarian class, it defined the duty of teachers as that of liberating themselves from the capitalist class by forming a common struggle with other revolutionary elements in the working class. Its demands, too, which went further than any previous teachers' union, were couched in similar terminology. Viewing the Japanese educational system as reactionary and controlled by capitalists and landowners for their own profit, the Educational Workers' Union proclaimed its opposition to all reactionary education. A mere glance at some of its more significant demands clearly reveals its position and draws an unhappy portrait of certain aspects of Japanese education in 1931.

1. Elimination of state textbooks.

2. Acquisition by teachers of the freedom to select their own textbooks and their own subjects.

3. Acquisition by teachers of the freedom to make their own decisions regarding class assignments and class management.

4. Abolition of tuition fees for all compulsory school children.

5. Extension of compulsory education.

6. Acquisition of the right of students to strike. (This was aimed particularly at the right of normal school students to strike.)

7. Elimination of the arbitrary power of principals to dismiss or transfer teachers.

8. Establishment of parents' organizations among the poor working classes.

9. Supervision by parents' organizations of school administration.

10. Acquisition of the freedom to establish a teachers' union and the freedom to participate in trade-union activities.

11. Acquisition by teachers of the right to join political parties and to participate in political activities.

12. Acquisition by teachers of the right to strike.

13. Establishment of a united front with other workers' unions and farmers' unions.

14. Opposition to the dismissal of substitute teachers and assistant teachers for military service.

15. Organization of a struggle against the peril of an imperialistic war.[27]

The different chapters of the union engaged in a variety of activities in order to achieve some of the above aims, although, as might be expected, they were met with determined opposition from the far more powerful governmental apparatus, including the police and educational administrators. The Tokyo chapter, for example, took the leader-

[27] *Ibid.*, pp. 89-90.

ship in organizing a strike by the students of the Toshima Normal School in protest against the firing of an instructor. At the same time, student leaders demanded improvement in the treatment of students by the school administration. The strike dragged on for nineteen days and, although the instructor was not rehired and all the student leaders were jailed, the treatment of students improved. The Kyoto chapter sponsored a number of study groups and attempted to organize a fund-raising campaign for the Communist Relief Organization (Sekishoku Kyūenkai), which led to the arrest of the entire group in June 1931. Six members of the Akita chapter were arrested on the charge that their group was a secret political organization that aimed at fostering a Marxist-type, class-based revolution. One of the leaders of the Kanagawa chapter was arrested in March 1931 for having organized study groups among his fellow teachers. In short, the government, through the police and educational administrators, cracked down on the members of the Educational Workers' Union and rendered it ineffective by jailing its top leaders and by dismissing or suspending scores of others from their positions as teachers. With the suppression of this union, no other teachers' union of importance emerged in the darkening decade of the 1930's.

The significance of the prewar teachers' union movement is contained in the fact that it existed at all, regardless of its extremely limited influence on or direct connection with the vast majority of elementary teachers. Harassed and suppressed, it nevertheless provided an experienced corps of leaders who were eager and able to organize teachers' unions in the postwar period when governmental restrictions were removed. It also managed to spread through the society at least some of its protests against "reactionary" education and some of its ideas concerning "democratic" education so that these concepts were not totally alien to teachers and the general public when they were vigorously propounded in the postwar period. In fact, with the Götterdämmerung of the defeat, "democratic" education and the leaders who had fought for it gained favor in the eyes of the teachers and the general public. Those who had argued in the 1920's and 1930's against the militarization of education, for example, were now seen to have been right. But perhaps a greater consequence of the prewar teachers' union movement was that it was forced to the radical left by governmental intolerance. This prevented the mainstream of the movement from developing along non-Marxist lines, and all but insured that the postwar movement would be radical. Of greater concern to this study, prewar intolerance on the part of the government prevented the growth of any kind of healthy relationship between the Ministry of Education and independent teachers' unions, thus laying the groundwork for the bitter struggles to be fought between the Ministry and the postwar teachers' unions and for the particular style of pressure politics engaged in by the JTU.

CHAPTER III

Postwar Origins and Struggles

THE JAPAN TEACHERS' UNION today bears the stamp not only of its prewar origins but also of its early postwar origins and succeeding years of struggle. The characteristics of the remarkable period of growth of the teachers' union movement from the end of the war until the founding of the JTU in June 1947 still have great influence on the union today. So, too, does the evolution during that period of the relationship between teachers' unions and the Ministry of Education. In addition, the subsequent great struggles in the 1950's and 1960's of the union against the government have contributed mightily to the behavior of the JTU today. A brief account of these early years and the subsequent struggles will provide the background for the more detailed analysis of the effectiveness of a selected few of these struggles that appears in Chapter VI. First, however, an understanding of the early postwar years of the teachers' union movement and the JTU's role in that movement will be aided if the major trends in Japanese left-wing politics and the labor movement as a whole during the first two years of the Occupation are briefly sketched.

THE NEW DISPENSATION

With the democratization of Japan as one of the primary goals of the American Occupation, the directives of the Supreme Commander for the Allied Powers (SCAP) quickly freed the Japanese political atmosphere from its wartime repressiveness. Under the new liberal dispensation, left-wing political parties, which had either been suppressed or illegal before the war, were allowed to reorganize and op-

40

erate legally. By mid-November 1945 both the Japan Socialist Party (Nihon Shakaitō, officially translated as the Social
Democratic Party of Japan) and the Japan Communist
Party (JCP) had been vigorously revived. Arguing for the
establishment of a common front of "democratic" forces in
the new Japan, JCP leaders tried to obtain the cooperation
of the JSP in proposing and fighting for a host of specific demands to the government. Not as aggressive or as tightly
organized as the JCP, the JSP was immediately plagued by
a split between the right-wing Socialists, who did not want
to participate with the JCP, and the left-wing Socialists,
who were ready to do so. In the immediate postwar years,
therefore, in the unhampered atmosphere in which left-
wing parties were free to challenge the government, there
was struggle within the left-wing leadership as a whole over
who was to lead: the right-wing Socialists, the left-wing Socialists, or the Communists? During these early years the
right-wing Socialists were able to dominate the JSP, but the
left-wing Socialists were by no means weak. And, measured
by the results of the first postwar elections to the House of
Representatives in 1946, the JSP as a whole proved to be far
stronger than the JCP, securing ninety-two seats to the
JCP's five.

The Communists, however, were more successful in the
labor movement than their showing in the first postwar
election suggests. Occupation policies, which encouraged
the formation of labor unions, together with desperate living conditions resulting from the devastation of the war, inflation, and food shortages led to "the meteoric rise of
labor unions, both numerically and politically."[1] By mid-
August 1946 two large labor federations had been established, each with its own political coloration and particular
member unions. On the right within the left-wing spectrum
and supporting the right-wing Socialists was the moderate

[1] Allan B. Cole, George O. Totten, and Cecil H. Uyehara, *Socialist
Parties in Postwar Japan* (New Haven: Yale University Press), 1966,
p. 10.

General Federation of Labor (Sōdōmei), consisting of 850,000 members "mainly from light industry and the smaller enterprises."[2] On the left was the radical Congress of Industrial Unions (Sambetsu), consisting of 1.6 million members, most of them government workers. Although the two centers occasionally worked together, the Sōdōmei was politically oriented toward the right-wing Socialists whereas the Sambetsu supported the left-wing Socialists and the JCP. In fact, the top officers of the Sambetsu were predominantly Communists, holding 30 of the 43 seats in the Sambetsu's Central Committee.[3] In size of membership the Sambetsu was twice as large as the Sōdōmei and by the end of 1946 it was clearly the more dominant federation.

In this brief sketch of the trends in the left-wing political and labor movements during the first two years of the Occupation, attention must be given to the abortive general strike of February 1, 1947, in which the Communists, through the Sambetsu, made their major bid to dominate the Japanese trade union movement—a bid that failed but nevertheless marks the high tide of Communist influence in the labor movement. With the background of the inability of the first Yoshida Cabinet (May 22, 1946 to May 24, 1947) to make significant gains in re-vitalizing the Japanese economy and reversing the depreciation of real wages, together with its generally antagonistic attitude toward labor as evidenced by its attempt to take away from governmental workers the right to strike, the two labor centers formed a joint struggle committee not only to seek wage increases but also to overthrow the Yoshida Cabinet. In this effort, on December 17, 1946 the Sōdōmei, the Sambetsu, and other union organizations mobilized half a million workers for a mass rally, with the demand that the Yoshida Cabinet be overthrown. Yoshida's "high posture" response as revealed

[2] Solomon B. Levine, *Industrial Relations in Postwar Japan* (Urbana: University of Illinois Press), 1958, p. 71.

[3] A. Rodger Swearingen, *Communist Strategy in Japan, 1945-1960* (Santa Monica: The Rand Corporation), 1965, p. 93.

in his New Year greeting only stiffened labor's determination. With Communist leaders in control of the joint struggle committee, it is not surprising that the committee soon called for a general strike, a standard Communist political weapon, to take place on February 1, 1947. As is well known, General MacArthur as the Supreme Commander for the Allied Powers outlawed the "use of so deadly a social weapon in the present impoverished and emaciated condition of Japan." MacArthur's prohibition of the general strike marked the beginning of a tougher attitude toward labor in general and toward the Communist leadership and organization within the labor movement in particular. By various means, from the removal of the right of government workers to strike and to bargain collectively, to the spread of the "democratization movement" (mindō) within labor unions, to the "red purge" of 1950, labor's power over the next several years was reduced and dominant Communist influence within the labor movement was checked and bested. It is within the context of these trends and events that the early postwar teachers' union movement and the creation of the JTU ought to be viewed.

IMMEDIATE CONDITIONS STIMULATING UNIONIZATION

In the first few months after Japan's surrender in August 1945, small groups of elementary school teachers, scattered in cities all over the country, reached out in a new direction. They joined newly created teachers' unions.[4] Within the brief span of two years over 95 percent of the elementary teachers had become members of the single, federated

---

[4] For thorough discussions of the early postwar unionization of teachers, see Sawada Fumiaki, Nikkyōso no Rekishi (History of the Japan Teachers' Union), Tokyo: Gōdō Shuppan, 1966; Japan Teachers' Union, Nikkyōso Jūnen-shi (The Ten-Year History of the Japan Teachers' Union) Tokyo: The Japan Teachers' Union, 1958; and Iwama Masao (ed.), Kyōin Kumiai Undō-shi (A History of the Teachers' Union Movement), Tokyo: Shūkan Kyōiku Shimbun-sha, 1948.

Japan Teachers' Union, the most powerful teachers' union to emerge in the postwar period.[5]

At the time this was a daring and formidable venture, for it meant a sharp break with the tradition that assigned teachers a passive role in public affairs and restricted their sphere of activity to the care of children in the classroom. The action on the part of the teachers also involved a repudiation of the notion that joining a trade union is undignified and unprofessional. What prompted this rapid large-scale unionization of teachers in the immediate postwar period? Particularly for the activists, but for some non-activists as well, there were of course the long-standing grievances against the government's unlimited authority over the teachers, which, as has been described in the preceding chapter, forced teachers into a "logic of subservience" and prevented them from developing strong organizations to protect their interests and improve their welfare. These activists, whether Communists, Marxist Socialists, or non-Marxist Socialists, wished to break the accepted patterns of meek subservience to authority and assert the independence of teachers. Of course, those leaders of the teachers' union movement who were members of the JCP as well as most of those who were left-wing Socialists saw the unionization and radicalization of teachers as a necessary and preliminary means for promoting a proletarian-socialist revolution that would, once successful, transform Japan's bourgeois-capitalist society. Such leaders wished to go further than merely creating teachers' unions as a countervailing force to the power of the Ministry of Education; instead, they wished to do away with the existing Ministry and the very governmental structure that lay behind it. One must be careful here, however, not to paint the totality of the early postwar teachers' union movement in such stark,

[5] In a report on its membership to the CIE, SCAP in October 1947, the JTU estimated that out of a total of 453,872 teachers, 446,151, or about 98 percent, were members of its union. SCAP, *Teachers' Unions in Japan*, Appendix J, pp. 75-80.

simplistic terms. When one remembers the considerable number of leaders who organized new teachers' unions at the prefectural level throughout Japan as well as the large number of teachers who joined these unions, objectives other than that of promoting revolution must be recognized. Much of the force that lay behind the movement stemmed from such determinations as the following: to abolish any interference by the government in the teachers' right to take part in labor or political activities; to establish and maintain the right of teachers to join independent nongovernmental teachers' organizations; to establish the right of teachers to bargain collectively through their own representatives for better salaries and working conditions; to secure for teachers the right to strike; and to revamp an educational system that had so easily lent itself to preparing children for war during the prewar period. Under the new encouraging policies of the Occupation, union organizers therefore set about establishing teachers' unions as quickly as possible.

The desire of the activists to organize teachers could scarcely have met with brighter conditions than those created by the initial Occupation policies. Perhaps the most significant aspect of the Occupation's democratization policy that contributed to the rapid postwar unionization of Japan's teachers, as well as of all workers, was the introduction into Japanese political values of the concept that an individual possesses legitimate private interests that he has the right to protect by joining associations of his choice. In contrast to the repressive conditions of the prewar period, in which freedom of association was limited by a series of police laws and peace preservation laws and in which an individual's private interests were subordinate to his duty to the Emperor, the postwar concept embraced unqualified freedom of association and the idea that private interests ought to be *protected* by law. The famous directive of the Supreme Commander for the Allied Powers (SCAP) of October 4, 1945, the so-called "Japanese Bill of Rights," ini-

45

tiated this policy by removing all prewar restrictions on political, civil, and religious liberties. A few days later, on October 11, General MacArthur personally handed to Prime Minister Shidehara Kijūrō a directive which called for "The encouragement of the unionization of Labor . . . that it may be clothed with such dignity as will permit it an initial voice in safeguarding the working man from exploitation and abuse and raising his living standard to a higher level."[6] It is impossible to overestimate the richness of the soil that SCAP's policy of emancipating Japanese workers provided for the subsequent mushrooming of teachers' unions, as well as all other unions. Statistics reveal this clearly. Whereas the total number of all trade union members in prewar Japan during the peak year of 1936 was only 420,589, it rose within one year after the war ended to 3,800,000.[7]

This tremendous growth in union membership was aided by the Diet's incredible rapidity in legitimatizing the trade union movement. Prodded by SCAP as well as by the demands of the newly created unions, the Diet, on December 22, 1945, seventeen months before the new Constitution went into effect, adopted Japan's first Trade Union Law, which had been drawn up by the government-created Labor Legislation Council (Rōmu Hōsei Shingikai), consisting of prominent leaders of the prewar trade union movement as well as authorities on labor law.[8] For the trade union movement this law was of historic significance. It clearly granted workers the right to form free and autonomous unions of their own, the right to engage in collective bargaining with employers on an equal footing, and the right to strike. The law gave the right of employees' representatives of a trade union to negotiate with an employer (Art.

[6] GHQ, SCAP, "Statement to the Japanese Government Concerning Required Reforms," *Political Reorientation of Japan* (Tokyo: SCAP), 1948, p. 741.

[7] Iwao F. Ayusawa, *A History of Labor in Modern Japan* (Honolulu: East-West Center Press 1966), p. 257.

[8] *Ibid.*, pp. 249-54.

10) and gave legal status to trade agreements arrived at by collective bargaining (Arts. 19-25). It granted these fundamental rights equally both to employees in private industry and to public workers. With the exception of certain categories of public workers such as firemen and police, all government employees, both national and local, such as teachers, postal workers, and employees of the state railways, who constituted at the time the largest membership of all unionized workers in Japan, enjoyed during these early postwar years, therefore, not only the right to organize but the crucial rights to bargain collectively and to strike.

The new liberal atmosphere and the possession of these three basic rights greatly stimulated the growth of the teachers' union movement, a growth that was only a part of the remarkable explosion of the trade union movement as a whole. Particularly meaningful to teachers, however, was the embodiment within the Trade Union Law of SCAP's principle that "trade unions should be allowed to take part in political activities and to support political parties."[9] Particularly by the prewar activists who had had to operate circumspectly or risk imprisonment and to a lesser degree by the ordinary elementary teachers long denied the right to participate in political activities, the new political freedom was welcomed and quickly used.

If the new political freedom created by the Occupation-inspired reforms was a powerful stimulant to the activists to organize teachers' unions, the psychological disillusionment and the immediate economic difficulties that all postwar teachers experienced were also potent forces in causing ordinary teachers to join the newly created unions. They were, in short, extremely ripe for unionization. The catastrophic defeat and its consequences—hunger, poverty, weariness, disillusionment, destroyed schools—were the im-

[9] This principle is stated in numerous Occupation documents. See, for example, "Principles for Japanese Trade Unions," adopted by the Far Eastern Commission, December 12, 1946, quoted in *ibid.*, pp. 243-44.

47

mediate conditions that signalled their response to the activists. Psychologically shattered by the total failure of the prewar Emperor-centered ideology, these ordinary teachers were disillusioned with the militaristic government and those forces in the society which had misled the country into the disastrous war; they were ready to join organizations that would represent their protest and their denunciation of the past. Long merely agents of the state, dutifully carrying out the orders of the Ministry of Education, they were anxious to play a more vital role in the formulation of educational policy and in the process of educating children. Having existed for decades on low salaries and never accorded the standard of pay of workers in prefectural or national bureaucracies, teachers felt the need for unionism. The early postwar elementary teachers, their energy consumed by weekend trips to the country to forage for food, their nerves racked from trying to make their inadequate salaries feed, clothe, and house themselves and their families, their schools in need of repair or reconstruction, their minds in chaos, no longer able to define truth, no longer able to instruct their students in what was right or wrong, and knowing only that the ideas they had been teaching with such conviction had led to nothing but the bleak reality of total colossal defeat, were ripe for joining organizations that promised them economic gains and a new sense of purpose and hope.

Economically, teachers were in dire straits and they hoped the new unions could achieve salary increases as quickly as possible. The fact that teachers' unions' campaigns, until the failure of the February 1, 1947 strike, were directed primarily toward the objective of winning wage increases, and the fact that the overwhelming majority of the teachers joined unions even though such action normally involved a breach with traditionally approved conduct, suggest that the economic situation had the most prominent influence in the early postwar development of teachers' unions in Japan.

Supporting the contention that the campaigns of teachers' unions until the February strike were primarily directed toward the improvement of teachers' wages is a list of the demands submitted by the National League of Teachers' Unions (Kyōin Kumiai Zenkoku Remmei) to the Minister of Education on October 15, 1946, a list typical of the demands a number of unions submitted to the Minister until February 1947:

1. Payment of the minimum salary of ¥600, not including allowances for the locality of service.

2. Abolition of differences in basic wages according to teaching localities.

3. Abolition of difference in pay between men and women.

4. Opposition to the discharge of teachers.

5. A 30-50 percent raise of locality allowances and readjustment of unfair allocations.

6. Raise of family allowances to the highest rate.

7. Raise of exemption points for income tax:

    a. A-class "classified income tax" exemption to ¥600.

    b. Surtax exemption point to ¥30,000.

    c. Family exemption point per dependent to ¥30.

8. All-around increase of educational appropriations:

    a. Establishment of a minimum basic salary according to the length of service.

    b. Increase of allowances for educational accommodations and equipment, as well as for research.

    c. Increase of the allocation of subsidies to private schools.

    d. Free distribution of clothes and other goods.

9. Speedy improvement of working conditions:

    a. Maximum working hours and teaching hours should be fixed definitely.

    b. The fixed number of children per class should be decreased.

    c. The number of teachers for each class should be increased.

d. A business administrative office should be placed in each national school beginning next year.[10]

A limited study of the livelihood of teachers conducted by the Operations Division of the Civil Intelligence Section of SCAP estimated in February 1946 that the average elementary teacher's salary barely covered one-third of his needs. The difference between the average total monthly salary of ¥143, which included bonuses and allowances, and the average total monthly expenses of ¥450 amounted to ¥307.[11] This serious deficit resulted from the fact that the average retail price index in Tokyo in May 1946 was fifteen times that of June 1937, and teachers' salaries, which had not increased from 1937 to 1942, had not kept up with this inflation at all.[12] Not only were salaries woefully inadequate, but food rationing was meager as well. "In Tokyo in November 1946 the government food ration could supply less than one-tenth of the fish, less than two-thirds of the rice, and merely one-fourth of the vegetables required for a minimum diet."[13] An indication of the teachers' distress is a directive of the Ministry of Education in April 1946 to the prefectural governors to prohibit teachers from requesting food from pupils.[14] In June 1946 teachers' salaries were delayed. Economic strife, therefore, was the primary reason the great mass of teachers joined the new teachers' unions, and for some of them their economic difficulties caused them to shed their old quiescent attitude and to take on a more militant one.

To a certain extent, the extremely high percentage of teachers who joined unions in the early postwar years may be attributed to sociological causes—that is, to the patterns of Japanese group behavior. Prewar values of paternalism,

[10] CIE, GHQ, SCAP, *A History of Teachers' Unions in Japan* (Tokyo: General Headquarters, 1948, quoting "Demands Submitted to the Minister of Education 15 October 1946," Appendix G, Part 1, p. 64).

[11] *Ibid.*, p. 10. [12] *Ibid.*, p. 11.
[13] *Ibid.*, p. 12. [14] *Ibid.*

which placed great stress on harmony within groups, did not die with the surrender. All teachers in a particular local school were accustomed to acting as a closely knit, harmonious group. They were reluctant to act in ways that might produce disharmony. Thus, teachers belonging to a particular local school were apt to join a teachers' union as a group and not as individuals. The attitude prevailed that a feeling of estrangement between teachers would develop if some entered a union and others did not. But this aspect of Japanese group behavior should not be overstressed. Although it is undeniable that some teachers joined unions merely because the majority of their group were doing so, it would be erroneous to interpret the wide-scale unionization of teachers as resulting primarily from this motive. And although some teachers, because of their lack of understanding of *demokurashii* coupled nevertheless with their desire to practice it, joined the new unions more in the sense of fulfilling a new "duty" to the new order than in the sense of exercising a new "right," it would also be erroneous to attribute the growth of unionism among teachers primarily to this factor. No doubt these attitudes played their part, but to overstress them would be to underrate the genuine desire on the part of most teachers to improve their own livelihood and to revamp the prewar educational practices that had played such a vital role in supporting the militarists' policies and in leading the country to war and defeat.[15] A final stimulant to the growth of teachers' unions in the immediate postwar period was the very fact of their initial success in winning certain demands. But this aspect of the story of the unionization of teachers is best told along with a description of the most prominent unions that emerged between December 1, 1945 and June 8, 1947, when almost all teachers' unions amalgamated into the JTU.

[15] This interpretation is not the result of any statistical study but was gleaned from numerous interviews I had in 1964-1965 with teachers who joined unions in the early days.

51

EARLY POSTWAR TEACHERS' UNIONS

Within four months after the surrender, two teachers' unions, one politically oriented around the JCP and the left Socialists and the other politically oriented around the right Socialists, had been formed in Tokyo. These two unions, although they were to change their names many times, constituted the two main strands, the warp and woof, of the early postwar teachers' union movement, later emerging as the two major factional groups within the amalgamated JTU. The first, the more radical All-Japan Teachers' Union (Zen Nihon Kyōin Kumiai, or Zenkyō) was founded on December 1, 1945, while the more moderate Japan Educators' Union (Nihon Kyōikusha Kumiai, or Nikkyō) was founded one day later. The kernel of the radical Zenkyō, a small group of elementary teachers, had first met at the home of one Ono Shunichi, an elementary teacher in Tokyo.[16] By the end of October, the Steering Committee of this group had met with four JCP members, Hani Gorō,[17] Kitamura Mago-

16 Ishii Kazutomo, *Ushinawareta Kyōiku: Nikkyōso Hakusho* (Education Lost: White Paper on the Japan Teachers' Union), Tokyo: Hobunsha, 1954, p. 506.

17 Hani Gorō, born in Gumma prefecture in 1901, graduated from the Department of Literature, Tokyo Imperial University before studying at Heidelberg University. In the prewar period he taught history at the Jiyū Gakuen (Freedom School), a Christian liberal school, and was active as a left-wing intellectual and publisher of radical books. He contributed to the famous symposium, *Nihon Shihonshugi Hattatsu-shi Kōza* (Lectures in the History of the Development of Japanese Capitalism). He was also the author of a number of books including *Fundamental Study of Shinin Sato, Study of Historical Change*, and *Political Thoughts of the People in the Last Days of the Feudal Government*. In the postwar period, besides becoming the Chairman of the All-Japan Teachers' Union (Zen Nihon Kyōin Kumiai, or Zenkyō), he was elected with the support of the Zenkyō's successor, the All-Japan Conference of Teachers' Unions (Zen Nihon Kyōin Kumiai Kyōgikai, or Zenkyōkyō), to the House of Councillors in 1947. To avoid the JCP label, he ran as an independent but quickly became associated with the doctrinaire Kuroda Hisao faction of the JSP, which in 1948 was expelled from the JSP and became a separate entity as the Worker-

mori,[18] Inagaki Masanobu, and Masubuchi Yuzuru,[19] who had just been released from prison on October 9, along with about three thousand other political prisoners, in compliance with SCAP's "Civil Liberties" directive of October 4. The significant fact about these four men is that they were Communist Party members, although this fact was not al-

Farmer Party (Rōdōsha Nōmintō, or Rōnōtō). Kuroda faction people have often been considered Communists in disguise. See Ishii Kazutomo, *Ushinawareta Kyōiku: Nikkyōso Hakusho* (Education Lost: White Paper on the Japan Teachers' Union), p. 506; Kurotaki Chikara and Itō Tadahiko, eds., *Nihon Kyōiku Undō-shi: Shōwa Shoki no Kyōiku Undō* (A History of Japan's Education Movement: The Education Movement in Early Shōwa), Vol. II, pp. 111 and 134; CIE, GHQ, SCAP, *A History of Teachers' Unions in Japan*, n. 19, p. 4; Iwama Masao (ed.), *Kyōin Kumiai Undō-shi*, p. 394; *Japan Who's Who: 1950-1951*; and Allan B. Cole, George O. Totten, and Cecil H. Uyehara, *Socialist Parties in Postwar Japan*, pp. 289-90.

[18] Kitamura Magomori, who became an elementary teacher in Tokyo in 1925, was active in the prewar teachers' union movement. Along with such leaders as Ueda Tadao and Ikeda Tsuneo (discussed in Chapter II), he was active in the League of Elementary School Teachers (Shōgakkō Kyōin Remmei) and was one of twelve teachers released from his teaching position for having participated in the January 1930 struggle against the government's suspension of increases in salaries. He then organized the New Education Institute (Shinkō Kyōiku Kenkyūsho) to help fight the legal battles of the radical Japan Educational Workers' Union (Nihon Kyōiku Rōdōsha Kumiai). Moving increasingly into the area of organizing industrial workers, he was arrested in 1941 for having organized the Workers' Committee of Industrial Machinists (Kikai Kōgyō Totei Iinkai). In 1958 he was indicted by the Prosecuting Attorney's Office of the Tokyo District Court for having participated in an "illegal" strike in connection with the anti-efficiency rating struggle. See Ishii Kazutomo, *Ushinawareta Kyōiku: Nikkyōso Hakusho* (Education Lost: White Paper on the Japan Teachers' Union), p. 506, and Munakata Seiya and Kokubu Ichitaro (eds.), *Nihon no Kyōiku* (Japanese Education) Tokyo: Iwanami Shinsho, 1962, pp. 23-27.

[19] Both men are referred to as JCP members in Ishii Kazutomo, *Ushinawareta Kyōiku: Nikkyōso Hakusho* (Education Lost: White Paper on the Japan Teachers' Union), p. 506. That Inagaki Masanobu was a JCP member is supported by a statement to that fact in CIE, GHQ, SCAP, *A History of Teachers' Unions in Japan*, n. 22, p. 13.

53

ways stressed by them in public. Hani Gorō, for example, the leader of the group, who was to become the first Chairman of the Zenkyō's Central Executive Committee, successfully ran as an independent for election to the House of Councillors in April 1947. But Hani had long been associated with Communist activities in the prewar period and his ideological position was no secret.

Because SCAP's October 4 directive guaranteed the right of organization to the people of Japan, the members of this "study group" were free to act, unhampered by police restraints. From November 18 they set out to organize a union. Letters were written to teachers who had been participants in social movements dissolved by the government before the war.[20] In response, nearly two hundred teachers gathered in Tokyo on December 1 to found the Zenkyō, which two years later was to amalgamate with other teachers' unions to form the JTU.[21]

Because the above-mentioned JCP members seized the leadership of the Zenkyō, it soon became identified in the minds of teachers and the general public with revolutionary, Communist ideology, in spite of its official welcome to all teachers of all political colorations, from ultra-nationalists to Communists. There appears to have been no significant participation in the formation of the Zenkyō by right-wingers, however. Instead, it became a rallying point for teachers discharged before the war for radicalism. Furthermore, the first issue of its weekly organ, the *Nippon Kyōiku Shimbun* (Japan Teachers' Journal), printed on the same day the union was founded, referred repeatedly to the theory of the class struggle and asserted that the union was to make a common front with the workers of Japan and to make "concerted efforts with international unions."[22] In one

[20] Japan Teachers' Union, *Nikkyōso Jūnenshi* (The Ten-Year History of the Japan Teachers' Union), Tokyo: The Union, 1958, p. 27.

[21] Iwama Masao (ed.), *Kyōin Kumiai Undō-shi* (History of the Teachers' Union Movement), p. 18.

[22] CIE, GHQ, SCAP, *A History of Teachers' Unions in Japan*, p. 16.

54

of the articles in the December 1 issue, Hani helped to stamp the Zenkyō as radical by attacking the Emperor for his failure to acknowledge his war guilt. Hani continued his attacks against the Emperor in the public press by portraying the Imperial Family as a political anachronism that served to hold the mass of people in subjugation.[23] Although this anti-Emperor posture was never officially endorsed by the Zenkyō, the fact that Hani, the Zenkyō's first chairman, published such revolutionary theories in the union's newspaper and in the public press served to identify the union with Communist thinking and tended to alienate the less radically minded teachers.

If the Zenkyō's radicalism on the question of the Emperor alienated some teachers, however, most of its initial economic and educational demands did not, even though they were also "radical." Few teachers objected to its demands to the Ministry of Education that their pay be increased five-fold or that a single salary schedule for men and women and for city and rural teachers be instituted. All teachers except a few extreme rightists favored the Zenkyō's demands that the government-sponsored Great Japan Education Association (called the Imperial Education Association until 1944) be abolished, that the school inspection system be discontinued, that militaristic and ultra-nationalist teachers be purged and re-educated, that textbooks compiled and published by the government be abolished, that a school lunch program be immediately instituted, that the union be designated as the sole collective bargaining agent for teachers, and that teachers and the public be educated for participation in democratic education and a democratic society.[24] Not all teachers agreed, however, with the

[23] See Hani Gorō, "The Position of the Emperor," *Mainichi Shimbun*, January 12 and 13, 1946.

[24] These demands are clearly outlined in the Zenkyō's "Report on Aims and Principles Adopted at the National Council," January 19 and 20, 1946. A copy of this Report was lent to the author by the Department of General Affairs of the Japan Teachers' Union.

Zenkyō's demand that principals should be elected by the general public. They feared that such a move would greatly enhance the Zenkyō's possibility of gaining control of school administration, a goal that the Zenkyō clearly desired. Such control would catapult the Zenkyō into a position of political power. Moderates feared such political power in the hands of the Zenkyō because they suspected that the Zenkyō, heavily influenced by Communist ideology, intended to use the teachers' union movement as an instrument for revolutionizing Japanese society. Nevertheless, most of the Zenkyō's radical ideas, along with the sensational demand for a 500 percent increase in salary, had tremendous propaganda value and served to attract the vast majority of the disillusioned and discontented postwar teachers into its fold.

Among those who feared that the Zenkyō intended to use the teachers' union movement primarily as an instrument for effecting a political and social revolution was Kagawa Toyohiko,[25] a well-known Christian reformer who, as a member of the Friendly Society (Yūaikai) in the prewar period, had devoted much of his life to the emancipation of the peasantry through peaceful means. Kagawa viewed the

25 Kagawa Toyohiko, a Christian and pastor, graduated from Kobe Theological School and preached the gospel to the poor before studying at Princeton University in 1916. A pioneer social worker, he became the Chairman of the Kansai Branch of the Friendly Society (Yūaikai), a labor union under the leadership of the Christian, Suzuki Bunji. In 1922, as a devoted Christian reformer in his early thirties, he organized the Japan Farmers' Union (Nippon Nōmin Kumiai) for the emancipation of the peasantry through peaceful means. After the war he organized the Union of Japanese Educators (Nihon Kyōikusha Kumiai), dedicated to the reform of education and the improvement of teachers' working conditions. He is the author of over fifty books; perhaps the two best known are *Shisen o Koete* (Before the Dawn) and *Hitotsubu no Mugi* (A Grain of Barley). See Iwao F. Ayusawa, *A History of Labor in Modern Japan*, pp. 162-63; Edwin O. Reischauer, John K. Fairbank, and Albert M. Craig, *East Asia: The Modern Transformation* (Boston: Houghton Mifflin Company, 1965), p. 569; and Sawada Fumiaki, *Nikkyōso no Rekishi* (History of the Japan Teachers' Union), pp. 109-20.

Zenkyō as a danger to Japanese society and determined to combat it by establishing a union of his own. Thus, on December 2, 1945, one day after the founding of the Zenkyō, he established the Japan Educators' Union (Nihon Kyōikusha Kumiai, or Nikkyō). Consisting chiefly of teachers of middle schools, colleges, and universities, the Nikkyō's economic demands were similar to those of the Zenkyō, but its political posture was less radical, as evidenced by its endorsement of right-wing Socialist Party candidates to the April 10, 1946 election to the House of Representatives. Fundamentally, the Nikkyō approved of the Emperor system and wished to accomplish educational reforms without violating the status quo of Japanese society. It is interesting to note, however, that, like the Zenkyō, it thoroughly disapproved of the Great Japan Education Association and demanded that it be replaced by a democratic organization independent of the Ministry of Education.

During January and February of 1946 great efforts were made to unite the two unions, but a formula for unification proved impossible. The Zenkyō, in order to appeal to the supporters of the JSP as well as the JCP, maintained that an amalgamated union should avoid party ties and that the president should be freely chosen. It refused to agree to the Nikkyō's proposal that only the Japan Socialist Party be supported and that Kagawa be elected president of the new unified union. Behind this squabble lay the deep ideological difference that the Zenkyō was prepared to revolutionize the society while the Nikkyō was not.

After the failure to unify, the moderate Nikkyō, never large in numbers in comparison to the radical Zenkyō, began to fade away when Kagawa and his faction, who favored alignment with the moderate General Federation of Labor (Sōdōmei), expelled an opposing faction further to the right that favored total abstention from the labor movement. This internal division weakened the Nikkyō and by July 1946, after changing its name to the Japan Teachers'

Union League (Nihon Kyōikusha Kumiai Rengō), it became, for all practical purposes, inactive. Most of its members were not lost to the teachers' union movement, however, because they quickly joined the newly organized National League of Teachers' Unions (Kyōin Kumiai Zenkoku Remmei, or Kyōzenren), founded on June 21, 1946. The Kyōzenren was the result of the unification of a number of teachers' unions in Tokyo and the prefectures that had sprung up in the first months of 1946. The four most important were: the Tokyo Youth School Teachers' Union (Tōkyōto Seinen Gakkō Kyōin Kumiai, or Seikyō), founded March 15; the Tokyo Middle School Educational Personnel Union (Tōkyōto Chūtō Gakkō Kyōshokuin Kumiai, or Chūkyō), founded March 19; the Tokyo Elementary School Teachers' Union (Tōkyōto Kokumin Gakkō Kyōin Kumiai or Kokkyō), founded April 25; and the Federation of Tokyo Educational Personnel Unions (Tōkyōto Kyōshokuin Kumiai Kyōgikai, or Tōkyōkyō), founded April 26. The immediate goal of all these unions, and consequently of the Kyōzenren into which they amalgamated, was the economic improvement of teachers. Equally important, however, was the Kyōzenren's demand for the democratization of education along the lines suggested by the Occupation, but, in contrast to the Zenkyō, the Kyōzenren did not regard democratization as a goal that could be achieved only through a class struggle. As did all teachers' unions, it strongly opposed the Great Japan Education Association or any other government-sponsored educational organization that teachers would be required to join.

Although the Kyōzenren united a number of minor unions, its membership was nevertheless only one-third that of the Zenkyō. This was primarily because the Kyōzenren consisted chiefly of teachers beyond the elementary level while the Zenkyō consisted chiefly of the far more numerous elementary teachers themselves. It was also partly because the elementary teachers, more rigidly controlled before the war than teachers of post-elementary schools, were more susceptible to the Zenkyō's radical program. Already by March 1946 the Zenkyō had about 60,000 members and, by setting up regional offices in Kobe, Kyoto, Nagoya, and Fukuoka, was making great efforts to incorporate the many independent prefectural teachers' unions that had sprung up throughout Japan. In July, however, in spite of the Zenkyō's efforts, the majority of the prefectural teachers' unions throughout the country still remained independent.

In connection with the initial difficulty of incorporating the prefectural teachers' unions into the Zenkyō, the "independence" of these prefectural unions is worthy of mention here. Even later in time, after joining larger federations and becoming at last part of the nationwide JTU, the prefectural unions displayed a taste for independent action. This propensity on the part of the prefectural unions, which still persists today long after federation with the JTU, stems from the fact that they were first established independently by prefectural leaders who built up their own unions without assistance or ties to any national center. Prior to the establishment of the JTU in June 1947, independent teachers' unions were already in existence in all forty-six prefectures. Many of them had been in operation for over a year. This independent inheritance of the prefectural unions has had great bearing on the JTU's style of "interest articulation" or its ability to mobilize the support, energy, and resources of its members.

At the Zenkyō's national conference of July 25 and 26, 1946, called to consider how to meet the threat of the newly created nationwide Kyōzenren, it was suggested that some prefectural unions were reluctant to join the Zenkyō because it had become Communist-dominated at the top, and that therefore it ought to change its name. Acting on this suggestion, the Zenkyō dissolved itself and reorganized on July 26 under the name of the Japan Educational Labor Union (Nihon Kyōin Rōdō Kumiai, or Nikkyōrō). In December, when this new union, still essentially consisting of the

59

elements that comprised the old Zenkyō, succeeded in incorporating the powerful Hokkaidō-Tōhoku Conference of Teachers' Unions (Hokkaidō-Tōhoku Kyōso Kyōgikai) and the Western Japan Conference of Teachers' Unions (Nishi Nihon Kyōso Kyōgikai), its name was again changed and it became the All-Japan Conference of Teachers' Unions (Zen Nihon Kyōin Kumiai Kyōgikai, or Zenkyōkyō). Table 1 diagrams this series of mergers. These two unions, the moderate and smaller Kyōzenren and the more radical and larger Zenkyōkyō, now opposed each other on a nationwide basis. They were to continue to do so until the failure of the February 1st general strike and the subsequent achievement of collective bargaining contracts with the Ministry of Education produced a situation in which the two unions began to work together, finally arriving at the conclusion that their movement would be strengthened if they merged. Consequently, at a Grand Amalgamation Meeting in Nara on June 8, 1947, one national organization, the Japan Teachers' Union, was formed.

RELATIONSHIP TO THE MINISTRY OF EDUCATION

Before proceeding with a brief sketch of the history of the JTU, outlining its major struggles and shifts in policy from 1947 to 1972, we shall give a brief account of the relationship that evolved between the teachers' unions and the Ministry of Education prior to the establishment of the JTU, as it has had considerable influence on the relationship between the JTU and the Ministry ever since. It will be remembered that the Zenkyō had not limited itself to activities designed solely to improve the economic welfare of teachers. With such Communists as Hani Gorō, Inagaki Masanobu, and Iwama Masao as members of its Central Executive Committee, it had increasingly become branded as a radical political organization. It had repeatedly attempted to justify its concern with politics by asserting that education could not be divorced from politics. Its argument

Chart Illustrating the Development of the Japan Teachers' Union

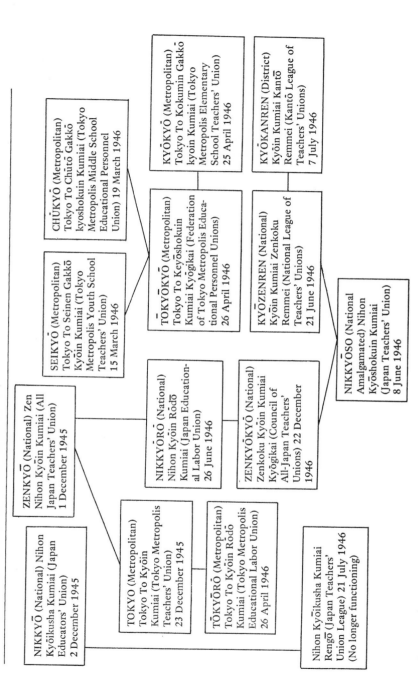

Source: Adapted from chart illustrating the establishment of the JTU, *Nikkyoso Junenshi* (Ten-Year History of the Japan Teachers' Union), Tokyo: Japan Teachers' Union, 1958, p. 9

ran that in the past education and teachers had been under the control of militarists, bureaucrats, and capitalists and in fact were still controlled by the bureaucrats and capitalists. If education was to be reformed, the Zenkyō argued, teachers had to be politically minded and identify themselves with the laboring rather than the ruling class. Thus, the Zenkyō had demanded time and again that the Ministry of Education recognize the right of teachers, who were considered by the Zenkyō as members of the laboring class, to control the schools. It had affirmed its belief in the theory of the class struggle and condemned the more moderate unions for speaking about fairness and moderation in a society in which the people were divided into classes and one class was exploiting the other for its own benefit. In short, the Zenkyō's educational reform implied social revolution.

The Zenkyō, which began to see its activities as "struggles," increasingly came to regard itself as a militant front in direct opposition to the Ministry of Education. Beginning in April 1946, a series of unpleasant confrontations between Zenkyō leaders and Ministry officials took place. For example, in that month, Zenkyō leaders, after the Vice-Minister of Education had declined to see them, forced their way into his office and demanded, among other things, that May Day be declared a holiday and that the Ministry recognize the right of teachers to control schools.[26] The rejection of these demands by the Vice-Minister created such an outburst of rage on the part of the Zenkyō leaders that the Vice-Minister was obliged to "escape from the Ministry."[27] Increasingly, the Zenkyō identified itself with the radical labor federation, Sambetsu, and on May Day 1946 its leaders and members joined the parade, carrying red flags and placards demanding decent wages and popular control of education.

Throughout the remainder of the year, Minister of Education Tanaka Kōtarō, taking the position that "unions which

[26] *Asahi Shimbun*, April 27, 1946.
[27] *Ibid.*, April 17, 1946.

aim at political or social movements are not recognized as real unions," continued to fence with the Zenkyō leaders.[28] On one occasion at the very beginning of Tanaka's tenure, Zenkyō leaders, including Inagaki Masanobu, spent the night in the Ministry in an effort to present their demands. Tanaka finally agreed to meet with them and later described the attitude of the Zenkyō leaders as "simply outrageous. . . . Inagaki read forth their resolution about teachers' pay increase with a volley of the most arrogant and insulting words absolutely beneath the dignity of educators, and denounced the Education Ministry, the Cabinet, and the Emperor. . . . He did not 'Mister' me, and even neglected the use of such common honorifics as daily social intercourse requires."[29] In the type of atmosphere created by such confrontations, little could be accomplished, although in July 1946 the Zenkyō, mounting a major struggle and joined by the efforts of the moderate Kyōzenren, succeeded in persuading the government to exclude teachers from the Labor Relations Adjustment Bill, which was to outlaw strikes by civil servants, such as postmen and state railway workers. The Zenkyō had attacked the bill not only as a government conspiracy against teachers but also as an attempt to "suppress all disputes" and "to put education again under the despotic rule of the bureaucrats."[30]

With the defeat of the anti-strike bill, the two national teachers' unions turned their attention to the question of increasing teachers' salaries. To gain the widest possible support and to dramatize the salary campaign, the Zenkyō, now the Nikkyōrō, organized a conference to which representatives of all independent unions not affiliated with either itself or the Kyōzenren were invited. According to some estimates, delegates representing three-fourths of the nation's 400,000 teachers attended this conference.[31] To

[28] CIE, GHQ, SCAP, *A History of Teachers' Unions in Japan*, p. 34, quoting Tanaka Kōtarō, "Reply to a Questionnaire," July 16, 1947.
[29] *Ibid.*, p. 35.   [30] *Kyōiku Rōdō*, July 17, 1946.
[31] *Yomiuri Shimbun*, October 27, 1946.

63

promote concerned action, a committee was formed to act as a spokesman for all unions in the salary campaign. The committee adopted the name of the National Council of Teachers' Unions to Secure a Minimum Standard of Living (Zenkoku Kyōin Kumiai Saitei Seikatsuken Kakutoku Kyō-gikai, or Zenkyōso). The Zenkyōso proposed that a ¥600 base pay be established, urged the raising of income tax exemptions, the abolition of discrimination against women teachers, the cessation of dismissals of teachers, and increases in allowances. Education Minister Tanaka received the Zenkyōso delegation on November 1, 1946. Although the interview was friendly, Tanaka's position of appearing to conciliate the delegation without meeting its demands concretely was interpreted as unacceptable.[32] Thus, on November 6, the Zenkyōso, apparently viewing negotiation with the Ministry as futile, announced its intention to resort to a strike. To strengthen its hand, the Zenkyōso decided to form a united front with other unions of civil servants, consisting of government office, railroad, and communication personnel, who were also engaged in a salary campaign. At the beginning of December, a joint campaign committee was set up to coordinate the activities of the unions. Even though the moderate Kyōzenren was having no more luck with the Ministry than the Zenkyōso, it declined an invitation by the Zenkyōso to participate in the strike. It was at this time, during the third week in December, that the unions that had cooperated under the leadership of the Zenkyōso, most noticeably the powerful Hokkaidō-Tōhoku Conference of Teachers' Unions and the Western Japan Conference of Teachers' Unions, convened in Tokyo to combine into one all-embracing organization. Representa-

[32] Tanaka, in a written reply to the Zenkyōso's demands, stated that (1) the raising of teachers' salaries without raising those of all public officials would be difficult, but that attempts to solve the salary question would be resumed "when the fiscal condition of the nation is improved"; (2) the raising of income tax exemptions would be referred to the financial authorities; and (3) the dismissals of teachers would be curtailed. *Jiji Shimpō*, November 3, 1946.

tives from 36 of the 46 prefectural unions attended and they established the new national union mentioned above, the Zenkyōkyō.[33]

A significant aspect of this amalgamation was the rise in power of a somewhat more moderate leadership within the Central Executive Committee of the Zenkyōkyō than had prevailed in the CEC of the Nikkyōrō. Iwama, for example, lost the chairmanship to the leader of the more moderate faction, Araki Masaburō, chairman of the Osaka Teachers' Union, which was affiliated with the Western Japan Conference of Teachers' Unions. In addition, the chairmen of the Hokkaidō-Tōhoku Conference of Teachers' Unions, emerged as the vice-chairman and secretary respectively. Iwama, however, retained his key post as leader of the salary campaign committee.[34] The day after the amalgamation, as teacher-demonstrators waited in the street before the Ministry of Education while Iwama conferred with the Minister, a truckload of police arrived and in the disturbance that followed several teachers were arrested. When Iwama emerged from the Ministry a few minutes later, he too was arrested. He was released, however, within a few hours.[35] The incident not only intensified the strained relations between the Zenkyōkyō and the Ministry but also thrust Iwama into the leadership of the Council of All-Japan Government and Public Office Employees' Labor Unions (Zen Kan Kocho Rōkyo, or Zenkanko), which had been

[33] One estimate states that 320,000 teachers were represented at the convention. *Shūkan Kyōiku Shimbun*, December 30, 1946.

[34] Iwama Masao (ed.), *Kyōin Kumiai Undō-shi* (History of the Teachers' Union Movement), p. 239.

[35] Varying accounts of this incident were reported in the December 24, 1946, issues of the *Mainichi Shimbun*, the *Asahi Shimbun* and the *Yomiuri Shimbun*. According to the *Mainichi* the arrests were made because the demonstrators had no permit for the public gathering and were blocking traffic. The *Asahi* stated that arrests were made following a dispute that flared up when a policeman pushed a demonstrator. The *Yomiuri*, commenting on Iwama's arrest, stated that he was taken into custody when he protested the arrest of some of his demonstrators.

65

formed to represent all unions of civil servants in the "struggle" to achieve pay increases. It was this Council, with Iwama as leader, which spearheaded the famous abortive "Ni-ichi Zene Suto," or "February 1st General Strike," the significance of which has been pointed out in the first section of this chapter.

On January 11, the Council sponsored a rally of its constituent unions to fix February 1, 1947 as the date for the general strike if its list of thirteen demands was not satisfactorily met by the government. In addition to the long-standing economic demands and those concerning unfair treatment of personnel, the list submitted to the government on January 11 contained no new demands other than that the police apologize for having arrested Zenkyōkyō members and that Prime Minister Yoshida apologize for a remark in his New Year's message warning the public against being misled by "malicious" labor leaders.[36] Although in the government's reply Yoshida apologized and promised to investigate the arrests of the Zenkyōkyō leaders, he gave no more than "assurances" that "investigations" concerning the minimum wage, allowances, and income tax reduction were being conducted. Consequently, the unions viewed the government's reply as unsatisfactory and made final preparations to carry out the general strike on February 1 as planned. As previously discussed, however, on January 31 General MacArthur issued his "Statement Calling Off General Strike."

The Zenkyōkyō immediately complied with General Mac-Arthur's "Statement," even though it informed its prefectural branches that the campaign against the Ministry would continue despite the suspension of the general strike. MacArthur's intervention, however, which dramatized the gravity of the situation, appears to have produced a more conciliatory attitude on the part of both the Zenkyōkyō and

[36] For this list of thirteen demands, see Iwama Masao (ed.), *Kyōin Kumiai Undō-shi* (History of the Teachers' Union Movement), pp. 269-70.

the Ministry. On February 13 the Ministry announced a temporary salary scale that would provide a 100 percent increase in the net pay of teachers earning ¥600 or less. On February 21 the Ministry promised to discuss the fixing of a permanent salary scale within a month. The Zenkyōkyō and the Kyōzenren accepted these measures but at the same time pressed separately for the conclusion of collective bargaining contracts. On March 8, 1947, the Zenkyōkyō finally achieved this aim by signing a contract with the Ministry that established the union as a bargaining agent for its own membership. (See Appendix A.) Three days later the Kyōzenren entered into a similar contract with the Ministry. This high point of the power of the postwar teachers' unions, marked by the historic conclusion of the first collective bargaining contracts in Japanese history between the government and the representatives of teachers' unions, was never to be reached again. To date, no further collective bargaining contracts have been signed between the government and the teachers' unions. The JTU, an organization that grew out of the amalgamation of the Zenkyōkyō and the Kyōzenren, looks back upon these contracts with great pride and points to them as examples of what can be achieved when collective bargaining is permitted.

The two unions won a series of demands that teachers' union activists had fought for ever since the 1920's. For example, based on the spirit of the Trade Union Law, the Ministry agreed to recognize each union as "an agent for collective bargaining" (Article 1) and agreed to encourage "collective bargaining agreements concerning vacations, personnel affairs, and the number of full-time union officers between prefectural chapters of the unions and prefectural governments" (Article xxi). In addition, the Ministry agreed to allow members of the contracting unions to engage full time in union affairs while maintaining their public service status as teachers (Article xiii), thereby enabling them to retain the prestige of the public servant and formal recognition as such by boards of education, even though working full time for the union and receiving their salaries from the union. Retention of their public service status as teachers also permitted union officers to continue to receive benefits from the government-as-employer, such as participation in the pension plan for teachers. The Ministry also agreed not to interfere with the political interests of the members of the unions (Article XXII) and agreed not to discharge any of the members of the unions for participating in union activities (Article XII). More concretely, the number of working hours per week was set at forty-two and the number of free study days per year at twenty (Articles V and VI). Women teachers were granted three physiological free days per month and sixteen weeks for childbirth (Article IX) and tubercular teachers were allowed three years with full pay for treatment (Article X). Each contract affirmed that the two parties would continue to negotiate in the future concerning salary schedules, the administration of personnel, working conditions, and "matters concerning education and culture" (Article XIX). An "understanding" that was written into the contracts pledged both the Ministry and the unions to work towards the unification of the teachers' unions into one single union, "so that it will be the only agent for collective bargaining with the Ministry."

FAILURE OF THE COLLECTIVE BARGAINING CONCEPT

If in March 1947 one had looked only at this final note of harmony achieved between the Ministry and the teachers' unions by the signing of the collective bargaining contracts, one might have concluded that the ensuing relationship between any newly created single national teachers' union and the Ministry would evolve on the basis of collective bargaining and that therefore this means of exerting pressure on the formulation of public policy in the fields of education and teachers' welfare would become one of the primary weapons in the union's arsenal. One might have assumed that the JTU, an amalgamation of the Zenkyōkyō and the

Kyōzenren, formed just four months after these two unions had completed separate collective bargaining contracts with the Ministry, would be able to continue to use the same tactic in reaching agreements with the Ministry. But such a conclusion would have been erroneous. The right of the new national teachers' union, the JTU, to bargain collectively at the national level as well as the right of its chapters to bargain collectively at the prefectural level was to die a quick death, as was the right to strike. The denial of the rights to bargain collectively and to strike precluded these methods as means of exerting pressure and forced the JTU to adopt different methods. However, in the light of the extreme difficulty, if not the impossibility, of the Ministry, on the one hand, to work cooperatively with a teachers' union led at the top primarily by men who wished to promote political and social revolution, and in the light of the unwillingness of many of these men, on the other hand, to work cooperatively with the Ministry without attempting to supplant its authority, it is surprising that any agreement was signed at all and perhaps not so surprising that collective bargaining as a means of settling disputes was soon discarded. In spite of the signing of the contracts, neither the Ministry nor the unions had any experience to guide them in their effort to define their respective areas of interest and to build some kind of constructive ongoing relationship. Furthermore, with the advantage of hindsight, it seems valid to interpret the Ministry's conclusion of the collective bargaining contracts in March 1947 as primarily the result of its temporary weakness vis-à-vis the unions. Certainly tradition ran counter to the acceptance on the part of Ministry officials of the necessity of independent teachers' unions. Furthermore, tradition was simply against effective use of collective bargaining as a means of settling disputes in the public sector.

Employer-employee relationships in Japan, both in governmental units and private industry, have traditionally been governed by the values of paternalism. In the *oyabun-*

kobun relationship, the *oya* or parent (employer) is in a position superior to the *ko* or child (employee). This hierarchical relationship of authority places the responsibility for the welfare of the employee upon the employer and dictates that this welfare be, in essence, the *employer's* concept of what that welfare ought to be. In such a relationship, the employee has little opportunity to participate in determining his own welfare. Collective bargaining, however, is a procedure that has evolved in democratic societies from the need for democracy on the economic side of man's life and is a procedure that gives the individual, through his representatives, the opportunity to participate in the determination of conditions of his own life. The concept of collective bargaining was foreign to the Japanese employer-employee relationship in another crucial aspect as well. Paternalism, as practiced in Japan, was based on the assumption that there were no inherent differences between the interests of the employer and employee. Collective bargaining, however, is based on the assumption that the employer-employee relationship *inevitably* generates problems between the employer and the employee because of the essential difference of interest between them. It is recognized that these differences arise because the employer wants to earn more money or keep costs down, while the employee wants to earn or save more money. The employer wants greater freedom in running his organization, while the employee wants greater freedom as an individual. The concept of collective bargaining asserts that there is nothing wrong with either position. Because differences of interest exist between them, it is recognized that neither side can be trusted to protect adequately the interests of the other. No employer, no matter how high-minded and well-intentioned, can adequately deal with his employee's interests on his own power. By the same token, no group of employees, no matter how idealistic they are, can adequately protect the employer's interests. These assumptions are in fundamental disagreement with those which lie behind the paternalistic

70

employer-employee relationship, in which theoretically neither side admits to basic differences of interest.

Since the Japanese pattern of paternalism in the employer-employee relationship has been essentially one in which the employer has assumed the responsibility for the employees and assumed that he knows what is best for them, the concept of collective bargaining is foreign to Japanese society and has not been easily assimilated. This is particularly true in the public sector of Japanese society, where the government is the employer. Even in the United States, where the concept and practice of collective bargaining has been most advanced, collective bargaining between governmental units and their respective unions has only lately come to be partially accepted. Until recently, the theory that the state is a sovereign employer and therefore by definition cannot bargain on an equal basis with its employees has retarded the use of collective bargaining in the public sphere. In Japan, where this procedure was hardly recognized in private industry before the war, and where government officials have traditionally occupied a higher status in the society than private citizens or public employees, it has been doubly difficult for the government to accept the principles and procedures of collective bargaining.

What is suggested above is that even if there had been no wide political gap between the government and the JTU, the process of developing collective bargaining machinery capable of handling disputes between the two sides would have been fraught with difficulties. Given the revolutionary color of the JTU and the Ministry's traditional attitudes, it is not surprising that the teachers' unions' rights to bargain collectively and to strike were denied them just two years after they had been granted. That these two basic rights were denied, however, greatly affected the JTU's "strategic" position in the society, thereby significantly influencing its style of pressure politics. This influence will be anlayzed in later chapters. First, however, a brief overview of the major

71

struggles of the JTU from 1947 to 1972 will help to place in context the analysis of the JTU's influence on educational policies that follows.

Major Struggles, 1947-1972

In addition to its constant demand that the rights to strike and bargain collectively be restored, the JTU has since 1947 engaged in a whole series of political, economic, and educational struggles.[37] While in the opinion of JTU leaders no struggle is wholly non-political, the term, "political struggles," as used here, is limited to those struggles against governmental domestic or foreign policies which have no direct or immediate bearing on teachers' wages, benefits, and conditions of work or on the content and administration of education. Political struggles refer, therefore, to those which arise primarily from the JTU's ideological orientation. They have been conducted throughout the postwar period against the government in concert with Japan's opposition Marxist-oriented left-wing labor unions and political parties. The overriding aim of these struggles, of course, has been to overthrow the conservative government, even though each struggle has also had more limited and specific objectives. Thus, a history of the JTU's participation in political struggles would be largely a history of Japan's postwar left-wing movement, which need not be recapitulated here. It will suffice to observe that most of the political struggles have involved foreign policy questions, stemming from the fact that the JTU, given its particular ideological bent, has consistently opposed the government's fundamentally pro-United States and pro-Western orientation. It has, for example, struggled against the retention

[37] For an excellent analysis of these struggles during the first decade, see Richard J. Smethurst, "The Origins and Policies of the Japan Teachers' Union 1945-1956," in Richard K. Beardsley (ed.), *Studies in Japanese History and Politics* (Ann Arbor: The University of Michigan Press), 1967, Occasional Papers No. 10.

of the United States-Japan Security Treaty, against the presence of American armed forces, against the Vietnam War, against the buildup of Japanese military forces, and against the signing of a treaty with South Korea. These struggles have involved hundreds of mass demonstrations and riots throughout the postwar period and have earned the JTU the bitter enmity of the government. Appealing to the people's desire for peace, however, they have had greater acceptance by the general public, although criticisms have arisen whenever tactics have become violent or disrupted education in the schools.

Participation in political struggles has been a double-edged problem for the JTU. Excessive concern with issues so remote from the daily lives of the rank and file has tended to create an almost unbridgeable gulf between the top leaders and the teachers and has led to the withdrawal of some teachers from the union. Excessive radicalism has tended to disaffect the moderates. On the other hand, weak leadership in political struggles has led to dissatisfaction among the radicals and to threats of forming splinter unions, which obviously would weaken the JTU as a whole. The latest such threat occurred over the anti-Vietnam War struggle. From 1965 to 1970 the moderate mainstream came under increasing attack from the radical anti-mainstream, particularly in certain prefectures, which demanded that the JTU conduct the anti-Vietnam War struggle with greater vigor and militancy. By capitalizing on anti-war sentiment, the anti-mainstream picked up strength, particularly at the local level. To retain the radicals within the union and avoid the possibility of an open split, the moderate leadership ordered anti-war demonstrations even in the face of criticism from both the majority moderate rank and file and the public. Because of the necessity to maintain the leadership of such political struggles, however, the moderate leaders have had little choice in such situations except to lead themselves. It is also true, nevertheless, that even without this problem, the union's fundamental disagreement with the government over the very nature of Japanese society would have assured the participation of the JTU in political struggles, to whatever degree of intensity.

In the economic sphere, the JTU has naturally demanded increases in the wages of educational personnel every year since its founding. Its economic struggle, however, has also included a host of additional related demands, such as increase in pay for teachers in remote areas, payment for overtime work, special allowance for attending education seminars, pregnancy and child-rearing leaves with pay, and payment of salary increases no later than April, the beginning of the school year. An interesting aspect of the economic struggle has been the insistence by the JTU on a single salary scale for all teachers from elementary through high school. High school teachers, who had traditionally enjoyed a higher pay scale than elementary and middle school teachers, objected to this idea, however. In addition, viewing themselves in Japan's hierarchically structured society as being higher in social status than elementary and middle school teachers, high school teachers objected to being identified with teachers of the lower levels. They also complained that their special problems as high school teachers were being slighted by the JTU because of the vast majority of lower level members. Consequently, in 1950 the Japan Senior High School Teachers' Union withdrew from the JTU.

As discussed fully in Chapter VI, the economic struggle climaxed in the great wage struggle of 1969-1970, in which the JTU finally won full implementation of the National Personnel Authority's recommendations regarding wages. A subsequent demand concerning wages takes a new and, in the light of the union's ideology, somewhat unexpected turn. Arguing that teachers are professionals and not merely laborers (in the class sense), the union is now demanding special compensation for teachers. Since this line of reasoning weakens the fundamental concept of teachers as laborers, a concept on which the JTU was founded, the orthodox anti-mainstream has opposed demands for higher wages for teachers on the grounds that they are professionals. In its view, to accede to such a concept would weaken the solidarity of teachers with the working class. So irate were members of the anti-mainstream that they physically attacked the headquarters of the JTU twice in March 1971. In spite of such problems, the economic struggle carried on by the union over the past twenty-five years has greatly benefitted the teachers of Japan.

But it has been in the field of education where the JTU has fought its fiercest struggles. Several of these are discussed in detail in Chapter VI in an attempt to analyze the JTU's influence as an interest group on educational policies. The purpose here is no more than to give a brief listing of the JTU's struggles from 1947 to 1972 in regard to the administration and content of education in order to alert the reader to the kinds of educational struggles that have engaged the union's attention and energy.

Regarding the administration of education, the first great struggle of the JTU against the educational bureaucracy was to prevent the government from changing the system of selecting boards of education members from an elective to an appointive one. Locally elected boards had been introduced by SCAP in 1948 in order to decentralize control of education. Through vigorous campaigning and propounding the view that teachers were best qualified to sit on the boards, one-third of the elected board members by 1952 were union-dominated teachers. Although the boards were actually controlled by conservative forces, the JTU was nevertheless able to bring a great deal of pressure to bear on them through the teacher members. Desiring, therefore, to reduce the power and influence of the JTU, the government passed in the Diet, in June 1956, despite JTU-led Socialist opposition of riotous proportion, a new school board bill that replaced direct election of members with appointment by the governor or local chief executive. When the new law went into effect in October 1956, teachers were reduced to occupying only eleven percent of board membership. Conservative control of education was thus assured.

A second major struggle in the field of education that has occupied the attention of the JTU throughout the postwar period has been that of opposing the re-centralization of textbook control. In the prewar period a tightly controlled system of uniform national textbooks published by the Ministry of Education had been in force. Democratization of this system after the war gave anyone the right to write and publish textbooks, but no textbook could be used in schools unless the Ministry had approved it as "suitable." Teachers were allowed to choose freely from among all approved textbooks. In 1956, along with the new school board bill, the government attempted to pass a textbook control bill that would have greatly tightened the Ministry's authority over the approval, publication, and selection of textbooks for classroom use. With the support of the JSP, Sōhyō, the majority of Japanese intellectuals, and the press, the JTU led a massive struggle against adoption of the bill and the government was successfully pressured into withdrawing it. The struggle against the re-centralization of textbook control has had to continue, however. Through Ministry practice and a series of directives, the limits of "suitability" have been considerably narrowed and final authority to choose textbooks has been shifted in effect from the teachers to the prefectural boards of education. The textbook approval system was again brought to public attention in July 1970, when the Tokyo District Court ruled that the Ministry had acted illegally and unconstitutionally in rejecting a textbook on Japanese history by the famed historian, Professor Ienaga Saburō.[38] The trial and the verdict received full

[38] For an exhaustive account of the Ienaga textbook trials, see Kyōka-sho Kentei Soshō Shien Zenkoku Renrakukai (All-Japan Council for Support of Litigation Concerning Textbook Authorization), *Kyōkasho Saiban* (Textbook Trials), Part I, Vol. 1 and 2; *Jumbi Shomen-hen* (Collection of Preliminary Documents), Part II, Vol. 1-9; *Hanketsu-hen* (Col-

press and television coverage. Basing its argument on Article 23 of the Constitution concerning academic freedom, the Court declared that "it is not permitted for the State unilaterally to require teachers to use certain textbooks, or to limit the participation of teachers in the choice of textbooks. . . ."[39] Since the Ministry has appealed to the Tokyo Higher Court, the struggle of the JTU against textbook control will necessarily continue.

A third struggle of the JTU in the educational field has been directed against the Ministry of Education Curriculum Outlines that have been sent down as detailed directives since 1958. Taking the fundamental view that curriculum changes—the content of education—ought to be the responsibility of teachers themselves and not that of the government, the JTU has opposed these changes in principle while teachers themselves have nevertheless accepted some of them in practice. Regarding curriculum change, however, the JTU, shut out from access to the Ministry, where the changes are made, has not been able to exercise any significant influence. It has instead attempted to persuade teachers not to adopt in the classrooms those changes it considers undesirable. It has been particularly insistent that teachers refuse to teach the morals courses that the Ministry began re-introducing into the compulsory school curriculum in 1958.

A fourth major struggle of the JTU against the government, one which is discussed in detail in Chapter VI and will therefore be mentioned only briefly here, was the violent and protracted struggle from 1957 on against the implementation of an efficiency rating system of teachers as

---

lection of Judicial Decisions), June 30, 1968 to June 30, 1971. See also the entire issue of *Hōritsu Jihō*, Vol. 42, September 1970, entitled *Kyōkasho Saiban Sugimoto Hanketsu* (The Sugimoto Decision Regarding the Textbook Trial), which contains interpretive articles by a number of lawyers and scholars.

[39] As quoted in Ronald P. Dore, "Textbook Censorship in Japan: The Ienaga Case," *Pacific Affairs*, Vol. 43, No. 4, Winter 1970-1971, p. 553.

demanded by the government. In a word, the JTU viewed the rating of teachers as a means of controlling them and of weeding out those thought politically undesirable. It therefore resisted the system as strongly as it could and later rendered it largely harmless through subtle means of noncooperation.

The JTU has also struggled vigorously against the nationwide achievement tests that were first administered in 1962. This struggle is also discussed in some detail in Chapter VI. Additional significant, yet low-keyed, struggles of the JTU regarding education and teachers have included the following: abolition of night guard duty for teachers and the hiring of regular guards, hiring of substitute teachers, expansion of compulsory education from nine to twelve years, retention of the comprehensive high school, increase in the number of public kindergartens and special schools for the handicapped, revision of the university entrance examination system, elimination of supplementary classes that have arisen because of the necessity for students to cram for university entrance examinations, and reduction in the teacher-pupil ratio.

A striking aspect of the JTU's major struggles has been their negative quality. They have been directed *against* governmental policies rather than *for* positive JTU-created policies. Until recently the JTU has been remiss in offering constructive alternative policies to those of the government which it opposed. Top leaders admit this lack of creativity and imagination within the JTU.[40] In the late 1960's, however, efforts were begun to correct this situation. In 1968, for example, the JTU set up a Committee for Wages and Shortening of Working Hours to provide the government with data on teachers' wage scales and working conditions in advanced Western and Communist countries. Essentially, the Committee reported that Japanese teachers are not paid as well and do not enjoy as favorable working condi-

[40] Interview with Makieda Motofumi, Secretary-General of the Japan Teachers' Union, December 4, 1970.

tions as teachers in other advanced countries and that they are not being paid in accordance with their status as professionals. A second example of the recent positive approach was the establishment in 1970 of a Special Committee for Studying the Educational System. Composed of professors, teachers, workers, women, journalists, and novelists, the Committee is charged with studying the administration of education and the 6-3-3 system of education and is to make recommendations from a constructive and comprehensive point of view on needed changes. Reflecting the new approach of the JTU is the new slogan, "Hantai teikō no undō kara sōzō no undō made" (from a movement of opposition struggle to one of creativity).

Evaluating the influence of the above-mentioned struggles requires insight into the JTU's dominant internal characteristics since they have so significantly contributed to the ability of the union to exercise effective influence. It seems appropriate, therefore, to examine in the following two chapters six important internal characteristics—ideology, objectives, organizational structure, membership, style of leadership, and degree of union consciousness—which have so greatly determined the JTU's style and effectiveness as an interest group in its effort to influence the formulation and implementation of public educational policies.

CHAPTER IV

Ideology and Objectives

ALL analysts of interest group behavior point to the importance of internal characteristics. Almond and Powell, for example, with their emphasis upon different "structures" that "perform the interest articulation function," assert that "some knowledge of the internal dynamics of interest-group behavior is useful in understanding the way certain groups perform their interest articulation functions," and that "a group's ability to mobilize the support, energy and resources of its members will surely influence its effectiveness."[1] Ishida Takeshi, Japan's leading analyst of Japanese interest group behavior, also points to the importance of internal characteristics in his hypothesis that the reliance of interest groups in Japan on the total commitment of members results in a "kind of apathy" of the members, in an absence of "active spontaneous participation" by the members, and in "carte blanche delegation of power."[2] Whether or not this hypothesis holds true for the JTU requires an analysis of its internal characteristics.

More than this, the internal characteristics of an interest group greatly affect its strategic position in society, which determines its ability to "gain access to one or more key points of decision in the government."[3] Depending on

[1] Gabriel A. Almond and G. Bingham Powell, Jr., *Comparative Politics: A Developmental Approach* (Boston: Little, Brown and Company, 1966), p. 78.

[2] Ishida Takeshi, "The Development of Interest Groups and the Pattern of Political Modernization in Japan," in Robert E. Ward (ed.), *Political Development in Modern Japan* (Princeton: Princeton University Press, 1968), p. 333.

[3] David B. Truman, *The Governmental Process: Political Interests and Public Opinion* (New York: Alfred A. Knopf, 1964), p. 264.

the relationship between the interest group and the government in power, the group may limit its exercise of pressure to institutionalized channels, may use both institutionalized and non-institutionalized channels, or may, if direct access is completely denied to it, be forced to use only non-institutionalized channels. Whatever the techniques a group uses, however, the very techniques themselves, the style with which they are used, and the degree of their effectiveness are largely determined by the nature of the group itself.

The situation in regard to the JTU is extremely complex not only because it is a "radical" interest group that nevertheless also behaves as a "regular" interest group but also because, as discussed in the following chapter, it behaves differently at its three distinct organizational levels: national, prefectural, and chapter. A number of the internal characteristics of the JTU, for example, have greatly weakened its strategic position in Japanese society at the national level and made the gaining of direct "access to key points of decision in the government" fraught with difficulty. As a result, at the national level, the JTU, while always using direct channels to the limit of its ability, has had to resort to a great extent to indirect channels in an effort to exert its influence. At the prefectural and chapter levels more direct access has been available although indirect and non-institutionalized channels have been used wherever and whenever necessary.

Before examining the specific techniques used to exert influence, however, we must analyze the internal characteristics of the JTU that have contributed so largely to the decisions to use specific techniques. The present chapter will consider the JTU's ideology and objectives, while the following chapter will consider its organizational structure, the nature of its leadership and membership, and, perhaps most important of all, the degree of union consciousness among its members.

IDEOLOGY

The obstreperous conduct of the Japan Teachers' Union has kept the educational world of postwar Japan in an uproar. That this uproar, which did not and could not have taken place under the prewar authoritarian system, has persisted and has by its noise attracted the attention and concern of the general public is an indication of the more liberal atmosphere created by the Occupation in contrast to the prewar days. It is also an indication of the rise of unions and left-wing political parties, which have blossomed in the more liberal atmosphere, and of the desire of the mainstream of the ruling Liberal-Democratic Party (LDP) not to revert to a prewar-type repressive monolithic political structure. Even though the early postwar rights of the JTU to strike, to bargain collectively, and for its members to participate in political activities have since been stripped away, the rights to organize and demonstrate, and for its leaders and members to express themselves freely, both in speech and in print, have remained. In spite of the sharp governmental crackdown on the JTU, its leaders have not been jailed for expressing views in violent disagreement with the government, as they certainly would have been under the prewar regime. Even unionists who have participated in what the government interprets as illegal strikes have for the most part not been jailed; instead, they have been arraigned in court and those found guilty have been either dismissed from their status as public service workers, fined, or warned. That the JTU, therefore, in spite of its fervent opposition to almost all governmental policies, both domestic and foreign, continues to maintain a healthy existence and is not suppressed outright is a measure of the distance Japan has traveled on the long road to democracy since the prewar days.

The JTU has been able to keep the world of Japanese education in an uproar throughout the postwar period because of its independent power and the various arguments its leaders have posed against the implementation of these policies. Their arguments against the government's educational policies and their basic posture of antagonism towards the government have stemmed from two sources: a Marxist-oriented ideology and a determination to prevent the re-creation of the prewar authoritarian educational system. These two springboards of the arguments of the JTU leaders are of course interrelated. They do, in fact, mean much the same thing for some activists, since adherence to a Marxist-oriented ideology precludes by definition the re-creation of the prewar Emperor-centered system of the society, in which education was authoritatively controlled by a reactionary government. There are, however, many rank and file who support the leadership's stand against governmental encroachment on the independence of education, not on the basis of an ideologically antagonistic view of the government, but more simply on the grounds of keeping education free of governmental control. Such individuals can readily support the JTU's position against various educational policies of the government without in the least endorsing a Marxist view of Japanese society. It is necessary to keep in mind this distinction between opposition to the government based on Marxist ideological grounds and that based on the desire to keep education free from excessive governmental control if one is to understand the high degree of support the JTU receives from its predominantly non-Marxist membership.

In explaining the adherence of the average non-Marxist teacher to a Marxist-oriented union, Robert E. Cole's analysis may be helpful.[4] Using his terminology, one may say that the vast majority of teachers support top JTU leaders not for their political beliefs but for their "value as symbols" expressing a willingness to oppose the educational bureaucracy. Since the average teacher is not class-conscious in the Marxian sense and does not feel oppressed by the capitalist

[4] Robert E. Cole, "Japanese Workers, Unions, and the Marxist Appeal," *The Japan Interpreter*, Vol. 6, Summer 1970.

class, his participation in union activities may be best understood as an "expressive" act designed to call attention to his discontent with specific aspects of his job as a teacher, and not as an "instrumental" act designed to secure the leadership's fixed political goal of revolution.

CODE OF ETHICS

The document of the JTU that most clearly expresses its Marxist-oriented ideology and its concern for protecting education from excessive bureaucratic control is the Code of Ethics (see Appendix B) adopted in 1952. The Code was written by fourteen left-wing intellectuals sympathetic to the JTU's ideological position in cooperation with the CEC of the JTU.[5] Eight of the fourteen members of the Drafting

[5] The fourteen members of the Drafting Committee were: (1) Sugō Hiroshi, graduate of the Faculty of Literature, Tokyo University, later Managing Director of the educational magazine, *Rokusan Kyōshitsu* (Six-Three Year System Schools), author of *Educational Reform, Juvenile Culture*, and *Educational Sociology*; (2) Miyahara Seiichi, graduate of Faculty of Literature, Tokyo University, later Dean of the Faculty of Pedagogy, Tokyo University, specialist in the history of education, author of *Kyōiku to Shakai* (Education and Society), *Katei to Gakkō* (Home and School), and others; (3) Katsuda Morikazu, graduate of Kyoto University, later Chairman of the Faculty of Education, Tokyo University; (4) Yanagida Kenjūrō, graduate of Kyoto University, later professor at Taihoku (Taipei) University and then at Saitama University, known for his study of philosophy and pacificism, author of *Shominshugi* (Democratism), *Gendai no Ryōshin* (Present-Day Conscience), *Nishida Tetsugaku Nyūmon* (Gateway to the Philosophy of Nishida), and others; (5) Ota Takashi, graduate of Faculty of Literature, Tokyo University, Assistant Professor of Pedagogy, Tokyo University when the Code was drafted, studied at the University of London (1956-1958), a member of Japan Pedagogical Society, Japan Educational Science Group, author of *Kindai Kyōiku to Riarizumu* (Modern Education and Realism), *Chiiki Kyōiku Keikaku* (Plans for Community Education), and others; (6) Kaigo Katsuo, graduate of the University of Literature and Science in Tokyo, Secretary-General of the Core Curriculum Federation when the Code was drafted, author of *Tōa Minzoku Kyōiku-ron* (Theories of Education of East Asian Peoples), and others; (7) Umene Satoru, graduate of the University of Literature and Science

Committee had either graduated from Tokyo Imperial University or were professors at Tokyo University in 1951 when the Code was drafted. Members also included professors at Hitotsubashi, Hōsei, and Keiō universities as well as the University of Literaure and Science at Tokyo. The po-

---

in Tokyo, appointed professor at Tokyo Education University in 1949, professor at the University of Literature and Science in Tokyo when the Code was drafted; (8) Shimizu Ikutarō, graduate of the Faculty of Literature, Tokyo University, once professor at Sophia University and editorial writer of the *Yomiuri Shimbun*, became Director of Gakushuin University after the war, sociologist and writer, author of *Shakaigaku Nōto* (Notes on Sociology), *Nihonjin* (The Japanese), and others; (9) Munakata Seiya, graduate of the Faculty of Literature, Tokyo Education University, professor at Tokyo University, Faculty of Pedagogy when the Code was drafted, specialist in educational administration, member of Japan Science Council, author of *Kyōiku Gyōseigaku Josetsu* (Introduction to Educational Administration), *Kyōiku to Kyōiku Seisaku* (Education and Educational Policy), and others; (10) Ukai Nobushige, graduate of Tokyo University, onetime professor at the Social Sciences Institute, Tokyo University, Professor of Constitutional Law at Tokyo University when the Code was drafted, later President of International Christian University, presently Professor of Constitutional Law at Aichi University; (11) Mutai Risaku, graduate of Kyoto University, onetime professor at the Taihoku (Taipei) University and later concurrently at the University of Literature and Science and Tokyo Higher Normal School, professor at Keiō University when the Code was drafted; (12) Uehara Senroku, graduate of Tokyo Higher Commercial School, became President of the same school in 1947, specialist on the history of the European economy, professor at Hitotsubashi University when the Code was drafted, author of *Rekishi-teki Seisatsu no Shin Taishō* (New Objects of Historical Study), *Doitsu Chūsei no Shakai to Keizai* (Society and Economics in Medieval Germany), *Heiwa no Sōzō* (For the Creation of Peace), and others; (13) Nakajima Kenzō, graduate of Department of French Literature, Tokyo University, organizer of the Japan Writers' Association established in 1946, professor at Tokyo University when the Code was drafted, a JCP member and frequent visitor to Communist China as President of the Japan-China Cultural Exchange Association, author of *Kaigi to Shōchō* (Skeptic and Symbol), *Hikaku Bungaku Josetsu* (Introduction to Comparative Literature), *Andore Jiido* (Andre Gide), and others; (14) Hani Setsuko, graduate of Jiyū Gakuen (Freedom School), onetime staff member of the magazine *Fujin no Tomo* (Women's Friend), and leader in the movement for the emancipation of litical views of the members of the Drafting Committee ranged from those of men like Ukai Nobushige, who later became the President of International Christian University and who in 1951 was Professor of Constitutional Law at Tokyo University, to men like Nakajima Kenzō, a JCP member and later a frequent visitor to Communist China as President of the Japan-China Cultural Exchange Association. The Committee also included Miyahara Seiichi, one of the union's most articulate and prolific defenders, who at the time the Code was drafted was an Assistant Professor in the Faculty of Pedagogy of Tokyo University; it also included progressive liberals as well. The final draft was cated exclusively at the Jiyū Gakuen (Freedom School) founded by her family and who was a social critic in 1951. The Drafting Committee, though predominantly Marxist, included progressive liberals as well. The final draft was discussed at the 19th meeting of the CEC in July 1951 and adopted as the official draft at the 20th meeting in August 1951. Between that date and the 9th annual convention in June 1952, the draft was reportedly submitted to the entire membership of the JTU for discussion. It was adopted at the 9th convention.[6]

The Code spells out the basic ethical lines that teachers ought to follow. Although the 1952 Code has been softened by an amended version adopted in 1961, which tones down some of the Marxist terminology, the original Code best

---

women, after the war organized and became the Director of the Japan Society for the Protection of Children, regarded as a social critic at the time the Code was drafted. See Japan Teachers' Union, *Nikkyōso Jūnen-shi* (Ten-Year History of the Japan Teachers' Union), pp. 208-11 and 225-32; *Nihon Meishi Nenkan*; Japan Teachers' Union, *Nikkyōso Nijūnen-shi* (Twenty-Year History of the Japan Teachers' Union) (Tokyo: Japan Teachers' Union, 1968), pp. 292-99; *Japan Biographical Encyclopedia and Who's Who, 1958; The Japan Who's Who, 1950-1951*; and "Biography," *JSPIJ*, Vol. 1, No. 3, December 1963, pp. 132-37.

[6] Japan Teachers' Union, *Nikkyōso Jūnen-shi* (Ten-Year History of the Japan Teachers' Union), pp. 208-11, 225-32.

illustrates the underlying ideological position of the JTU leaders that has governed their actions throughout the postwar period. While refraining from using the term "class struggle," the Code nevertheless clearly reflects the Marxist view of history as one of class struggle by declaring that the teachers of Japan "at the present stage of history . . . shall be aware of their position as laborers" whose responsibility it is to work with the laboring class as a whole "for the realization of a new society" (Article VIII). The Marxist view of history is further evident in the Code in the second paragraph of the introduction, which, in its definition of the term "code of ethics," refers to the "historical tasks that have been bestowed upon a people within a specific historical period." Other sections of the Code stress the "historical tasks of protecting peace" (Article I), the creation of a "new culture of the working man" (Article VII), and the unity of the teachers of Japan "with the teachers of the world and . . . with all laborers" (Article X).

That the Code was drawn up and adopted in 1951 and 1952 can be explained by the growing conviction of the JTU leaders that the Japanese government was once again leading the country towards war. In their eyes the government by 1951 had shifted from peace to preparation for war and was pressing for rearmament and for revision of the "peace" Constitution. The outbreak of the Korean conflict, the possibility of the conclusion of a peace treaty without the signature of the Soviet Union, the possibility of Japan's becoming closely allied to the United States through a mutual security agreement, the establishment of the Police Reserve Force, the expansion of American bases in Japan, and the upsurge of divisive arguments over revision of the Constitution to allow rearmament, had resulted in the adoption by the National Convention of the JTU in May 1951 of the firmly stated policy "to fight to the finish to eliminate reactionary forces that would spark a war."[7] It was this same

[7] Miyahara Seiichi, "The Japan Teachers' Union and Its Code of Ethics," *JSPIJ*, Vol. 1, No. 3, December 1963, pp. 102-05, quoting the

convention that, dominated by a fear of what the delegates interpreted to be a growing governmental reactionary movement, resolved that a Code of Ethics should be written that would embody the aim of fighting reactionary forces and adopted the extremely appealing slogan, still in use today, "Never again send children to the battlefield."

It should be emphasized that this hardening of JTU policy was consistent with the shift at the time in the Japanese labor movement as a whole. In this sense the JTU was acting in harmony with the mainstream of the left wing. In fact, the delegates at the May 1951 JTU National Conference pledged to adhere to the Four Principles of Peace as previously adopted by Sōhyō: (1) the signing of a peace treaty with all of the Allied Powers, including the Soviet Union, (2) the withdrawal of foreign bases from Japanese soil, (3) the adoption of a policy of neutrality for Japan, and (4) opposition to Japan's rearmament. The Code of Ethics may be viewed, therefore, as a reaction to what JTU leaders considered an ominous trend in Japanese domestic and foreign policies and as an instrument for protecting the Four Principles of Peace. To the union activists in 1951 peace could best be achieved by opposing Japan's "monopoly capital, which was trying at the expense of the workers to make Japan into a war plant in order to protect the interests of the capitalists."[8] Consequently, the Code is a blend of the JTU's genuine desire to maintain peace and its firm belief that the best way to do so is for teachers to recognize their "historical tasks"; that is, for teachers to realize that they are laborers and that they must unite in order to resist "stagnation and reaction," which are their enemies, and to create a "new society of mankind that respects fundamental human

---

policy statement issued by the Eighth National Convention of the JTU that met at Kinosaki, Hyōgo Prefecture, in May 1951.

[8] Imamiya Kohei, *Nikkyōso: Kikō to Sono Seikaku* (The Japan Teachers' Union: Its Organization and Characteristics), Tokyo: Shin Kigensha, 1957, p. 14.

rights . . . and that utilizes resources, technology, and science for the welfare of all men" (Article VIII).

But the Code reflects much more than this Marxist view of history and definition of contemporary Japanese society for which its enemies criticize it so severely. Quite clearly, it cannot be understood solely in Marxist terms and certainly its appeal to Japanese teachers cannot be explained solely on the basis of its Marxist-oriented ideology. Much of the appeal of the Code stems from the fact that it articulates the antipathy of many of the teachers to the prewar authoritarian educational system, in spite of its Marxist-tinged terminology. Article VI, for example, states: "Successive governments, under the pretext of making education politically neutral, have long deprived the teachers of Japan of their freedoms and have forced them to serve in whatever way the government has desired. After the war, having been given the freedom to participate in political activities, teachers banded together and fought for proper government, but now such political freedom is again being taken away from them. . . . Teachers, together with all working men, shall participate in political activities and shall pool their resources in seeking proper government." Although "proper government" in this sixth precept of the Code is interpreted by the Marxist-oriented believer to mean government by the laboring class, it means to non-Marxist believers in the Code merely any government that is responsive to the will of the people. Both Marxists and non-Marxists are able to support this precept therefore.

The Code also has appeal to many non-Marxist (as well as Marxist) teachers because it stresses the postwar rights and duties of teachers in such a way as to express their disapproval of the status and behavior of teachers in the prewar period. Article IX, for example, forcefully makes the point that teachers have the right to protect their own livelihood: "Having been forced thus far to live in noble poverty under the proud name of educator, teachers have been ashamed to voice their demands for even the minimum material benefits necessary for their existence. To demand just recompense for their own labors would have been unthinkable to teachers of the past. . . . Teachers shall consider it their right and duty to protect their own right to maintain a minimum standard of living and to fight for optimum conditions under which to live and labor." As corroborated statistically in the following chapter, perhaps the greatest achievement of the JTU in the light of the prewar role of teachers is that the vast majority of teachers have come to believe that the above statement is true, that teachers do have the right and duty "to demand just recompense for their own labors."

SHIFT IN INTERPRETATION

During the decade of the 1960's the JTU leaders' interpretation of the union's ideology as expressed in the 1952 Code of Ethics underwent slight but significant changes. Regarding the fundamental concept that teachers are laborers, JTU leaders began to play down the class aspect of the word *rōdōsha*, the term normally used for laborers in the Marxist sense and used in the Code when defining teachers as laborers, and to stress instead the "wage earner" nuance of the word. Having met resistance from the general public, the Ministry of Education, and the teachers themselves, the JTU leadership began to emphasize not so much the class aspect of teachers but rather their function as wage earners. Secretary-General Makieda stated in 1965, for example, "The JTU has dared to define teachers as people who work for their living, rather than as people who participate in a 'sacred mission' as was done before the war."[9] The reinterpretation of the Code went slightly further. Chairman Miyanohara broadened the JTU's definition of teachers by advancing his well-known "two wheel" theory in which he argued that teachers are not only laborers or wage earners but also professionals. Teachers have two as-

[9] Interview with Makieda Motofumi, February 13, 1965.

90

pects, argued Miyanohara: as laborers, they have the right to demand better wages and working conditions; as professionals, they have the right to participate in the formulation of educational policies and to prevent the distortion of education by the government. In the chairman's view, the fact that teachers are professionals obligates them to become involved in political struggles, since they must not permit their authority as professionals to be undermined by unfavorable educational policies pursued by the government. Miyanohara's main point is that the JTU is not only a union limited merely to the objective of winning higher salaries, a function related to the aspect of teachers as laborers, but one vitally concerned with the right of teachers to make their own decisions regarding educational policies, a function related to their aspect as professionals.[10]

That the JTU's ideology has come to stress that teachers are not only *rōdōsha* (laborers), but also *kyōiku rōdōsha* (educational laborers), placing much emphasis on *kyōiku* (educational, or for the purpose of the discussion here, professional), stems from the realization by union leaders that the Japanese public, including the teachers themselves, has not responded favorably to the idea that teachers are merely laborers. Although the concept has been accepted to a degree, the limitation of teachers to this definition has gone against the historical attitude of the Japanese people toward the teacher. Given this reality of Japanese society, it became imperative for the JTU to distinguish teachers from ordinary workers. For this reason, JTU leaders came to emphasize the professional aspect of teachers while insisting at the same time that they were also laborers.

In spite of this emphasis, however, in 1970 JTU leaders still adhered firmly to their original ideology based on class consciousness. They still expressed their ideas within the limited framework of Marxism-Leninism and appeared, particularly at the national level, unable and unwilling to

[10] Tominaga Kenichi, "Semmon Shokugyō no Shakai-teki Chii" (The Social Status of Professionals), *Chūō Kōron*, February 1966.

91

break away from this framework and its terminology. Their position was against the direction in which the Japanese labor movement as a whole was moving. For by 1970 two factors had become apparent: first, that the leadership of the labor movement, which had been dominated since the war by public workers' unions, was being challenged by private unions; and, secondly, that, as the private unions increased their power, the possibility of the unification of labor not based on class consciousness was becoming greater. In short, the labor movement as a whole was moving to the right and losing its class consciousness. This long-talked-about movement, one which the JTU was firmly against, was gaining momentum and paralleled the decline in the strength of the JSP, which suffered a disastrous defeat at the polls in December 1969 by losing fifty seats in the House of Representatives. Reflected against this development, the ideological stance of the JTU leaders caused its political position within the labor movement to appear further to the left than it had been throughout the 1960's. The position of the JTU leaders cannot be attributed solely to ideological rigidity, however, as it was evident in 1970 that they were attempting to prevent a major split in the union by radical prefectural unions centered in Kyushu, particularly Fukuoka. Nevertheless, their position posed the possibility that in the decade of the 1970's the mainstream of the Japanese labor movement would pass them by. Miyanohara, speaking for the JTU at its National Convention in June 1970, was clear on the JTU's position: "We oppose the unification of labor on an anti-Communist basis. We do not agree with any unification of labor that would be based on the cooperation of labor and capital. We have severe criticisms of the JCP but it is not our enemy when we confront monopoly capitalism."[11]

11 *Kōan Jōhō*, "Nikkyōso Taikai no Jōkyō to Tokuchō-ten ni Tsuite" (The General Situation and Distinctive Features of the Japan Teachers' Union Annual Conference), June 1970.

To date, therefore, the general tenor of the JTU's Marxist-oriented ideology that has been espoused by its leaders and that has demanded the establishment of a new social order by eliminating the present rule of monopolistic capital, has caused the JTU, at least at the national level, to be an anti-status-quo interest group and to remain within the mainstream of left-wing Japanese politics. Thus the JTU as an interest group within the renovationist camp has been constantly plagued, particularly at the national level, by its inability to gain ready access to governmental leaders and agencies concerned with education that have been in power since 1947 and that are still reluctant to accept the notion that an *independent* teachers' union is necessary or ought to exist. In the context of Japanese politics and society, therefore, this particular internal characteristic of the JTU —its ideology—has placed it in an unfavorable strategic position that, in turn, has caused it to resort to a variety of non-institutionalized channels to achieve its objectives. But first, the objectives themselves need clarification.

OBJECTIVES

The objectives of the JTU, which flow naturally from its ideology, are numerous, but perhaps can be best discussed under three rubrics: (1) to establish "democratic" education, (2) to raise the economic, social, and political status of teachers, and (3) to contribute to the construction of a "democratic" country, loving peace and freedom.[12] Regarding the first objective, democratic education, it has been defined by Secretary-General Makieda as "education of, by, and for the people. It is education that is not controlled by any existing government or by the particular political party that happens to possess the reins of government. Democratic education is education that is con-

[12] Japan Teachers' Union, *Japan Teachers' Union: Its Organization and Movement* (Tokyo: Japan Teachers' Union), 1966, p. 2.

93

trolled by the 'people' and not by the 'bureaucracy.' "[13] A similar view is reflected by the former chairman of the JTU, Kobayashi Takeshi, who has written that "democratic education is education that belongs to the people and does not reflect only the policies of the government in power at any particular time. Education should not be used for the purpose of executing the government's policies."[14] This definition is also given by Munakata Seiya, a leading spokesman for the JTU, who has written that democratic education is tantamount to "autonomy in education," or education that is not "controlled by outside political authorities."[15]

With this definition of democratic education and with the JTU's belief that the present content and the present administrative system of education in Japan is non-democratic and essentially for the benefit of the ruling class, it becomes understandable that the establishment of democratic education by the JTU would be tantamount to overturning the existing state of affairs and placing the control of education in the hands of the "people." In this sense, democratic education is "people's education" and the aim of the JTU is to create a new political situation through political means that will enable the "people" to control education. This makes the establishment of democratic education a political movement; therefore, the JTU naturally takes the position that education and politics cannot and ought not to be separate. It does not agree with the government's argument that education should be "politically neutral." It takes the position that "political neutrality in education" is theoretically impossible. It argues that the government, in the name of political neutrality, actually fosters the partisan views of the

[13] Interview with Makieda Motofumi, February 13, 1965.

[14] Letter from Kobayashi Takeshi to Minister of Education Araki Masuo, August 18, 1960, quoted in *Kyōshokuin Dantai-ra Kankei Shiryō* (Data Concerning Educational Personnel Organizations) (Tokyo: Ministry of Education, February 1964), an unpublished report lent to the author by Sawada Michiya in 1965.

[15] Munakata Seiya, *Watakushi no Kyōiku Sengen* (My Declaration on Education) (Tokyo: Iwanami Shoten, 1958), pp. 4-11.

LDP while at the same time ignoring the views of the opposition parties and the JTU. While this is no doubt true to a large extent, the reverse is also true, for what makes the assertion by the above-mentioned JTU leaders that democratic education is "education not controlled by any particular party" ring somewhat hollow is that the JTU itself, as will be discussed more fully in Chapter VI, is closely tied to a particular political party, the Japan Socialist Party. The JTU argues, however, that the close association between the JTU and the JSP does not mean that the JTU is subject to JSP partisan views. In fact, argues the JTU, the educational policies of the JSP are dictated to it by the JTU. Since it is the belief of the JTU that it in turn represents the voice of the people in educational matters, it follows that the JSP educational policies are not narrowly partisan but desired by the "people" themselves. The fallacy of this argument lies not in the assertion that the JSP's educational policies are determined by the JTU but in the JTU's contention that it represents the voice of the whole people. Given the JTU's ideology, which too simply divides Japanese society into the ruling class and the "people," categorizes teachers as laborers, and sees itself as the vanguard of the people in the world of education, the assertion is understandable but it is highly questionable. The JTU by no means represents the voice of the whole people and in the real world, as opposed to the JTU's ideological world, such an assertion is preposterous. Teachers are only one of many groups in the society concerned with education, and for the JTU to claim that it represents the voice of the whole people is an unhappy example of how ideology can obfuscate reality.

The JTU bases its argument that education is not at present democratic on Article x of the 1947 Fundamental Law of Education (see Appendix C), which states: "Education shall not be subject to improper control but it shall be directly responsible to the whole people. School administration shall, on the basis of this realization, aim at the adjustment and establishment of the various conditions required

95

for the pursuit of the aim of education." The JTU's interpretation of this article,[16] as expressed by Munakata Seiya, rests on its interpretation of the phrase "various conditions required for the pursuit of the aim of education." To Munakata, "various conditions" refers only to the physical facilities "required for the pursuit of the aim of education" and not to the *content* of education. Therefore, "school administration" ought not to be concerned with "internal matters," but only with "external matters." When "school administration" does concern itself with "internal matters," or the *content*, of education, it violates the spirit of Article x and engages in exercising "improper control."

Munakata justifies his contention that "school administration" that concerns itself with the content of education constitutes "improper control" by the following argument: "First, to have the state decide on matters relating to our value system, or to be more concrete, on what the contents of a course on ethics should be, is in conflict with our Constitution, which guarantees freedom of thought and conscience. Second, it would be contrary to the intent of Paragraph 1 of Article x of the Fundamental Law of Education to have the administration of education controlled by a value system decided on by the National Diet."[17] Munakata reinforces this argument by pointing to Article xix of the 1947 Constitution, which states that "Freedom of thought

[16] See, for example, Adachi Kenji, "Kyōiku Kihonhō Daijūjō no Kaishaku" (An Interpretation of Article x of the Fundamental Law of Education), *Gakkō Keiei*, November 1960, pp. 12-19; Educational Laws Study Circle, *Kyōiku Kihonhō no Kaisetsu* (Commentaries on the Fundamental Law of Education), Tokyo: Kunitachi Shoin, 1947, p. 150; Munakata Seiya, *Kyōiku to Kyōiku Seisaku* (Education and Educational Policies), Tokyo: Iwanami Shoten, 1961, pp. 65-110; Rōyama Masamichi, "Seiji to Kyōiku" (Politics and Education), *Rōyama Masamichi Hyōron Chosakushū* (Collection of Rōyama Masamichi's Critical Essays), Vol. iv, Tokyo: Chūō Kōronsha, 1962, pp. 2-30; Tanaka Kōtarō, *Kyōiku Kihonhō no Riron* (The Theory of the Fundamental Law of Education), Tokyo: Yūhikaku, 1961, pp. 1-230.

[17] Munakata Seiya, *Kyōiku to Kyōiku Seisaku* (Education and Educational Policies), p. 56.

and conscience shall not be violated." In his view, if the government were to determine the content of courses, it would be in violation of this article. Thus, his basic point is that "improper control" remains improper even when legalized. Supposedly, democratic education, as defined by the JTU, would not tolerate the use of such "improper control."

The JTU's underlying objective of establishing democratic education has shaped its educational policies and determined its fierce struggles against all governmental policy initiatives that, in its view, might result in "improper control" over education by the Ministry of Education. Thus it fought vigorously against the creation of appointive boards of education that it felt would establish Ministerial control over the boards, resisted fiercely the implementation of an efficiency rating system for teachers and principals that it felt would establish Ministerial control over principals as well as over teachers, refused to cooperate with the reimposition of special classes for moral education that it felt would establish Ministerial control over students, and struggled against the carrying out of the nationwide achievement tests and revisions in the textbook approval system that it felt would confirm the Ministry's control over the content of education. The techniques of the JTU in resisting these Ministry-initiated policies will be discussed in Chapter VI. It is sufficient to point out here that resistance, on the one hand, to increasing bureaucratic control and the establishment, on the other hand, of a truly decentralized administrative system of education have been the two sides of the same coin of establishing democratic education.

In its effort to establish democratic education the JTU has talked consistently of *kokumin kyōiku*, or people's education, which is concerned with the development of a new kind of person, in contrast to the prewar person, whom the JTU considers the present and future society of Japan requires.[18] In the JTU's view the prewar *kokumin* were mere-

[18] For a thorough discussion of the JTU's interpretation of *kokumin kyōiku*, see *Kokumin Kyōiku*, (People's Education), edited by the Nikkyōso Sengen-bu (Propaganda Section of the JTU), Tokyo: Gōdō Shinsho, 1958.

97

ly subjects of the Emperor who were taught not to think of themselves as independent members of society possessing their own thoughts and political power. They were left purposely unaware of their rights and were not conscious of the evils capitalism produced in their society. Consequently, unable to perceive events as they really were, they unwittingly served the interests of the imperial regime and the militarists. The aim of *kokumin kyōiku* is to change the prewar consciousness of the Japanese people and to create *atarashii kokumin* or "new people."[19] This process is referred to as the revolutionizing of the people's consciousness.

Atarashii kokumin are individuals who see the conditions of society as they really are, who are fully aware of their value as independent members of the society, and who are able to recognize and judge Japan's domestic and foreign problems by themselves. There is an assumption among the JTU writers that an individual who has become an *atarashii kokumin* will be different from individuals in prewar Japan who were not able to "see" clearly what was happening. There is general agreement that once the new person's vision of Japanese society is clarified, he will view the existing government as reactionary and dangerous. Once again, the whole concept of the "new person"—both how to create him and the type of individual he will be—borrows much from Marxist thinking. There is therefore the tendency among JTU writers to expound on the notion that the *atarashii kokumin* will hold a "correct" view of Japanese society and the world, a phenomenon that, if achieved, would make the "new person" as blind as was the old prewar stereotype. But the effort to create the "new person" is nevertheless at the heart of the JTU's desire to establish democratic education.

As an additional aspect of its objective to establish democratic education, the JTU has been concerned with intro-

19 For a discussion of *atarashii kokumin*, see Uehara Senroku, "Kokumin Kyōiku ni Tsuite" (Concerning People's Education), in *ibid.*, pp. 31-47.

ducing into Japanese education new teaching methods. In its effort to wipe out "feudal" practices in which the teacher accepted course outlines as decided by superiors and in which the teacher in his relationship to students assumed the role of an absolute judge of good and bad and of right and wrong, the JTU, especially since instituting the annual Educational Study Conferences in 1952, has stressed relating education to the personal experience of the child. Advocating a method that has come to be called "life guidance," the JTU urged teachers to build courses around student compositions about their daily life activities. The underlying idea was to change the student's reliance for knowledge on his teacher and textbook, which was the essence of the prewar approach, to a new situation in which, with the guidance of the teacher, students would begin to learn by analyzing their own lives and by sharing ideas with each other. The goal of this method of education was to benefit the student rather than to indoctrinate him. At the same time, however, it must be acknowledged that JTU activists who put this method of teaching into practice indulged in their own indoctrination techniques. One famous teacher, Muchaku Seikyō, who practiced this method in Yamagata Prefecture in 1952 and 1953, collected a number of children's essays and had them published under the title *Echoes from a Mountain School*. In explaining his technique, Muchaku wrote: "I am most anxious that these children should know about social conditions in their country and especially in their own community and that they should become interested in improving them. Simply reading their textbooks on Social Science did not seem sufficient, so I conceived the idea of having the pupils write school compositions about their own special problems and their thoughts on life in general."[20]

This collection of little essays immediately became a best seller as well as a successful movie. The particular essays

[20] Muchaku Seikyō, ed. *Echoes from a Mountain School* (Tokyo: Kenkyūsha, 1953), p. iv.

selected for publication, however, blatantly reveal the political bias of Muchaku. One cannot read these compositions without wondering how much red penciling Muchaku did before they were published. Without strict "guidance" from Muchaku, which would be tantamount to the rigid indoctrination imparted by teachers before the war, it is unbelievable that these students in a remote area of Yamagata would uniformly write of death, disease, poverty, the horrors of war, the inequities of the existing society, and their determination to improve society when they grow up.

Further indication that many of these efforts were marred by an ideological rigidity just as onerous although different from that of the prewar days was revealed by the famous Yamaguchi Diary incident, which exploded on the educational scene in 1953 when the Yamaguchi Teachers' Union collected, edited, and published the diaries of primary and junior high school students for use in the classroom. It selected various student compositions that the Yamaguchi Union, then part of the heavily Communist-influenced mainstream of the JTU, considered appropriate for its "peace education." The following editorial passage from the book of collected diaries clearly reveals the ideological bias of this particular union-supported educational technique. (The passage is quoted from the *JSPIJ* and the editorial comments in the parentheses are by the editor of *JSPIJ*.) "Every year we are spending a lot of money to make the padlock called military rearmament bigger and bigger but the burglars [meaning the Soviet Union and China—Ed.] haven't come yet. While we were concentrating on making the lock on the front door bigger and bigger we left the back door wide open and a fine gentleman [meaning America—Ed.] came in in his muddy shoes and took 806 [the number of American military installations in Japan—Ed.] valuable articles out of our house."[21]

21 Editorial Staff, *Asahi Jānaru*, "The Altered Image of Teachers," *JSPIJ*, Vol. 1, No. 3, December 1963, p. 107.

Although the ideological bias revealed in both *Echoes from a Mountain School* and *The Yamaguchi Diary* may not have reflected the views of the majority of the members of the JTU, they clearly suggest that in the early 1950's the activists were using the "life guidance" technique of teaching in order to promote a particular political viewpoint. On this score the JTU appears to be even more guilty than the Ministry of Education, although in recent years it has become less strident and has placed less emphasis in its Educational Study Conferences on ideology, on its point of view regarding the present nature of Japanese society, and on its vision of the kind of society the JTU ought to help Japan create. It now places greater, but not nearly enough, stress on the practical problem of making lesson plans, creating units of study, and improving teaching techniques, even though it is still concerned with the solving of present-day social problems and even though it still publishes a teacher's handbook for each course discussing the point of view from which the course ought to be taught.[22]

The goal of the JTU, therefore, in establishing democratic education is to establish an educational system that will not be "improperly controlled" by the governmental bureaucracy and that will, to quote Munakata again, "teach the truth about Japanese society," all of which, still to a number of activists if not to the average teacher, means to teach students how to struggle against the present undesirable social, economic, and political realities in Japan.

The second major objective of the JTU is to raise the economic, social, and political status of the teachers of Japan.

[22] Interview with Fukushi Shunro and Ōsawa Toshinari, English teachers at Iwate University Attached Junior High School, October 14, 1964. A single copy of the JTU's handbook for a particular course is sent to each school. It is not geared to a particular text, but to the nature of the course in general, clarifying from the union's point of view the problems that exist in the particular field. Few teachers look at the handbook, since most of them use the teacher's manuals that are invariably published simultaneously with the textbook.

101

In an effort to improve the economic welfare of teachers, the JTU over the past twenty years has made a wide range of demands. In addition to struggling annually for across-the-board wage increases, it has demanded increases in remote area salaries, in retirement pay, in bonuses, in tax exemptions, and in the number of days with pay for sickness, childbirth, and study time. It has also demanded that the number of years it takes to reach maximum salary be reduced. Although the specific methods used by the JTU at the national and local levels to win salary increases and fringe benefits for teachers are discussed in Chapter VI in the context of the JTU's techniques of exerting pressure upon governmental bodies, it is necessary to point out here, in connection with the objectives of the JTU, that these methods have apparently produced results. To what extent the general postwar rise in teachers' salaries would have occurred without the persistent demands of the JTU is, of course, impossible to determine. What is evident, however, is that salaries have increased. An indication of this improvement may be gleaned from the rise in the national average of public elementary school teachers' salaries from ¥21,500 ($60) a month in 1959 to ¥48,000 ($133.33) a month in 1966.[23] What is also evident is that most education officials[24] as well as an overwhelming percentage of teacher-union members are convinced that the JTU has been instrumental in bringing about such increases. This is substantiated by the fact that of 222 elementary and lower secondary teacher-union members in Tokyo, Sendai, and Morioka who completed a questionnaire submitted by this writer in the summer of 1965, 97.3 percent, in answering the

23 Ministry of Education, *Education in Japan: A Graphic Presentation* (Tokyo: Ministry of Education), 1961 and 1967.

24 All Ministry of Education officials as well as prefectural boards of education officials with whom this writer has had contact admit that teachers' salaries certainly would have improved throughout the postwar period without the existence of the JTU but that salaries have risen much faster because of JTU pressure. (See bibliography for list of officials interviewed.)

102

question, "Do you think the JTU is necessary for the protection of the teachers' livelihood?" responded that the JTU was either "very necessary" (62.6 percent) or "necessary" (34.7 percent). This extremely high percentage is a strong indication that the members of the JTU are fully aware of the union's economic objective of raising their salaries and that they believe its influence has been indispensable. Awareness of this aspect of the JTU's activities helps to explain the willingness of many of the teachers to support the JTU even though they may not agree with the ideological convictions espoused by its leaders.

In its effort to raise the social status or prestige of teachers, the JTU has harped on the viewpoint, contrary to that held in Japan's traditional society, that teachers who agitate for increased wages do not degrade themselves. In refuting the charges that teachers are degraded by defining themselves as laborers and by participating in union activities, including demonstrations, Kobayashi Takeshi, Chairman of the JTU for eight years, has stated that "to call a teacher a laborer is not to degrade him and to think in such a way is the fault of the Japanese society."[25] Enhancement of the prestige of teachers has also been attempted on the part of the JTU by demanding improvement in their working conditions and expansion of their rights. For example, the JTU has consistently demanded that the teacher-pupil ratio in elementary and lower secondary schools be decreased, that the number of teaching hours per week in the elementary schools be reduced from 30 to 24 and in the lower secondary schools from 26 to 21, that teachers not be transferred from one teaching post to another against their will, that teachers be permitted to select their own textbooks, that machinery be provided for the protection of teachers against unjust administrative action, and that the Ministry

[25] Kobayashi Takeshi, "Nikkyōso's View of Education," *Kingu*, March 1957, as translated in *Summaries of Selected Japanese Magazines* (Tokyo: American Embassy, Translation Services Branch), February 18, 1957.

of Education negotiate with the JTU at the national level. The achievement of these aims, particularly the last, would contribute considerably to increasing the prestige of the elementary teachers of Japan.

The JTU has also taken the position that the social status of teachers would be increased if all teachers were made aware of their rights and exercised them fully. Consequently, the national union as well as the prefectural unions have placed a great deal of emphasis upon informing teachers of their rights. The Iwate Prefectural Teachers' Union, for example, in a pamphlet prepared annually for all new teachers, discusses these rights in considerable detail.[26] Under a section entitled "Watakushitachi no Kenri" (Our Rights), the pamphlet stresses: (1) the maximum number of hours per week a teacher can be compelled to work, (2) the regulations governing overtime pay, (3) the number of minutes of recess a teacher is entitled to in an eight-hour working day, (4) the number of annual paid holidays, (5) the number of days off with pay women teachers may have for childbirth, (6) the regulations regarding time off for further education, (7) the right of teachers to organize and to negotiate with local public bodies, and (8) the right to file claim if a teacher feels he has been unjustly treated. In Iwate prefecture at the beginning of each new school year, time is set aside at union chapter meetings to clarify these rights, to explain the history and purpose of the Iwate Teachers' Union as well as the national JTU, and to encourage teachers to give the union their support. These efforts are made not only to gain new members, but also to instill in teachers the concept that they are public service employees who have certain clearly defined rights. Compared with the prewar teacher who, trained to believe he had no right to question educational authorities, the postwar teacher, thanks to the JTU, has come to consider himself much more than a

[26] Iwate-ken Kyōin Kumiai (Iwate Prefectural Teachers' Union), *Shin Kumiaiin Kōza Shiryō* (Material to be Studied by New Teachers), Iwate-ken Kyōso, 1963.

mere pawn in an enormous bureaucracy. He has become much more willing and capable of questioning and evaluating educational policies as they come down from the Ministry of Education and is much more apt to ignore policies he judges to be unsound. This is an extremely healthy sign that the JTU has gone a long way towards raising the social status of teachers, at least in their own eyes, if not always in the eyes of the community at large.

In addition to raising the economic and social status of teachers, the JTU has sought to raise their political status. Although Chapter VII will discuss in some detail the role of the JTU in postwar Japanese politics, focusing particularly on the relationship between the JTU and the JSP and on the considerable commitment the union has made to the election of its own candidates to public office, it is necessary to point out here that one of the primary aims of the JTU since its inception has been the politicization of teachers. At the same time, and as part of the same aim, it has fought vigorously to prevent teachers from becoming politically neutralized as they were before the war. It is axiomatic that the direct acquisition of political power through the election of ex-JTU officers to public office has contributed not only to the attainment of the JTU's larger objectives but to the politicization of teachers as well. Undeniably, the voting of teachers of their own union leaders into public office has heightened their political awareness and involved them more closely with the political process than was ever possible in the prewar period. In spite of the enactment in 1956 of a law providing for the political neutrality of teachers,[27] which spells out in greater detail than the Fundamental Law of Education the illegality of teachers' teaching from the point of view of any particular political party, the JTU has been able to make the great mass of Japanese teachers

[27] Law No. 157, June 3, 1956, *Gimu Kyōikusho Gakkō ni okeru Kyōiku no Seiji-teki Chūritsu no Kakuho ni Kansuru Rinji Sochi-hō* (Law Governing Provisional Measures for Securing Political Neutrality of Compulsory Education).

more politically aware, partially through campaigns to elect its own officers to public office but also through a series of major struggles (to be discussed in Chapter VI) against specific policies of the Ministry of Education. If the great bulk of Japanese teachers can maintain their considerable degree of political independence from both the government and the JTU, this heightened political awareness augurs well for the future democratic health of Japan.

The third major objective of the JTU is "to contribute to the establishment of a democratic country, loving peace and freedom." As has already been made clear in the discussion of the JTU's ideology as well as in the discussion of the first objective—that of establishing democratic education—the JTU's definition of a democratic country is Marxist-tinged and is related to the question of which class has controlling power. As is obvious by now, in the eyes of the JTU Japan cannot become a "democratic" country, which by definition will be dedicated to the "preservation of peace and freedom," as long as it is controlled by Japanese monopoly capital, which, in turn, is closely tied to, if not controlled by, the capitalist, imperialist United States. From the JTU's ideological viewpoint, a "democratic" country is ipso facto a force for peace, while a capitalist country is a force for war. The ideology dictates that the United States, as an imperialist, capitalist country, inevitably initiates wars. Genuinely desiring peace, the JTU has consequently been forced by its ideology into an anti-United States posture, even though it has supported all the major educational reforms stimulated by the Occupation. While the JTU ever since its founding in 1947, when it called for the purge of all militarists and ultra-nationalists from education,[28] has fought for the establishment of a peace-loving Japan, it was not until 1949, after the so-called "reverse course" was well-established, that the "peace movement" within the union began to take on its anti-American flavor. From this time

[28] JTU, *Nikkyōso Jūnen-shi*, p. 60.

forward, the attainment of peace was concomitant with resistance to the United States. Hence, throughout the decade of the 1950's the JTU was one of the leading groups in Japanese society to organize and participate in numerous anti-American demonstrations directed against such policies as the enlargement of United States military bases (the famous Sunakawa case) and the signing of the U.S.-Japan Security Treaty in 1952 and its revision in 1960.

The JTU's concern for establishing a "democratic country loving peace and freedom" also caused it to oppose all measures of the ruling conservative government that, in its view, might lead once again to militarism. Ever since the famous ninth national convention of June 1952, which adopted the Code of Ethics discussed above, the JTU's annual action policies have called for the following kinds of measures that, from the JTU's viewpoint, have been vitally related to the question of peace: (1) the revision of the pro-American Peace Treaty, (2) the abolition of the U.S.-Japan Security Treaty, (3) absolute opposition to rearmament and conscription, (4) immediate withdrawal of American troops from Japan, and (5) protection of the "peace" Constitution —that is, absolute opposition to the revision of Article IX, the so-called "no war" Article. The preservation of peace has been perhaps the most important objective of the JTU. Certainly, as a leading participant in the left-wing "peace movement" (heiwa undō), the JTU has been able to appeal to the anti-militaristic, pacifist sentiment of the Japanese people throughout the postwar period. As nationalism rises, however, partly as a result of the anti-American flavor of the "peace movement" itself, the appeal of a strictly anti-militaristic "peace movement," one that will not even condone the existence of military forces necessary for Japan's minimum defense needs, will undoubtedly decline. Of course, the specific policies of the JTU designed to establish a peace-loving "democratic" country cannot be divorced from the JTU's concepts of "democratic" education. In this context, the JTU has urged the propagation of "peace education," or education that teaches the "truth" about Japanese society and Japan's relation to the rest of the world.

It should be noted also in discussing this third objective that the JTU has not forgotten the word "freedom." In fact, its argument against revision of Article IX of the Constitution is based not only on its belief that the unaltered retention of the article will best preserve peace for Japan, but also on its fear that if the conservatives can muster enough strength to amend one section of the Constitution, they might be able to amend other sections as well, particularly those which explicitly guarantee the Japanese people a long list of particular freedoms.

This discussion of two of the internal characteristics of the JTU, its ideology and its objectives, reveals that it is in the mainstream of the left wing of the Japanese political spectrum. From the point of view of the teacher members themselves, this is a rather remarkable position for them to be in. Trained in the prewar period to be loyal supporters of the status quo—in fact, trained as individuals responsible for the very transmission of the prevailing value system—teachers were by no means conversant with the role of the dissenter. Now, in the postwar period, as members of a union that is determinedly against the status quo, teachers find themselves strongly urged to be dissenters and protesters. Unaccustomed to this role, many of them, not surprisingly, feel uncomfortable. Habits ingrained from decades of automatic subservience to an authoritarian Ministry of Education cannot be broken overnight. Teachers' attitudes towards the JTU are therefore ambivalent; their loyalty is not total. This ambivalence, which cuts into the JTU's strength as a pressure group, will be more fully analyzed in the following chapter, when the problem of union consciousness is explored more thoroughly. From the point of view of the JTU as an interest group that must find ways to exert pressure on public policy makers, this position in the left wing of the Japanese political spectrum presents staggering problems. It has made the attainment of access to key points in the governmental decision-making process extraordinarily difficult and has forced the JTU to resort in large measure to techniques not fully approved by Japanese society and not even fully approved by the teacher members themselves. But the effectiveness of these techniques, as well as those approved by society, such as the election of ex-JTU officers to public office, have depended upon a number of other internal characteristics, such as the JTU's organizational structure, its size and wealth, its style of leadership, and the degree of union consciousness of its members. It is therefore to these characteristics we now must turn.

CHAPTER V

Organizational Structure and Union Consciousness

ALTHOUGH an interest group is a living organism of many parts subject to constant change, an analysis of its dominant prevailing traits and their effect on its ability to exert influence is essential in order to evaluate the group's effectiveness as a whole. Four important internal characteristics, in addition to ideology and objectives already discussed, which bear considerably on the JTU's effectiveness as an interest group, are: the nature of its organizational structure, the size and distribution of its membership, the style of its leadership, and the degree of union consciousness of its members.

ORGANIZATIONAL STRUCTURE

The most important principle underlying the organizational structure of the JTU is that of democratic centralism, a principle that embodies the contradiction of "democracy," or impulses coming from below in an organization, and "centralism," or impulses coming from the top. According to the principle, higher bodies are supposed to have authority over lower bodies and the rank and file, while at the same time incorporating the views of the lower bodies and the rank and file into policy decisions. Final authority is to rest at the top. In the organizational structure of the JTU, however, because the prefectural unions possess a greater degree of autonomy than the principle of democratic centralism would suggest, the top level, while it has the authority to *formulate* the JTU's national policy, does not in many instances have the authority or the power to see that such policies are *implemented* at the prefectural and lower levels. Nevertheless, the bodies that normally exist in organizations structured according to the principle of democratic centralism, such as the Central Executive Committees (CEC), which in the JTU exist at the national, prefectural, and local branch levels, and the Central Committee (CC) and the National Conference at the national level, have combined with the autonomous prefectural unions to produce a federated type of structure with a high degree of decentralization.

FOUR ORGANIZATIONAL LEVELS

Perhaps the clearest way to view the organizational structure of the JTU is to recognize four distinct levels. At the top level is the national headquarters of the JTU, referred to by the government of Japan as an extra-legal body (the question of its legality is discussed in more detail in Chapter VI), which is itself a federation of the next lower level, the forty-six *kenkyōso*, or prefectural unions. In turn the prefectural unions are themselves federations of *shibu kyōso*, or local branch unions that are organized on a regional basis within each prefecture. The Iwate Teachers' Union, for example, has sixteen local branch unions organized on a geographical basis within the prefecture of Iwate. Below this are the *bunkai*, the fourth and lowest level of the organizational structure, the union chapters within the schools. These four organizational levels of the JTU correspond to the nationwide structure of the educational bureaucracy. The JTU at the national level, with its headquarters in Tokyo, its national leaders, and its elected representatives in the Diet, corresponds to the Tokyo-based apex of the educational bureaucracy, the Ministry of Education, with the Minister himself a member of the Cabinet and his immediate subordinates the top policy-makers in the educational field. At the prefectural level, the prefectural teachers' union and the chairman correspond to the prefectural board of education and the superintendent, if not the governor. A similar correspondence normally occurs at the branch level between the local branch teachers' union and the local board of education. At the chapter level in each school a correspondence exists between the school leader of the union, or chapter head, and the principal, while the teacher members themselves are, of course, both employees of the prefectural or local boards of education and members of the union. Thus, organizationally, the JTU is well-structured for exerting pressure upon the crucial decision-making levels within the educational bureaucracy as well as at the base level where educational policies are implemented.

At the national level the three most significant organizational bodies are the CEC, the CC, and the National Conference. The latter, a delegate body of approximately 500 members, usually meets once a year in May to consider such matters as the union's annual action policy, the selection of officials, the allocation of funds, the affiliation and withdrawal of JTU membership from other organizations, the disciplining of members, and a host of additional union matters. Although in theory the National Conference is the JTU's supreme decision-making body, which sets the general policy for the JTU, in practice, because of its large size and infrequent meetings, it normally does little more than ratify policy decisions already determined by the CEC or CC. Ratification, however, is preceded by vigorous and open discussion in which contrary views, especially those of the anti-mainstream faction, are fully aired. The CC, like the National Conference, is also a delegate body but considerably smaller. Its responsibilities are similar to those of the National Conference but are more detailed in nature; hence, it normally meets about three times a year, although in times of crisis it may meet as often as six to eight times.

That body which is most important in determining the direction of JTU policy and its daily operation at the national level is, however, the CEC. The members of the CEC formulate policies to be ratified by the National Conference and do their best to see that these policies are implemented by the prefectural unions. More than this, the members of the CEC are the kingpins of the union at the national level, deeply involved in the day-to-day decisions of all facets of the national union's activities, from its election campaigns, wage struggles, and struggles against particular governmental educational policies to its participation in anti-governmental political demonstrations, in international labor conferences, and in programs to win favorable public opinion. The mainstream members of the CEC define the union's political role at the national level, determining on the one hand the JTU's position vis-à-vis the government on all domestic and foreign policy issues with which the union is concerned, and carving out on the other hand the JTU's working relationship with Sōhyō, the JSP, and the JCP in the left-wing movement. In essence, the top leaders of the CEC, assisted by the staff members at national headquarters, lead the JTU in all of its political activities.

Until 1962 the members of the CEC numbered 66, 1 member elected from each prefecture and the remaining 20 appointed by the CEC and approved by the National Conference. Among the 20 appointees were normally the national officers of the JTU, consisting of the chairman, 2 vice-chairmen, the secretary-general, 2 assistant secretaries, the treasurer, and 1 inspector for each of the 9 geographical blocs into which the whole of Japan was then divided. The remaining posts were filled by directors of the most important departments of the Secretariat, such as the Departments of General Affairs, Organization, Joint Struggles, and Information and Press. At the 24th National Conference in Toyama in 1962, however, in line with the structural reform introduced by the victorious moderate mainstream, the number of members of the CEC was reduced from 66 to 47. In 1969 the number of CEC members was reduced again from 47 to 36.[1]

[1] The political and economic reasons for the reduction of the num-

Within the JTU's organizational structure, a Central Executive Committee exists not just at the national level. Each prefectural union has its own CEC as does each local branch union within each prefecture. Teacher members normally elect all the members of their prefectural CEC, their own branch chairman, vice-chairman, and secretary-general, as well as their own chapter leader, although the "election" at the school level is more apt to be by consensus than by a clear-cut vote. Although the principle of democratic centralism underlies the organizational structure of the JTU and has provided the nomenclature of the executive bodies within that structure, an important aspect of the principle that in practice has not held true for the JTU is the concept of the strict subordination of all lower bodies to the dictates of the CEC at the top. In fact, the prefectural unions, although they are on paper subordinate to the national CEC, are to a great extent autonomous. Partly because of their independent origin but more importantly because of their high degree of financial independence and their primary concern with educational problems within their own prefectures, which differ widely depending upon the socio-economic nature of each prefecture, the prefectural unions do not permit themselves to be dictated to by the national JTU. Prefectural teachers' unions plan, budget, and administer their own programs largely without formal interference from the national JTU. Participation in programs advocated by the JTU at the national level is voluntary and advice is usually obtained on an informal basis. This is not to say that the national JTU does not urge the prefectural unions to participate in particular struggles or "strikes," or that it will not move in with financial aid and personnel if a particular prefectural union finds itself in need, as was the case in Ehime in 1958 during the anti-efficiency rating struggle and in Iwate in 1962 during the

---

ber of national CEC members is discussed more fully in this chapter under the section, "Style of Leadership."

114

anti-achievement test struggle. Nevertheless, prefectural unions participate in "nation-wide" struggles as announced by the national JTU on a voluntary basis, their leaders making the decision whether or not to participate in an analysis of their own union's needs, abilities, and objectives rather than on the feeling that they ought to fulfill a request merely because it has originated from headquarters in Tokyo. The national CEC does have a restraining influence on certain activities of the prefectural unions, however. JTU headquarters will not, for example, extend relief funds to prefectural unions that have gone out on strike without the national CEC's approval. This policy has a dampening effect on the more radical prefectural unions.

The degree of autonomy from higher union authorities lessens, however, as one proceeds down the organizational structure from the prefectural level. Local branch and chapter leaders, while by no means unable to adjust their actions to the realities of their corresponding local boards of education and principals, are nevertheless primarily responsible for transmitting and implementing union policies determined at the prefectural level. Even union leaders in the schools who are not in agreement with union policies are apt to do their best to fulfill this role.[2] At the school level teachers are informed of union policies at meetings held about once a month. The head of the chapter usually presides at these meetings although in some schools it has become the practice to allow a different teacher to preside at each meeting.[3] To assist the chapter head in administrative matters there are in most schools union representatives of each grade level, each with an assistant or two. Topics for discussion at chapter meetings may originate, of course, at any of the four structural levels of the JTU. As discussed in greater detail in the section in this chapter on "Union

[2] John Singleton, *Nichū: A Japanese School* (New York: Holt, Rinehart and Winston, 1967), p. 112.

[3] For a discussion of the attitudes of teachers toward their chapter meetings, see the section in this chapter on "Union Consciousness."

Consciousness," teachers in their typical Japanese search for harmony within the group display in their discussions at chapter meetings a strong tendency either to side with the union point of view or remain silent. The few teachers who openly dare to oppose the union on a particular issue almost always do so by espousing the view of their board of education. Only extremely rarely does a teacher express an independent point of view, one that may not agree with either the union or the board, a phenomenon that suggests that teachers are still too dependent in their thinking, whether upon the union *or* the educational bureaucracy.

At this base level of the JTU organizational structure, the conflict between the union and the educational bureaucracy becomes highly personal. What happens at this level is different in every single school and depends to a very great extent upon the personal relationship between the principal and the chapter head. Principals themselves run the gamut from being adamantly opposed to the union to being strong supporters. On the other hand, some chapter leaders are more activist than others. But, by and large, it can be said that within each school the union leader constantly exerts pressure upon the principal, although normally not to such an extent as to disrupt classroom teaching. As a result the principal is placed in the position of either exerting pressure in return or forfeiting his authority.[4] Thus, pressure at the school level constantly flows in both directions, even though the relationship between the principal and the union leader may be very close. It ought to be remembered that these two in the course of their daily work are apt to meet each other a dozen times and thus are usually able to sit down together and talk over all problems, even though they represent two opposing views. The principal is there to administer, while the union leader is there to oppose

---

[4] One principal of a lower secondary school in Morioka remarked to the writer that he was constantly afraid of his own teachers. Interview with Oda Hajime, Principal of Semboku Lower Secondary School in Morioka City, November 9, 1964.

116

many of the programs the principal is attempting to administer. Although each of these two men tries to implement the policies of his respective superior, at the same time each understands the position of the other and is therefore usually reluctant to push too far. For these reasons what is actually done at the school level concerning major policies and programs announced by the Ministry and opposed by the union is worked out between the principal and the chapter head and depends to a great extent upon the personal relationship between these two men.

Consequently, although the JTU is a hierarchically structured federation of national, prefectural, branch, and chapter unions well organized to exert pressure on the educational bureaucracy at all levels, much of what actually takes place in schools throughout the country is the product not only of the nature of the relationship between the prefectural union and board of education but also of the personal relationship between the school principal and chapter head. In this respect the relationship between the union and the educational bureaucracy may be viewed as two pyramids, one representing the educational bureaucracy from the Minister of Education down to the principal and the other representing the union bureaucracy from the chairman down to the chapter head. As in the following diagram, the two pyramids overlap considerably at the base and at the middle level but are separated at the top:

Relationship Between the Japan Teachers' Union
and the Ministry of Education

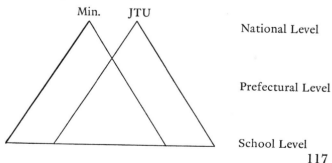

For this reason, JTU demands are taken more seriously and are therefore more often met at the bottom and middle levels, where the two sides must work together if education is to proceed harmoniously, than at the top, where the gap does not appear to be immediately harmful to the education of children.

THE MUTUAL AID SOCIETY

Of recent significance to the internal organizational strength of the JTU was the creation in 1965 of a Mutual Aid Society. By joining the Society, JTU members can purchase at extremely low premiums across-the-board insurance for such disasters as death, fire, and flood. The Society claims that since its purpose is not to make a profit, it is able to offer greater cash benefits at lower premiums than can commercial insurance companies. Legally and financially separate from the JTU, the Society is nevertheless the child of the union, sharing executives as well as office space with the parent body at Tokyo headquarters, and utilizing the JTU's organizational structure at the prefectural, branch, and chapter levels for canvassing, collecting shares, and paying benefits. Established to strengthen the ties of the rank and file to the union itself, the Society would appear to have contributed to this aim. By January 1971 over 380,000 teachers were participating in its various mutual aid programs. Table 2 shows a breakdown by prefecture of the percentage of union members who had joined the Mutual Aid Society by January 1971.

MEMBERSHIP

The size and distribution of the membership of any interest group has a direct bearing on its ability to exert effective pressure on public decision-making bodies. Statistically, the JTU is without question the only organization that can claim to represent the interests of teachers. Even if one accepts the statistics of the Ministry of Education, which are misleading (for example, Ministry statistics make the percentage of educational personnel who are JTU members appear less than it is by including principals and vice-principals in its total number of educational personnel even though they are no longer permitted to become members of the union), the JTU remains the only giant in the field. According to the Ministry, in 1970 membership of the JTU stood at 505,509, while the next largest single teachers' organization claimed only 29,421 members.[5] All sources agree that the total membership of the JTU since 1948 has fluctuated somewhere between 500,000 and 600,000, making the JTU the undisputed leader among teachers' organizations.[6] With this number of members the JTU is not only a significant proportion of Japanese organized labor as a whole, which in 1970 numbered 11.6 million, but also the second largest union in the public sector in the nation. As the second largest union in Sōhyō, the General Council of Japanese Trade Unions, whose membership of 4.2 million contains 2.6 million public service workers, the JTU exercises considerable influence over Sōhyō's educational and cultural policies.[7]

If we accept the 1970 Ministry of Education figure of 505,509 as the total membership of the JTU, it must be remembered that it represents all educational personnel, including clerks, throughout the entire educational system

[5] Japan, Ministry of Education, Local Affairs Section, *Kyōshokuin no Soshiki Suru Shokuin Dantai no Gaikyō* (Profile of Employees' Groups Organized by Educational Personnel) (Tokyo: Ministry of Education, November 1970), p. 27.

[6] The Ministry of Labor reported the total membership of the JTU to be 589,664 as of June 1964. Japan, Ministry of Labor, *Basic Survey of Trade Unions* (Tokyo: Ministry of Labor, March 1965). According to the Ministry of Education the total figure in 1964 was 566,281. Ministry of Education, *Kyōshokuin Dantai-ra Kankei Shiryō*, pp. 245-46.

[7] The 1970 statistics on labor as a whole come from Hara Takashi, Trade Union Section of the Ministry of Labor, interviewed on December 17, 1970.

Table 2

Number of Mutual Aid Society Members
(Statistics as of January 1971)

	Elem., Mid., & H.S. Union Members	Univ. Union Members	Total	Number in Mutual Aid Association	% in Mutual Aid Ass'n
Hokkaidō	30,251	1,100	31,351	25,990	83
Aomori	6,642	30	6,672	6,566	98
Akita	7,943	40	7,983	8,157	102
Iwate	12,795	212	13,007	11,779	91
Yamagata	10,143	134	10,277	9,683	94
Miyagi	12,557	1,200	13,757	8,385	61
Fukushima	13,140	160	13,300	10,335	78
Tochigi	307	208	515	261	51
Ibaraki	12,668		12,668	10,653	84
Fumma	6,690	400	7,090	5,767	81
Saitama	11,151	94	11,245	8,119	72
Chiba	18,579		18,579	11,583	62
Tokyo	36,850	2,420	39,270	14,183	36
Kanagawa	16,508		16,508	5,937	36
Yamanachi	4,348	60	4,408	4,180	95
Nagano	10,253	40	10,293	8,231	80
Shizuoka	14,846	400	15,346	13,932	91
Niigata	18,021	300	18,321	18,271	99
Toyama	4,473	140	4,613	4,579	99
Ishikawa	5,243	510	5,753	5,228	91
Fukui	6,148	120	6,268	5,931	95
Aichi	22,828	1,040	23,868	20,210	85
Gifu	2,628	200	2,828	1,472	52
Mie	10,863	130	10,993	8,917	81
Shiga	2,771		2,771	2,250	81
Kyoto	8,697	1,000	9,697	2,892	30
Nara	4,171	80	4,251	1,541	36
Wakayama	4,286	160	4,446	2,942	66
Osaka	30,230	1,138	31,368	21,009	67
Hyōgo	25,612	512	26,124	17,246	66
Tottori	4,665		4,665	3,345	72
Okayama	9,985	60	10,045	3,646	86
Shimane	3,502	60	3,562	2,489	70
Hiroshima	13,454	18	13,472	9,270	69
Yamaguchi	2,053	436	2,489	1,823	73
Kagawa	337	50	387	210	54
Tokushima	405	120	525	292	56
Ehime	483	60	543	427	79

Table 2—*continued,*

	Elem., Mid., & H.S. Union Members	Univ. Union Members	Total	Number in Mutual Aid Association	% in Mutual Aid Ass'n
Kōchi	3,875	72	3,947	3,120	79
Fukuoka	25,523	1,450	26,973	20,842	77
Saga	4,008	120	4,128	3,480	84
Nagasaki	7,401		7,401	5,862	79
Ōita	7,752	90	7,842	9,141	116
Kumamoto	9,428	180	9,608	7,614	79
Miyazaki	6,887	174	7,061	6,273	89
Kagoshima	10,822	60	10,882	10,205	94
Okinawa	13,038		13,038	11,776	90
JTU Hqs.	77		77	129	168
Total	495,437	14,778	510,215	381,164	75

*Percentages above 100 percent occur because of a number of principals and vice-principals who joined the Mutual Aid Society before they were forced by law to give up their membership in the JTU. The JTU has nevertheless permitted them to remain in the Mutual Aid Society. The high percentage at JTU headquarters is explained by the large number of full-time union officers who have lost their status as public service employees yet remain members of the Mutual Aid Society.

Source: Prepared by the staff of the Mutual Aid Society headquarters in Tokyo, February, 1971.

from the elementary schools through the universities, or 56.2 percent of the total. If we consider, however, only the percentage of teachers at the compulsory school level alone, 74 percent are members of the JTU.

Teachers are not legally bound to join the JTU; the school is not a closed shop. Nevertheless, except in areas where severe struggles against Ministry of Education policies have resulted in large-scale withdrawals, in most schools the majority of teachers are union members. But some of them are not. In spite of the well-known Japanese tendency to practice harmonious group behavior and of the union's desire for solidarity, it would be erroneous to assume that in any particular school either all or none of the teachers are union

121

members. Particularly in urban areas, in almost every school there are a few teachers who are not union members. This phenomenon leads to the tentative hypothesis that the traditionally oriented threat of being ostracized from one's fellow teachers for behaving non-cooperatively and non-harmoniously may be weakening, especially in urban areas. If so, however, the process has not yet attained significant proportions.

Although approximately three-fourths of all elementary and lower secondary school teachers remain members of the JTU, the union has nevertheless suffered a decline in membership over the past decade. Withdrawals have resulted from a number of severe clashes with the Ministry of Education over such issues as the efficiency rating system, the nationwide achievement tests, and the wage struggles conducted from 1966 through 1970. After participating in these struggles, teachers left the union for a variety of reasons: dissatisfaction over the use of violent tactics that disrupted classrooms, capitulation to pressures from boards of education to leave the union, and frustration from the excessive concern of union leaders with national and international politics while slighting the more immediate concerns of teachers with education and their own welfare. Decline in union membership is indicated by comparing Tables 3 and 4, which rank the prefectures according to the percentage of educational personnel in the JTU as of February 18, 1964 and June 1, 1970. Although these figures are somewhat misleading because they include all levels of education as well as principals and vice-principals who were forced out of the union by law in 1969, they nevertheless reveal a gradual decline in union membership. It is interesting to note, however, that even though the percentage drop from 72.9 to 56.2, or 16.7 percent, suggests considerable weakening of the union, the absolute number of total members fell only by 60,772, or 10.7 percent. When it is considered that much of this decline resulted from the compulsory withdrawal of principals and vice-principals, the actual decline in union membership is slight, despite Ministry efforts to make it appear otherwise.

Nevertheless, it cannot be denied that the percentage of the total number of educational personnel who are union members has declined as the total number of educational personnel has increased. Over the past decade new educational personnel have been entering the union at a declining rate. According to Ministry statistics, the percentage of new personnel entering the JTU declined from 76.6 percent in 1961 to 61.5 percent in 1970.[8] JTU Secretary-General Makieda warns that here again the Ministry, in its desire to portray the JTU as weakening, draws a misleading picture because statistics on the percentage of new teachers who join the JTU are compiled in April and May at the beginning of the academic year. This does not result in an accurate percentage since the Ministry urges new teachers not to join unions or teachers' associations during their first six months. Nevertheless, fewer new teachers are joining the union. If this pattern continues, it does not bode well for the JTU's future strength.

Tables 3 and 4 reveal that there is a wide range of participation in the JTU from prefecture to prefecture. Why these differences? While it is not possible to discuss each prefecture in turn, the observation can be made that the extremely low membership rate in such prefectures as Yamaguchi, Ehime, and Tochigi has resulted from two main factors: the alienation of the teachers from the uncompromising political views and violent tactics of these prefectural union leaders, and the pressure from the boards of education for teachers to withdraw. In Yamaguchi, for example, rapid decline followed the famous Diary incident of 1953 (see pages 100-01 above), which alienated all but the most radical teachers from the union's leadership. Unable to embrace the ideological extremism of the Yamaguchi union leaders, teachers withdrew by the thousands. Some

[8] Ministry of Education, *Kyōshokuin no Soshiki Suru Shokuin Dantai no Gaikyō*, 1964-1970, p. 12.

Table 3

Ranking of the Prefectures According to the Percentage of Educational Personnel* from Elementary Schools Through Universities Who Are JTU Members (as of Feb. 18, 1964)

Rank	Prefecture	Total Educational Personnel	JTU Members	%
1	Fukui	6,570	6,519	99.2
2	Chiba	18,090	17,465	96.0
3	Miyagi	14,816	13,938	94.1
4	Tottori	5,637	5,227	92.7
5	Mie	22,208	20,227	91.1
6	Ibaraki	17,717	16,011	90.4
7	Hiroshima	17,404	15,583	89.5
8	Osaka	34,395	29,827	87.8
9	Kyoto	13,755	11,679	84.9
10	Miyazaki	10,342	8,600	84.1
11	Shizuoka	10,098	16,788	84.0
12	Kumamoto	18,170	14,993	82.5
13	Kagoshima	18,736	15,336	81.9
14	Gifu	13,364	10,924	81.7
15	Aichi	28,317	23,183	81.6
16	Ishikawa	8,209	6,690	81.4
17	Hyōgo	31,868	25,639	80.4
18	Kanagawa	24,057	15,060	79.8
19	Fukuoka	34,027	27,034	79.4
20	Hokkaidō	47,854	37,854	79.2
21	Iwate	13,952	11,012	78.9
22	Aomori	13,667	10,750	78.7
23	Akita	12,749	9,840	77.2
24	Saitama	19,461	14,904	76.6
25	Toyama	9,156	6,953	76.0
26	Ōita	11,362	8,549	75.0
27	Shiga	6,901	5,028	72.8
28	Niigata	25,503	18,474	72.4
29	Nagano	17,686	12,715	72.0
30	Shimane	8,612	6,159	71.5
31	Nagasaki	15,344	10,860	70.8
32	Yamanashi	7,195	4,947	68.6
33	Yamagata	12,338	8,383	67.9
34	Fukushima	21,310	14,348	67.3
35	Tokyo	58,772	38,168	67.2
36	Wakayama	8,596	5,207	60.6
37	Okayama	17,111	10,386	60.0
38	Kōchi	8,153	4,572	56.0

124

Table 3—*continued,*

Rank	Prefecture	Total Educational Personnel	JTU Members	%
39	Gumma	13,604	7,575	55.7
40	Saga	8,416	4,661	55.4
41	Nara	6,026	2,832	47.0
42	Yamaguchi	13,455	3,537	26.3
43	Kagawa	7,894	1,235	16.0
44	Tokushima	8,030	819	10.0
45	Ehime	13,218	1,275	9.6
46	Tochigi	14,939	525	3.5
Total		777,094	566,281	72.9

*The term "educational personnel" includes principals, vice-principals, teachers and clerks.

Source: Ministry of Education, Local Affairs Section, *Kyōshokuin Dantai-ra Kankei Shiryō* (Data Concerning Educational Personnel Organizations), (Tokyo: Ministry of Education, February 1964) pp. 245-46.

formed a new and more moderate union known as the Prefectural Federation of Teachers. Similarly, in Ehime the withdrawal of teachers began after the sharp confrontation between the union and the Ehime Board of Education, backed by the Ministry of Education, over the implementation of the efficiency rating system in 1958 (see pages 191-95 and 205-09 below). Teachers were alienated by the intransigence of union leaders who clashed with the police. At the same time, the Ehime Board of Education brought great pressure to bear on teachers to withdraw. Although the situation was different, the stimulus for large-scale withdrawals in Tochigi was essentially the same. Without question the single most important reason for withdrawals in such prefectures has been poor leadership that at times of crisis has proved to be inflexible and uncompromising. By contrast, prefectural unions that have managed to retain high membership rates, such as Iwate, Osaka, and Aichi, have done so by adopting realistic, flexible attitudes in their struggles. In

Table 4

Ranking of the Prefectures According to the Percentage of
Educational Personnel from Elementary Schools through
Universities Who Are JTU Members (as of June 1, 1970)

Rank	Prefecture	Total Educational Personnel	JTU Members	%
1	Fukui	7,494	6,436	85.9
2	Tottori	6,108	4,719	77.3
3	Iwate	16,326	12,462	76.3
4	Osaka	48,422	36,030	74.4
5	Aichi	35,773	26,351	74.0
6	Mie	14,466	10,660	73.7
7	Fukuoka	34,679	25,343	73.1
8	Yamagata	13,801	10,117	73.0
9	Hyōgo	34,452	24,772	71.9
10	Miyagi	17,504	12,466	71.2
11	Chiba	25,682	18,168	71.0
12	Ibaraki	20,478	13,928	68.0
13	Niigata	27,434	18,565	67.7
14	Ōita	13,727	9,222	67.2
15	Kyoto	16,249	10,770	66.0
16	Miyazaki	10,739	6,870	64.0
17	Yamanashi	7,948	6,064	63.7
18	Kanagawa	32,868	20,866	63.5
19	Hiroshima	21,796	13,861	63.5
20	Akita	13,016	8,161	62.0
21	Fukushima	22,012	13,228	60.1
22	Hokkaidō	49,784	29,442	59.1
23	Nara	8,561	5,018	58.6
24	Shizuoka	25,983	15,190	58.5
25	Nagano	19,240	10,658	55.4
26	Okayama	17,147	9,286	54.2
27	Kumamoto	17,866	9,688	54.2
28	Ishikawa	9,917	5,211	52.0
29	Tokyo	77,585	40,090	51.7
30	Kagoshima	22,672	10,508	46.3
31	Wakayama	9,820	4,512	46.0
32	Aomori	15,693	6,997	44.6
33	Gumma	14,854	6,575	44.2
34	Toyama	10,728	4,596	42.8
35	Kōchi	9,099	3,882	42.7
36	Saitama	27,192	11,558	42.2
37	Nagasaki	17,313	7,284	42.0
38	Saga	9,732	3,952	40.6

Table 4—*continued*,

Rank	Prefecture	Total Educational Personnel	JTU Members	%
39	Shimane	9,398	3,432	36.5
40	Shiga	8,011	2,911	36.3
41	Gifu	16,267	3,288	20.0
42	Yamaguchi	14,632	2,036	13.8
43	Tokushima	8,012	411	5.1
44	Kagawa	9,119	279	3.0
45	Ehime	14,969	421	2.8
46	Tochigi	15,703	225	1.4
Total		900,271	505,509	56.2

Source: Ministry of Education, Local Affairs Section, *Kyōshokuin no Soshiki Suru Shokuin Dantai no Gaikyō* (Profile of Employees' Groups Organized by Educational Personnel), Tokyo: Ministry of Education, Nov. 1970, p. 27.

addition, certain prefectures, such as Iwate, have succeeded in tying the interests of their members closely to the union by establishing special programs, such as aid for retired teachers.

On balance, the JTU as a nationwide organization has retained its great numerical strength and by no means has suffered a knockout blow in spite of Ministry pressure, although the great loss of members in the late 1950's in a few prefectures was a clear warning to the emerging mainstream, led by the moderate Miyanohara Sadamitsu, that the union was in danger and would have to shift its tactics, if not its fundamental policy, if the downward trend in membership was to be halted and the union's strength preserved. The JTU responded to the threat of increased resignations by a shift in leadership from the radical faction, led by Hiragaki Miyoji, to the more moderate faction, led by Miyanohara, which adopted a more flexible, less doctrinaire attitude in its struggles against the Ministry and switched its emphasis from politics to economics. It may be too early to state categorically that the new emphasis, which includes the creation of the Mutual Aid Society in 1965, is going to be successful over the long run in maintaining a high membership percentage, although certainly to date the union remains statistically a giant without rivals.

With reference to Tables 3 and 4, it is extremely tantalizing to assert that the JTU is strongest in those prefectures where the percentage of its membership is greatest. If strength is measured by the ability to influence significantly the formulation and implementation of educational policies and to resist effectively those policies of the Ministry of Education considered undesirable, however, high membership percentages do not necessarily correlate with strength. No evidence was found in 1964, for example, that the Miyagi Prefectural Teachers' Union, which then comprised 94 percent of all educational personnel, was any stronger vis-à-vis the Miyagi Prefectural Board of Education than was the Iwate Prefectural Teachers' Union, which then comprised 80 percent of all educational personnel, vis-à-vis the Iwate Prefectural Board of Education. In fact, the reverse was found to be closer to the truth. An extremely high membership percentage may coincide with ability to exert influence effectively, as is true of the Osaka and Hiroshima Teachers' Unions, but at the same time it may not, as is apparent in the Chiba and Fukui Teachers' Unions. Without other factors, such as strong leadership and imaginative programs, a high membership percentage in a particular prefecture may only reflect expected group behavior. Generalizations on this point are extremely dangerous. Even the urban-rural (or progressive-backward) variable provides no correlation with this particular measurement of strength. One can only make the observation that some prefectural unions with high membership percentages have shown a considerable degree of effectiveness vis-à-vis their respective boards of education while others have not. The difference is attributable more to leadership and programs than to a high membership percentage, although it is recognized that no prefectural union without a decisive majority of the teachers can possibly be effective.

If there is no close correlation in the prefectures between the size of the unions and their effectiveness vis-à-vis the boards of education, there is a high correlation between size and the ability of the JTU to elect its own candidates to public office. The sheer total number of members is highly significant to the voting strength of the union, particularly in its ability to elect nationwide candidates to the House of Councillors. This significance of the JTU's large membership is explored fully in Chapter VII. Furthermore, in regard to elections, of equal significance to the total number of members is the fact of their widespread distribution. Teachers who staff the nation's schools are spread throughout all election districts. This gives JTU candidates a horizontal sweep that candidates from other unions, concentrated in particular areas in an election district, do not enjoy. The surprising number of candidates the JTU has been able to elect to public office compared to other unions in Japan attests to the importance of the union's large and widespread membership.

STYLE OF LEADERSHIP

Only a small percentage of the members of any interest group may be termed activists and the JTU is no exception. This does not belittle the importance of the activists' role, however. No matter how few, activists within the JTU have been essential in developing union consciousness among the teachers and in guiding the union at its various levels towards fulfilling its objectives. In fact, because of the traditional tendency among Japanese teachers to believe that whatever the state does regarding education is right, activists have been particularly necessary to the strength and effectiveness of the JTU. It is extremely difficult to estimate the number of activists among the JTU membership, however, and the estimation naturally varies depending upon which teachers are included within the definition of the term. Even Nakakōji Kiyō, Chairman of the Department of Organization at JTU headquarters in Tokyo in 1965, and Inaba Takashi, Vice-Chairman of the same department in 1971, were hesitant (or reluctant) to cite any figures.[9] If only full-time union officers are considered activists, the figure is extremely small; in 1964 there were 969 officers or one per 568 members, while in 1970 there were 905 or one per 558 members, in each instance far fewer than one percent of the membership.[10]

Limiting the definition of activists to full-time union officers is not realistic, however, as it does not include union leaders within the schools who spend a considerable amount of time on union activities while carrying a full teaching load. At the same time, not all union leaders in the schools would be termed activists by full-time union officers. As previously mentioned, some union leaders in the schools merely perform their roles perfunctorily and publicly while privately disagreeing with union policies. Such teachers, in spite of their participation in union activities, would not be termed activists by JTU leaders. Instead, as defined by Nakakōji, the term is reserved for leaders engaged in union activities at all levels who have a "deep understanding of JTU policies," and who "reflect most faithfully the opinions of the ordinary teacher-members."[11] Although the degree to which activists reflect the opinion of the rank and file is open to question and is discussed in greater detail in the following section, Nakakōji and Inaba made it absolutely clear that the present national leadership

[9] Interviews with Nakakōji Kiyō, Chairman of the Department of Organization, JTU Headquarters, Tokyo, February 16, 1965, and Inaba Takashi, Vice-Chairman of the Department of Organization, JTU Headquarters, Tokyo, February 12, 1971.

[10] Ministry of Education, *Kyōshokuin no Soshiki Suru Shokuin Dantai no Gaikyō* (Profile of Employees' Groups Organized by Educational Personnel), 1964, p. 10 and November 1970, p. 11.

[11] Interview with Nakakōji Kiyō, February 16, 1965.

does not wish to include extreme radicals within the definition of the term "activist." In fact, they asserted that the present mainstream of the JTU CEC recognizes that the vast majority of the teacher members are not extreme left-wingers and that therefore the promotion of radical leaders of this ilk, which would only lead to a widening of the gap that already exists between the leaders and the rank and file, is not condoned by the national JTU. Consequently, although the dividing line may not be clear in every instance, at present the creation and promotion of activists as encouraged by the mainstream of the JTU CEC is not the same as the creation and promotion of extremists, even though such activists stand in opposition to most governmental educational policies. As Nakakōji phrased it, "The JTU cannot exist if it goes against the wishes of the majority of the teachers." Of course the national JTU is not able to dictate to the prefectural unions who should or should not be promoted as union leaders within the prefectural structure. Consequently, in some prefectures where the more radical anti-mainstream remains dominant, the promotion of radical activists is still encouraged. This goes against the nation-wide trend, however, in which in prefecture after prefecture during the 1960's the radicals were bested by the moderates, although by 1970 and 1971 there were signs that the radicals in certain prefectures, increasingly disenchanted with the moderate Miyanohara-Makieda leadership, were gaining some strength. A group of such teachers broke into a meeting of the national CEC in March 1971; the CEC called in the police, who arrested several offenders. In any case, estimating the number of activists remains difficult. With Nakakōji's definition of an activist in mind, if one makes the arbitrary assumption that there is an average of one activist in each elementary and lower secondary school—which, according to Inabe, is the aim of the JTU— the total number would be about 40,000, or 8 percent of the JTU membership at those levels. This percentage may not be too wide of the mark.

Even though the exact number of activists cannot be ascertained, JTU leaders are very much concerned with increasing that number. Both Nakakōji and Inabe affirmed that the ongoing creation of activists was absolutely essential to the continuing work of the JTU because the traditional paternalistic nature of the employer-employee relationship in Japan has worked against a high level of union consciousness among all workers, not only teachers. The recent exclusion of principals and vice-principals from the union has compounded the problem and made it even more imperative that strong union leaders be created in the schools. With this in mind, although the JTU does not run a leadership school per se, it does attempt to foster the emergence of activists through the meetings and activities of specific groups, particularly through the young male teachers (the so-called Youth Division, which includes all male teachers up to age thirty-five), and the young women teachers. Apparently the JTU leaders do not select individuals from these groups in any specific way; rather, they emerge and become activists through the process of attempting to solve various educational and teachers' problems. Although JTU headquarters does not publish any overall guide for the training of activists, the Department of Organization sends procedural suggestions to the prefectural unions, which they may or may not follow, whenever the JTU as a whole is engaged in a particular struggle.

Why do some teachers become activists? First, it ought to be remarked that the teachers who become activists are usually the best teachers, the ones who are most energetic, who wish to improve the educational system, who are forward-looking. During the 1950's such teachers sympathized with the ideological stance of the JTU and were excited by the prospect of participating in a teachers' union that possessed real power and influence. At the same time, young teachers saw the possibility of advancing up the "union ladder," in time to a position within the prefectural and then national JTU CEC and perhaps climaxed by election to the

Diet. In short, the union offered the opportunity to combine ideological conviction with self-advancement. As is discussed in greater detail in Chapter VII, in the early days the route up the union ladder to national prestige was very popular and was travelled by all of the present members of the JTU CEC and the JTU representatives in the Diet. No individual has transferred into the top level of the JTU leadership structure laterally.

At present, however, becoming an activist with the dream of advancing up the union ladder is no longer the lure it once was. Ebata Kiyoshi, Editor of the *Asahi Shimbun*, has rightly pointed out that all the top executive posts in the JTU at the national and prefectural levels are virtually closed to newcomers because of the relative youth of the present leadership.[12] As shown in Table 5, this assertion is

Table 5

Age of Full-Time Union Officers

Age	1964	1970
	%	%
30 and under	7.2	3.4
31-41	68.2	47.3
41-50	20.3	44.9
51 and above	4.1	4.4

Source: Ministry of Education, Local Affairs Section, *Kyōshokuin no Soshiki Suru Shokuin Dantai no Gaikyō* (Profile of Employees' Groups Organized by Educational Personnel), 1964, pp. 9-10 and November 1970, pp. 40-41.

borne out by Ministry of Education statistics, which disclose that in 1964 68 percent of the 969 full-time union officers were between 30 and 40 years of age, and that in 1970 47 percent of the 905 officers were between 30 and 40 while 92 percent were between 30 and 50. Even the average age

[12] Ebata Kiyoshi, "Mombudaijin to Tairitsushi" (History of the Confrontation with the Minister of Education), *Asahi Journal*, Vol. 7, No. 12 (March 21, 1956), pp. 102-08.

of the 47 members of the National JTU CEC remains youthful. In 1965 the average age was only 41, while that of the top 7 leaders was only 45. By 1970 the average age of the 36 members of the JTU CEC was only 45 while that of the top 5 leaders was only 49.

In spite of the relative youth of the leaders, many have nevertheless remained full-time union officers for long periods of time, further exacerbating the lack of upward mobility for young activists. For example, in 1965 the top 7 leaders in the JTU CEC had served as full-time union officers an average of 12 years. By 1970 the top 5 leaders had served an average of 20 years. Also, by 1970 the chairman had been a full-time officer at various levels of the union's organizational structure for 23 years, the secretary-general for 22 years, and one of the vice-chairmen for 24 years. Twenty-seven, or three-fourths, of the 36 members had been full-time officers for 10 years or more, and 13 for 15 years or more. All 36 members had served for an average of 14 years. The situation was not much better for aspiring young activists at the prefectural level either. For example, in the Iwate Prefectural Teachers' Union the average age of the 14 members of its CEC in 1965 was only 40 while the average length of service was 7 years, with the 2 top leaders having each served for 20 years ever since the founding of the union. Consequently, given the relative youth of the JTU leaders and their tendency to remain in office for long periods of time—even ex-JTU Diet representatives are repeatedly re-elected—advancement up the union ladder has lost the attraction it once had because it simply is not as possible as it once was.

Another decisive factor contributing to the difficulty of advancing upward within the union organization is the decision of the national CEC to reduce the number of full-time union officers. This decision was a consequence of the revision in the Local Public Service Law resulting from Japan's ratification in 1965 of ILO Article 87 regarding freedom of association. The revision prohibits a full-time union officer from retaining his public service status beyond three years. This forecast an added financial burden for the union. Although the JTU has always paid the salaries of teachers who worked full time for the union, the prefectural governments as the employers of teachers continued to pay retirement and other benefits to full-time officers as long as they retained their public service status, which prior to the revision of the LPSL was indefinitely. With the revision of the law, however, the JTU itself will have to take on the burden of paying retirement and other benefits to all full-time officers who remain on the job beyond the three-year limit. With this professionalization of the union leaders, the projected expense when the first year beyond the three-year limit began in December 1971 is considerable.

Consequently, mainly as an economy move but also because the union has become over-staffed in certain prefectures (and under-staffed in others), the JTU CEC has worked out a nationwide plan determining the ideal number of full-time union officers in each prefecture at both the prefectural and branch levels. The ideal number varies, of course, from prefecture to prefecture, depending on the number of union members. In most prefectures, however, the ideal number is less than the present actual number. To place pressure on these prefectures to reduce the actual number to the ideal number, the national JTU refuses to pay fifty percent of the salaries, as it normally does, to those officers who exceed the ideal number. Table 6 indicates that in 1967 the actual number of full-time officers at the prefectural level exceeded the ideal number by 164 and at the branch level by 121. The total number of actual full-time officers exceeded the ideal number by 285. With this kind of pressure to reduce the total number of officers, the opportunity for young activists to advance up the union ladder is slimmer than ever. Also, of course, such a situation makes it more difficult to recruit activists at all.

Faced with this scarcity of opportunities to advance within the union structure, a number of young full-time union

135

Table 6

Ideal Versus Actual Number of Full-Time Union Officers

	Prefectural Level	Branch Level	Total
Actual	514	479	993
·Ideal	350	358	708
Excess:	164	121	285

Source: Interview with Inaba Takashi, Vice-Chairman, Department of Organization, February 12, 1971.

activists have deserted and climbed aboard the ladder of the educational bureaucracy. They have actually used the JTU structure as a springboard towards higher positions in educational administration. This has been possible because activists at the prefectural level who are in close touch with boards of education are in an excellent position to hear of good opportunities and to take advantage of them. At the same time the process has been encouraged by the boards, who are not above wooing union leaders to their side. In Iwate, for example, several past full-time members of the CEC are now principals or superintendents and no longer union members. This has, of course, opened up a few positions within the union bureaucracy but only at a rather low level.

THE MIYANOHARA LINE

Since the founding of the JTU, the most significant change in its national leadership was the emergence of the moderate mainstream, led by Miyanohara Sadamitsu, over the radical former mainstream, led by Hiragaki Miyoji. The emergence of the moderates, which has been discussed in Chapter IV from the point of view of its significance to the JTU's change in ideological emphasis, began in 1958 but did not culminate in decisive control over the national JTU

136

CEC until 1962. Although many factors contributed to their victory, perhaps the three most significant were the movement toward moderation within the left wing as a whole in the first half of the 1960's, the unfavorable reaction of the general public and many teachers themselves to the "total confrontation" tactics the JTU had pursued from 1955 to 1960, and the extraordinary ability of the emerging moderate leaders. First, it is important to point out that the seizure of the leadership of the JTU by the moderates in the early 1960's clearly shows the political position of the JTU as very much within the mainstream of the Japanese left wing, since similar changes were common in other leftist groups at the time. The JTU, closely tied to the Left Socialist Wada faction in the JSP, moved with the Wada faction's modification of its position in 1960 to support the more moderate structural reformers. In addition, the mainstream of the JSP, which had been controlled by the Left Socialists from 1955 to 1960, came under the control of the Right Socialists, led initially by the structural reformist, Eda Saburō, from late 1960 to 1965. Failure of the JSP to increase its strength at the polls after the peak year of 1958 had begun the trend toward moderation and opened the way for the adoption by the party of the structural reform doctrine, which held at its core that Socialism could be established gradually through piecemeal changes in the existing capitalist society, not requiring revolution through direct confrontation, as preached by the Left Socialists. Within Sōhyō too a shift occurred. Having taken part only in negative campaigns of *opposition* and *resistance* to governmental policies, it shifted its emphasis from political action to workers' economic interests.

Secondly, the increase of withdrawals from the JTU and of dismissed personnel from their public service status as a result of the confrontation tactics of the Hiragaki faction, as well as the sharp criticism from the public that the JTU was concentrating too heavily on political struggles to the detriment of economic and educational issues, contributed to the victory of the moderate leaders. Thirdly, they were ultimately successful in their bid for power because of their leadership skills. From 1958 to 1962 the moderates worked tirelessly and skillfully at the national and prefectural levels to overcome the power of the radical former mainstream within the national JTU CEC, a power that was not truly representative of the rank and file nor of the majority of the prefectural unions. Miyanohara's personality contributed greatly to his success. Coming from Kagoshima Prefecture and known as the "Saigō Takamori" of the JTU, he is a man who exudes sincerity, calmness, and inner strength. He is widely respected, not for any domineering leadership, but for his fairness, his willingness to listen, and his ability to work out compromises. A pacifist, he unequivocally repudiated violence in the campus disputes in the late 1960's. In 1971 he ran as a nationwide candidate to the House of Councillors and was elected. But perhaps Miyanohara's secret weapon has been his great friend, Makieda Motofumi, former Secretary-General of the JTU who became its Chairman in 1971. Makieda was the brain behind Miyanohara's winning personality and has been the author of the JTU's strategy and policies ever since the moderates seized the leadership in the early 1960's.

There have been two persistent tactical differences between the radicals and the moderates that can be traced all the way back to the differences discussed in Chapter III between the radical Zenkyōkyō and the moderate Kyōzenren before the JTU was formed. The first has concerned the relationship between the JTU and the Japan Communist Party (JCP). Although there has been much controversy among scholars and members of SCAP and the Ministry of Education, to say nothing of JTU leaders themselves, over whether or not the JTU national leadership was Communist dominated from 1947 to 1958,[13] there has been no contro-

[13] See, for example, Richard J. Smethurst's discussion of this point in "The Origins and Policies of the Japan Teachers' Union 1945-1956," *Studies in Japanese History and Politics* (Ann Arbor: The

versy over the inescapable fact that since 1958 the radical anti-mainstream has favored a policy of cooperation with the JCP while the moderate mainstream has not. Although the mainstream was not strong enough to make this policy stick until mid-1961, it has always shied away from full-scale co-operation with the JCP. The second major point of difference between the two factions, previously alluded to, has concerned the relationship between the JTU and the educational bureaucracy. The two factions have differed over the correct tactics in carrying out the union's struggles against the Ministry of Education and the prefectural and local boards of education. On the one hand, the radical Hiragaki faction favored a policy of total confrontation and absolute opposition to Ministry policies, which led in many prefectures to the boycotting of classrooms by teachers. This policy, of course, was most harmful to the students. On the other hand, the Miyanohara faction decried the policy of absolute opposition and called for central negotiations at the national level between JTU leaders and Ministry of Education officials and the opening of talks at the prefectural and local levels between union leaders and members of boards of education and principals.

The fight between the two factions came to a head at the seventeenth National Conference held in Kitayama in June 1958 when both Hiragaki and Miyanohara ran for election to the position of Secretary-General of the JTU, a position that Hiragaki had held since 1953 and from which he was able to lead his then mainstream faction, which had a slight majority in the CEC even though the CEC Chairman, Kobayashi Takeshi, was a member of the moderate faction.[14] In the first vote taken by secret ballot Hiragaki lost

University of Michigan Press, 1967), Occasional Papers No. 10, pp. 151-53.

[14] For this recapitulation of the factional fight from 1958 to 1962 I am indebted to the following participants who were kind enough to grant me interviews: Kobayashi Takeshi, former Chairman of the JTU and now a member of the House of Councillors, interviewed at

by a single vote. He demanded a recount, but Suzuki Riki, the then Chairman of the Iwate Teachers' Union, a member of the emerging moderate Miyanohara faction, suggested that the National Conference adjourn and that a re-vote be taken at a succeeding extraordinary conference. Amid considerable confusion, this was decided. At the succeeding conference, which opened the following month in Tokyo, Miyanohara won more decisively and his faction captured three out of the five top posts in the CEC, although it fell slightly short of a majority of the total number (66) of CEC members.

Clearly, the national leadership of the JTU was going through a very crucial transition in 1958, one in which the radical leadership, which was to decrease gradually in strength in the succeeding years, was nevertheless still powerful, as can be seen by the inability of the emerging moderates within the CEC to have the CEC call off a nationwide boycott of classes on September 15, 1958, a product of Hiragaki's radical policy, and their inability at a meeting in January 1959 to have the CEC come to any decision concerning the "Kanagawa formula," a compromise proposal concerning the efficiency rating system that had been put forth by the Kanagawa Board of Education on the previous December 9. In June of 1959 at the twenty-first National Conference held in Kōchi, however, the Miyanohara faction captured all of the top five executive posts and emerged as

---

JTU headquarters in Tokyo, March 8, 1965; Hiragaki Miyoji, former Secretary-General of the JTU CEC, interviewed at the Osaka Prefectural Teachers' Union headquarters, May 3, 1965; Miyanohara Sadamitsu, former Chairman of the JTU and now a Diet member, interviewed at JTU headquarters in Tokyo, February 13, 1965; Makieda Motofumi, former Secretary-General of the JTU and now Chairman, interviewed at JTU headquarters in Tokyo, February 13, 1965; Ogawa Jun-ichi, former Chairman of the Iwate Teachers' Union, now Vice-Chairman of the JTU, interviewed in Morioka, December 16, 1964. In addition, some of the statistics were obtained from the staff of the JTU Department of Organization.

the mainstream within the CEC by a slight majority. By this time 43 of the 46 prefectural unions had submitted to the implementation of the efficiency rating system even though they had not given up their struggle against it. The subtlety with which they were able to defeat the intent of the efficiency rating system, attributable to the leadership of the Miyanohara faction, is discussed in detail in the following chapter.

At the Kōchi Conference when the question of supporting political parties came up for a vote, as was the annual procedure, the Hiragaki faction, as it had done in the past, demanded that the JTU give its support to both the JSP and the JCP. The Hiragaki supporters argued that only through the cooperation of labor unions, which naturally included the JTU, with the JCP could the conservative Japanese government be overthrown, the efficiency rating system be eliminated, and, of even greater importance to these extremists, the U.S.-Japan Security Treaty, up for revision the following year, be abolished. The Miyanohara faction, not yet strong enough in 1959 to force through its policy of non-cooperation with the JCP, argued for the postponement of any decision on the question of political support in view of the sharp differences within the union and of the large number of withdrawals in a few prefectures. The mainstream Miyanohara faction won by a vote of 206 to 170, thus postponing the decision on party support, a significant victory in itself. If the Miyanohara faction did not feel strong enough to force through a decision concerning party support, a year later in January 1960 it did feel strong enough to call together all the prefectural chairmen and secretary-generals in order to effect an official change in the JTU's fundamental policy vis-à-vis the Ministry of Education. The leaders pointed out that the number of teachers dismissed for having participated in illegal strikes had risen sharply, causing the relief funds supplied by the national JTU for the strikers to skyrocket. In sloganistic terms they therefore proposed to change the JTU's policy from "Kimpyō Zettai

141

Hantai" (absolute opposition to the efficiency rating system) to "Chūō Kōshō ni yoru Kaiketsu" (settlement through central negotiations). The change in policy was approved and led shortly thereafter to talks, albeit nonproductive, with Education Minister Matsuda Takechiyo.

This change in policy by no means signalled that the new Miyanohara-led mainstream was giving up struggles against those policies of the Ministry of Education which it considered undesirable. Rather, the policy change may best be interpreted as a tactical change, one designed to be more effective vis-à-vis the Ministry and to preserve the strength of the union by maintaining the support of the rank and file. Still, in 1960 the Miyanohara mainstream was not able to change the policy of the JTU in regard to the political parties, even though thirty of its members announced in that year that they would become full-fledged members of the JSP, an act followed by the affiliation with the JSP of a large number of the full-time union officials at the prefectural level. The policy of supporting only the JSP was not accomplished until more than a year later at a special conference one month after the twenty-third National Conference, which met in Miyazaki in June 1961. The mainstream and the anti-mainstream continued to disagree violently over whether the JTU should give its support to both the JSP and the JCP or only the JSP. To the mainstream the matter was crucial in view of the upcoming election to the House of Councillors in July of the following year, an election in which Chairman Kobayashi Takeshi would run as a nationwide candidate and in which the JTU hoped to elect as many candidates as possible.[15] The stark question that confronted the mainstream leaders was whether the JTU could elect more candidates by retaining its policy of cooperation with the JCP or by abolishing it. Would close connection with the JCP be political poison? Results of all the elections to both the House of Councillors and the House of Representatives since the end of the war had

[15] See Chapter VII for a discussion of the JTU's electoral politics.

shown that the JSP was far more capable of drawing votes than the JCP. More than this, the JSP itself had not fared well in the previous year's general elections to the House of Representatives held on November 20, 1960, and there was general agreement that the voters had turned against the JSP to a certain extent because of its association with the JCP during the anti-Security Treaty struggle in the spring. In 1961 it appeared, at least to the members of the mainstream, that association with the JCP would lose the JTU votes. Opposition to supporting only the JSP was so strong, however, that a decision on party support was again postponed. A month later, however, at a conference convened in Tokyo, the mainstream for the first time in the history of the JTU was finally able to push through the policy of supporting only the JSP and not the JCP.

Decisive victory of the Miyanohara mainstream over the Hiragaki faction did not occur, however, until a year later in July 1962 at the twenty-fourth National Conference held in Toyama, when the Miyanohara mainstream gained 40 seats on the CEC to the anti-mainstream's 26. In addition, at this conference, Miyanohara was elected chairman (the previous chairman, Kobayashi Takeshi, had just been elected on July 1 to the House of Councillors) and Makieda Motofumi was elected secretary-general. By this time Miyanohara's "gradualism" had superseded Hiragaki's "absolute confrontation" in most of the prefectural unions. Furthermore, the moderate mainstream began to place increasing emphasis on the economic well-being of the teachers and less overt emphasis on political struggles. The victory of the Miyanohara faction was crowned by its successfully implementing structural reform within the JTU, the most significant aspect for our purposes here being the reduction of the number of members of the CEC from 66 to 47. However valid were the reasons given by the mainstream for carrying out this reform, the most cogent being the necessity to reduce the total number of full-time officers at all levels of the union because of the possible passage of the government's proposed revision of the Local Public Service Law, which would not permit full-time officers to maintain their public service status for more than three years, the effect of the reform was to increase the strength of the Miyanohara faction markedly. This can be shown clearly by comparing the number of members in the mainstream and the anti-mainstream before and after the reform:

JTU CEC (1962)

	Number of Mainstream	Number of Anti-Mainstream	Total Number
Before reform	40	26	66
After reform	37	10	47

As a result of the reform, the Miyanohara faction lost only 3 members, while the Hiragaki faction lost 16 members. In percentage terms, the strength of the anti-mainstream in the national CEC fell from 39 percent to 21 percent. By 1968 the mainstream had increased its number to 41 while the anti-mainstream had dropped to 6. With the further reduction in 1969 of the total number of national CEC members to 36, the ratio stood 30 to 6, leaving the mainstream in indisputable control. Over the last decade the ratio between the mainstream and the anti-mainstream in the national CEC has been as follows:

	Mainstream (moderate)	Anti-Mainstream (radical)	Total Number in National CEC
1962	40	26	66
1963	37	10	47
1967	40	7	47
1968	41	6	47
1969	30	6	36
1971	30	6	36

Thus, finally, after years of determined effort and great struggle, the Mivanohara-Makieda moderate faction

144

emerged in a position of decisive control within the JTU CEC. The "red-crested white-bodied crane" lost much of its color at the top and became more truly reflective of the prefectural leadership, although in 1970 and 1971 rumblings from discontented radical groups were increasing at the local level. In addition, the gap between the top leaders and the great body of teachers, while persisting, narrowed somewhat. Though still not reflecting the views of the average teacher, as will be discussed in the following section, the new leaders moved in the direction of becoming more sensitive to the needs of the rank and file than had been true of the previous radical leadership. Of greater significance, the new leaders recognized the essential reactive and negative nature of the JTU's past policies and struggles and began to offer their own positive policies for the improvement of education.

Union Consciousness

Measuring Union Consciousness

One of the problems in analyzing the JTU as an interest group is that of measuring the degree to which the rank and file feel a part of the union and are ready to participate in its activities. As has already been indicated by the statistics on membership, a high percentage of elementary and lower secondary teachers are members of the JTU, but the question is whether this statistical fact reflects a high degree of union consciousness, a strong awareness of union goals, and a willingness to participate in union activities or whether it merely reflects the social fact that teachers who work in the same school feel close to each other, would feel left out if they did not join the union, and are apathetic about union goals. Naturally, if the majority of the rank and file have an apathetic attitude, the strength of the union would be reduced and its effectiveness as an interest group greatly curtailed. In an effort to measure union consciousness and the willingness of members to participate in union activities, the writer prepared and distributed a questionnaire of 40 questions to 222 teachers in 7 elementary and 7 lower secondary schools in Tokyo, Sendai, and Morioka. (See Appendix D for the Japanese version of the questionnaire that was used and an English translation.) Certain questions were designed to elicit attitudes toward a number of factors common to all interest groups, such as the frequency of meetings, the amount of dues, the benefits of the group to the member, and so forth. Other questions, however, elicited attitudes towards a number of the specific problems and activities of the JTU, for example, whether teachers should have the right to strike and whether the JTU should have the right to negotiate with the Ministry of Education at the national level.

By arrangement with the principal and the chapter head of each school, the writer met with all of the teacher members prior to distributing the questionnaire in order to identify himself and explain the purpose of the study of which the questionnaire was a part. The teachers were assured that the results of the questionnaire would be used solely for academic purposes.

The prefectures in which the questionnaire was given were not chosen at random, but rather upon the basis of the reputation of the prefectural union as being either "strong" or "weak." Since the Iwate Teachers' Union is well known for its "strength" and the Miyagi Teachers' Union for its "weakness," schools in the capitals of these respective prefectures, Morioka and Sendai, were chosen in an effort to obtain a more balanced response. The same principle was followed in selecting the nine schools within the city of Tokyo, since the teachers' unions in the poorer wards, such as Katsushika and Edogawa, are reputedly stronger and more active than those in the wealthier wards, such as Nakano and Shinjuku. The list of schools at which the questionnaire was given along with the number of teachers at each school who responded is:

Name of School	Number of Respondents
Tokyo	
Nakano Kuritsu Daigo Chūgakkō	11
Nakano Kuritsu Daiyon Shōgakkō	19
Shinjuku Kuritsu Ōkubo Shōgakkō	18
Shinjuku Kuritsu Higashi Toyama Shōgakkō	15
Katsushika Kuritsu Aoto Chūgakkō	6
Edogawa Kuritsu Komatsugawa Daisan Chūgakkō	11
Itabashi Kuritsu Shimura Daini Chūgakkō	15
Itabashi Kuritsu Daiyon Shōgakkō	18
Suginami Kuritsu Daiichi Shōgakkō	13
Sub Total	126
Sendai	
Sendai Shiritsu Kamisugiyama Chūgakkō	38
Sendai Shiritsu Aramachi Shōgakkō	13
Sub Total	51
Morioka	
Iwate Daigaku Gakugei Gakubu Fuzoku Chūgakkō	6
Iwate Daigaku Gakugei Gakubu Fuzoku Shōgakkō	16
Morioka Shiritsu Ueda Chūgakkō	23
Sub Total	45
TOTAL	222

The analysis of the results of the questionnaire that appears below rests largely on the statistical information obtained from submitting the raw data to Fortran Programming, in which there were 222 units (the total number of cards) and 36 variables. In addition to merely totalling the answers to each question and gaining the percentages, the

147

computer was programmed to compute cross tabulations for 194 contingency tables. Because some questions, for reasons unknown, were not answered by certain teachers, these blanks have been treated as missing and tabulated as such in the total percentages. The author has not treated these unanswered questions as meaning "I don't know," simply because leaving a question blank does not necessarily mean that the teacher "doesn't know." Also, certain questions did provide an "I don't know" answer and the author wished to distinguish clearly between this response and the leaving of a question unanswered. Thus, the reader ought to be aware that the total number of teachers responding to a particular question does not always add up to the total number of 222 nor do the percentages always add up to 100.

Brief Profile of Teachers Who Completed Questionnaire

A brief composite portrait of the teachers who completed the questionnaire will be useful background information for the interpretation of the data that follows. Of the 222 teachers, 110 were elementary and 112 lower secondary teachers. This almost equal split between the two levels is, of course, not an accurate representation of the nationwide division, in which at the time of the questionnaire there was naturally a larger number of elementary teachers (295,594) than lower secondary teachers (211,138). Nevertheless, since there was almost no difference in the percentage of teachers at each level who belonged to the JTU, both percentages being very close to 86 percent, and since differences in opinion between elementary and lower secondary teachers were found to be too slight to be meaningful, the almost equal split in number between the two levels does not misconstrue the findings. The male-female ratio of the 222 teachers in which 143 (64 percent) were men and 79 (35 percent) were women was about consistent with the national average at the time if both the elementary and lower secondary levels are taken into consideration. As to their

148

age, over half (57 percent) fell within the 30-39 age group, with the next largest percentage (23 percent) falling within the 40-49 age group. By contrast, only 12 percent were in their twenties and 8 percent in their fifties. The average age was 36 while the average number of years of teaching was 16. Concerning their educational background, approximately two-thirds of the teachers completed their higher education under the prewar system, with about half of these attending technical schools and the other half normal schools; the remaining one-third completed their higher education under the postwar system. Of the latter group all attended two-year colleges, except for five who attended four-year universities. From the above facts, it is not too grossly inaccurate to say that the average teacher of this particular survey, taken in 1965, was an elementary or middle school teacher, male, in his mid-thirties, who had completed his higher education under the prewar system, and had taught for 16 years and been a member of the JTU for 13 years.

The following analysis of the results of the questionnaire are compared, where appropriate, to those of a survey carried out by the JTU itself in 1969.[16] In the JTU survey 6,864 teachers were polled in 9 prefectures stretching from Hokkaido to Kagoshima. Consisting of 21 questions, the JTU survey attempted to elicit teacher attitudes toward four major areas of their lives: teaching, the union, educational policies, and politics. In spite of the limitations of any questionnaire or survey, an analysis of the responses of these two polls permits certain generalizations to be made concerning the degree of union consciousness among the teacher members and their willingness to support and participate in union activities.

Attendance and Participation in Union Meetings

After requesting such personal information as age, sex, and educational background, the writer's questionnaire at-

[16] JTU, *Kumiaiin Ishiki: Chōsa no Matome* (Consciousness of Teachers' Union Members: Results of a Survey) (Tokyo, JTU, August 20, 1969).

tempted to ascertain the attitude of the teachers toward their union meetings. The average number of chapter meetings per year was found to be 9. When asked about the frequency of these meetings, 73 percent responded that the number was "about right," 21 percent "too few," and only 3 percent "too many." Thus, 94 percent of the teachers indicated that about 9 meetings per year was either "about right" or "too few," indicating their strong support for this reasonable number of chapter meetings. In addition, worthy of note is that a far greater percentage (21 percent) of teachers desired an *increase* in the number of meetings than a decrease (3 percent). More than this, when correlated with the age groups, 34 percent of all of the teachers in the 20-29 age group thought the meetings were "too few," while this percentage declined in the older age brackets from 25 percent of the 30-39 age group to only 7 percent of the 40-49 group. This suggests a greater desire for participation in union activities on the part of the younger teachers than on the part of the older teachers, a trend that augurs well for the JTU's future.

That teachers are willing to participate in union activities at least to the extent of attending chapter meetings is further substantiated by the response to question 14, which asked teachers to indicate to what extent they preferred to attend such meetings rather than do something else. Eight percent responded that they "would rather go to a chapter meeting than almost anything else," and 70 percent that they "usually prefer to go to a chapter meeting," while only 21 percent answered that they "sometimes prefer a chapter meeting; sometimes prefer to do other things," and no teacher checked "usually prefer to do something else." The response to this question in which 78 percent of the teachers indicated that they were more than willing to participate in chapter meetings certainly suggests that the teachers are far from apathetic about their union. This suggests a rather high degree of union consciousness.

If the above statistics reveal the teachers' willingness to

attend school union meetings, they do not, of course, reveal to what extent teachers participate in the discussions that take place at these meetings. In an attempt to measure this, teachers were asked in questions 15 and 16 how often they speak up at chapter meetings and how often they thought their fellow teachers do. Thirty-seven percent responded that they speak up "often" or "occasionally," while a majority 59 percent indicated that they "seldom" or "never" speak up. Interestingly, however, in answer to how often they thought their fellow teachers speak up, 47 percent thought that "most of" or "about half of" them do and 49 percent that "very few" do. This response indicates that about half of the teachers thought that about half of the teachers participate in the discussions. Consequently, even though 59 percent responded that they themselves "seldom" or "never" speak up, teachers do not feel that the meetings are being dominated by a small handful of activists. There is enough participation to dispel such a feeling.

The quality of this participation may be something else again, however. It was frequently asserted to this observer by individual Japanese teachers that the average teacher does not dare oppose publicly in chapter meetings any policy that the prefectural union leaders strongly support. Again and again teachers made the point in private conversations that only rarely did teachers openly argue against the announced policy of union leaders and that, when they did so, as previously stated, they were apt not to offer their own opinions but rather that of their boards of education.[17] Whether the quality of the discussion is such that opposing views are thrashed out or whether announced policies are merely clarified through discussion to enable almost every-

[17] Interviews with Numakunai Shimpei, English teacher, Ueda Lower Secondary School, Morioka, November 13, 1964; Fukushi Shunro and Ōsawa Toshinari, English teachers, Iwate University Attached Junior High School, Morioka, October 14, 1964; Ōshima Masao, history teacher, First Senior High School, Morioka, November 30, 1964; Oda Hajime, Principal, Semboku Lower Secondary School, Morioka, November 9, 1964.

151

one to come to agreement is not as significant here, however, as the fact that, as far as the attitude of the teachers is concerned, half of the teachers felt that half of the teachers *do* participate in discussions. Again, this indicates a high degree of participation and, consequently, of union consciousness.

Teachers have also participated in a different type of union meeting, the so-called educational study conferences, which were first begun by the JTU in 1952. Although initially the emphasis of these conferences was ideological, attempting to inform the participants of the JTU's view of Japanese society and its problems, in recent years, largely because of the challenge of more practical Ministry of Education-sponsored conferences that began in 1962, the emphasis has shifted to the more immediate problems of teaching, such as the making of lesson plans, the learning of new teaching techniques, and the creation of new units. Ideology still plays its role at union educational workshops, but it has lessened. At any rate, there are now educational workshops and seminars of all kinds that have developed out of the educational study conferences, and frequently teachers have the opportunity to attend those sponsored by the JTU as well as by the Ministry. A comparison of the number of times they have attended each kind of meeting and their opinion of the usefulness of each kind of meeting in improving their classroom teaching ability will help complete the portrait of the teachers' attitude toward union meetings.

The results of the questionnaire revealed that 63 percent of the teacher members had attended union-sponsored educational study meetings an average of 1.75 times during the calendar year of 1964, while 77 percent had attended study meetings sponsored by the Ministry of Education or Board of Education an average of 2.45 times during the same period. This suggests that the government is somewhat more active in this area than is the union. When asked how useful the meetings were in improving their teaching ability, however, both fared about equally and neither walked off with overwhelming percentages, as can be seen by the following:

	JTU-sponsored educational study meetings %	Ministry-sponsored educational study meetings %
Extremely useful	10	4
Fairly useful	41	51
Not very useful	31	34
Not applicable	18	11

Although the JTU topped the Ministry 10 percent to 4 percent in the "extremely useful" category, it fared less well than the Ministry in the "fairly useful" category, 41 percent to 51 percent, results that place the JTU and the Ministry very close if these two categories are added together: 51 percent for the JTU and 55 percent for the Ministry. On the whole, the teacher members considered both government- and union-sponsored educational study conferences about equally useful although clearly they were not overly impressed with either. Significant is the fact that about one-third of the teachers thought neither of the conferences very useful.

Consistent with the responses of the 20-29-year-olds to other questions already discussed, this age group showed a slight preference for the JTU-sponsored conferences over the Ministry-sponsored ones:

20-29-year-old age group

	JTU-sponsored educational study meetings %	Ministry-sponsored educational study meetings %
Extremely useful	3	0
Fairly useful	38	38
Not very useful	27	42
Not applicable	32	20

153

As can be seen, a slightly higher percentage of 20-29-year-olds thought the JTU-sponsored conferences more useful than the Ministry-sponsored ones. Consistent with this, 15 percent more placed the Ministry-sponsored conferences in the "not very useful" category than the JTU-sponsored conferences. As might be expected, a similar pattern appears when the prewar-postwar education variable is applied to these two questions, with the postwar-education teachers indicating a slight preference for the JTU workshops.

In the JTU survey of 6,864 teachers, when asked in question 12 if they would be willing to attend seminars sponsored by the Ministry and the Boards of Education, the teachers revealed a decided reluctance to do so. Only 14 percent responded clearly in the affirmative that they would be "willing to attend," while the rest displayed various degrees of unwillingness: 49 percent "unwilling but would attend anyway," 30 percent "unwilling to participate," and 5 percent "absolutely unwilling." Although the question was not asked specifically, the response implies that teachers would prefer to attend seminars sponsored by the union.

On the basis of the above findings concerning the attitude of teachers towards attending various kinds of union meetings, from chapter meetings to education seminars, there appears to be substantial willingness to attend and to participate in discussion. Such a response indicates a fairly high degree of union consciousness and a fairly strong desire to participate in union activities.

Union Dues

A further index for measuring the willingness to participate in JTU activities is the attitude of the members toward the amount of their union dues. Since each prefectural union determines independently the monthly rate, the amount varies considerably from prefecture to prefecture, as can be seen in Table 7. Based upon the above statistics, the average monthly dues in 1964 were ¥534. Happily for

Table 7

Amount of Union Dues
(as of June 1, 1964) (These figures include special assessments.)

Monthly Rate Yen	Prefectures	Total Number of Prefectures
- - - -350	Ibaraki, Chiba, Tokyo, Nagano, Aichi, Nara, Okayama, Tokushima	8
351-450	Tochigi, Kanagawa, Fukui, Yamanashi, Kyoto, Hyōgo, Ōita	7
451-550	Aomori, Miyagi, Yamagata, Gumma, Niigata, Toyama, Osaka, Shiga, Shimane, Yamaguchi, Kagawa, Fukuoka	12
551-650	Fukushima, Saitama, Gifu, Mie, Hiroshima, Nagasaki, Miyazaki, Kagoshima	8
651-750	Akita, Hokkaidō, Ishikawa, Tottori, Ehime, Saga, Kumamoto	7
751-1,100	Iwate, Shizuoka, Wakayama, Kōchi	4

Source: Ministry of Education, Local Affairs Section, *Kyōshokuin no Soshiki Suru Shokuin Dantai no Gaikyō* (Profile of Employees' Groups Organized by Educational Personnel), 1964, p. 33. The above table is adopted from Table 12.

this study, the union dues in the three prefectures of Tokyo, Miyagi, and Iwate ranged from the lowest to the highest category. In fact, the monthly dues of the Iwate Teachers' Union were ¥1,053, twice as high as the average prefecture, while the dues in Tokyo were below average and those in Miyagi about average. Therefore, the attitude of the teachers sampled should correspond closely to that of the members of the union as a whole.

In response to question 20 concerning their attitude toward the amount of their union dues, 44 percent of the teachers thought them "about right," while 56 percent thought them "too high." None thought the dues "too low."

155

Where the pocketbook is concerned, the fact that 44 percent thought the dues "about right" indicates substantial willingness to pay them, although the fact that 56 percent thought the dues "too high" is certainly a warning that a majority of the teachers do not feel they are getting their money's worth. As might be expected, in Iwate, where the dues were unusually steep, 77 percent of the teachers indicated that they thought them "too high," whereas in Miyagi, where the dues were about the same as the national average, this figure dropped to 63 percent. In Tokyo, where the dues were below the national average, only 43 percent thought them "too high." These percentages suggest that there is definitely a limit to the amount of dues teachers will pay willingly but at the same time that they are certainly willing to pay a reasonable amount of dues in order to support the union and its activities.

Awareness of Goals

As an interest group within the renovationist camp of Japanese politics that has been denied the right to strike, the JTU has from time to time resorted to tactics, such as "simultaneous leaves of absence," which have been regarded by the government as illegal strikes. Such "strikes" entail the refusal to teach or the boycott of classrooms during regular teaching hours, normally lasting no more than a few hours or half a day. On rare occasions "strikes" have lasted an entire day, or a certain percentage of teachers have been asked to stay away for a two or three-day period. When urged by the national JTU to engage in such "strikes," each prefectural union determines whether or not it will participate and, if so, the number of hours the teachers will be asked to boycott classrooms. Rallies and demonstrations are not considered "strikes" when they occur during non-teaching hours. Although it is probably true that not all teachers who participate in the frequent rallies and demonstrations called by the leadership of the JTU are fully aware of the purposes of such acts and participate in

156

them only on a rotation basis simply because it is their turn to do so, the same cannot be said for "strikes." "Strikes" have been far less frequent than demonstrations and have occurred after months, if not years, of confrontation between the JTU and the Ministry of Education over a specific issue, such as the efficiency rating system. They have also occurred after weeks of discussion over the specific issue at chapter meetings in the schools and long after the issue has received full coverage by press, radio, and television. Consequently, by the time the "strike" date arrives, it is inconceivable that any teacher member could be unaware of the issue involved or of the union's position. Decision by the teacher whether or not to participate in the "strike" is made, therefore, with full knowledge of the JTU's objective, as well as, it may be added, of the possible legal consequences of "striking." A decision to "strike" would therefore indicate not only full awareness of the specific goal of the JTU in regard to the immediate issue but also a high degree of willingness to participate in union activities even at some risk.

To measure teacher members' attitudes regarding strikes, the questionnaire first asked (question 21) whether teachers should have the right to strike, now illegal, and, second, whether they would participate in a strike, if necessary, even though it was illegal (question 22). To each question teachers were asked to check "yes" or "no" or "I don't know." Fifty-eight percent responded that teachers ought to have the right to strike, 25 percent that they should not, and 12 percent that they did not know. These findings, when compared with the results to question 9 of the 1969 JTU survey, reveal that the percentage of teachers who believe teachers ought to have the right to strike may be increasing. Although teachers may have responded as they did because they knew the answer the JTU wanted, it is nevertheless impressive that 80 percent of the 6,864 questioned thought that teachers ought to have the right to strike. This reflects not only the success of the JTU leaders

157

in educating teachers to their way of thinking in the post-war period but also the desire on the part of the teachers to possess stronger means for the protection of their rights.

A third survey, conducted by the Osaka Teachers' Union in May 1964, substantiates this conclusion. In this survey 5,000 educational personnel, including union and non-union members from principals down to clerks, were polled. Their opinions regarding strikes were elicited by questioning their understanding of the relationship between the Constitution and the laws, on the one hand, and the striking of teachers, on the other. The question and results were as follows:

"Apart from your approval or disapproval of the strikes conducted by the JTU in order to protect the status and labor conditions of teachers and to have the contents and conditions of education improved for the benefit of the people, what do you think about the relation between the Constitution and the laws on the one hand and the carrying out of strikes on the other?"[18]

	%
a. Striking by teachers is lawful under Constitution and the laws	23.4
b. Striking by teachers is against the Constitution and the laws	8.0
c. Striking by teachers is against the laws but legal under the Constitution	52.6
d. I don't know	16.0
TOTAL	100.0

Those who checked "a" and "c" above, a total of 76 percent, believed that striking by teachers is legal under the Constitution, if not under the laws. This implies that 76 percent of the respondents would be in favor of teachers' pos-

[18] The results of this survey were supplied to the author by Ichikawa Taishirō, Secretary-General of the Osaka City Teachers' Union, in an interview on March 2, 1965.

sessing the right to strike, a position that corroborates the results of the author's questionnaire and the JTU nationwide survey.

This fundamental conclusion is substantiated by the results in the writer's questionnaire to the second question regarding strikes, which asked whether the teachers would participate in a strike, if necessary, in spite of its illegality. Fifty-five percent (only 3 percent less than those who thought teachers ought to have the right to strike) responded that they would be willing to participate in such a strike. Twenty-seven percent responded that they would not participate in an illegal strike and 17 percent checked the "I don't know" answer. Thus, a majority of the teachers indicated their willingness to participate in an illegal strike. It is interesting that in the JTU survey of 1969 the exact same percentage of teachers, 55 percent, thought that it was "all right" for the JTU to engage in *political* strikes (the question was so worded that it did not refer necessarily to educational policies) to assert its opinion if the government persisted in political policies neglecting the JTU's view. At the same time, however, 39 percent, a rather high percentage, either thought that such strikes were "not all right" or found themselves in a dilemma and could not say whether or not they were right. When it is remembered, however, that teachers are subject to administrative punishment whenever they participate in an illegal strike, the willingness of 55 percent of the union membership to do so is a strong indication of their belief in the necessity to strike to achieve specific union goals.

On the assumption that Japanese male teachers would be more inclined to act in order to protect their job security and their rights than would Japanese female teachers, one might conclude that the majority of the teachers who responded to the writer's questionnaire favored participating in illegal strikes if necessary simply because 64 percent of them were male. It is extraordinarily interesting to note, however, that the percentage of female teachers who were

159

willing to participate in an illegal strike was greater than that of the male teachers. Fifty-eight percent of the female teachers indicated their willingness to do so as compared with 52 percent of the males. This may be highly significant for the future vitality of the JTU. A number of observers have suggested that the JTU will become weaker as the proportion of female teacher members increases, as is happening particularly at the elementary level, but this finding suggests that such gloomy prognostications may not be valid. The explanation for this greater willingness of women teachers to participate in illegal strikes may be that they fear sanctions less than do men teachers, simply because for many of them teaching is not a necessity but a luxury, an additional salary to their husbands'. Or, the explanation may lie in the importance the women teachers attached to the words, "if necessary," in the question. This latter interpretation suggests itself from the fact that while a higher percentage of female teachers than male teachers were willing to participate in an illegal strike if necessary, a lower percentage of female teachers (48 percent) than of male teachers (62 percent) thought that teachers, who are public service workers, should have the right to strike in the first place. These percentages suggest that male teachers, while strongly desiring the legal right to strike, are somewhat reluctant to strike illegally, while female teachers, rather less concerned about the legal right to strike, are more willing to strike illegally if necessary. Women may feel that teachers ought not to have the right to strike since strikes interrupt the education of children, while, at the same time, they feel that, in spite of this temporary undesirable result, they must participate in strikes when absolutely necessary for the good of the children's future education.

At any rate, the point that the vigor of the JTU may not necessarily be diminished by the steady increase in the proportion of female teachers is reinforced by the fact that a greater percentage of younger teachers favored the right of teachers to strike and were willing to participate in illegal strikes. Broken down by age groups the results were as follows:

Those who thought teachers should have the right to strike:

> 65 percent of the 20-29 year olds
> 63 percent of the 30-39 year olds
> 50 percent of the 40-49 year olds
> 41 percent of the 50-59 year olds

Those who indicated their willingness to participate in illegal strikes:

> 69 percent of the 20-29 year olds
> 56 percent of the 30-39 year olds
> 47 percent of the 40-49 year olds
> 38 percent of the 50-59 year olds

These percentages reveal clearly the difference in attitude between the 20-29 age group and the 50-59 age group. As might be expected, a similar pattern emerges when the education variable is cross-tabulated with these two questions. Of the teachers who attended postwar junior colleges or universities, 75 percent thought teachers should have the right to strike and 68 percent indicated their willingness to participate in illegal strikes. By contrast, of the teachers who completed their education in the prewar period, only 51 percent thought teachers should have the right to strike and only 43 percent indicated their willingness to participate in illegal strikes.

That teachers have such willingness is reinforced by the results to question 7 of the JTU survey. When asked how they would act if ordered by the JTU to go on strike, 22 percent responded that they would obey the strike order automatically while 61 percent responded that they would consult their union leaders first. The implication is that they would strike if necessary since teachers were given the option of responding that they would obey the authority of the board of education, which, by definition, would be

161

against a strike. Hence, 83 percent of the teachers indicated a willingness to strike if necessary.

The findings discussed above in regard to the attitudes of teacher members towards the whole question of strikes suggest that teachers have a high degree of union consciousness as well as a high degree of willingness to participate in union activities. Furthermore, the findings strongly suggest that these attitudes will not decrease in the future but will probably increase, since it was discovered that women, the young, and the postwar-educated teachers all had these attitudes to a greater degree than did the men, the older, and the prewar-educated teachers.

Indication that teacher members are fully aware of specific union goals is strongly supported by the results to question 26, which asked the respondents whether or not they thought the JTU should "have the right to negotiate" with the Ministry of Education at the national level, a right that the JTU has been demanding ever since it was taken away in 1948, or only the right to negotiate with the boards of education at the prefectural level and below.[19]

Of 222 teachers, 193 or 87 percent thought that the JTU should have the right to negotiate at the national level, while only 8 teachers, or roughly 4 percent, thought that the JTU should negotiate only at the prefectural level and below. Fifteen teachers, or 7 percent, responded that they did not know. This overwhelmingly favorable response to the JTU's point of view, along with the very small percentage of teachers who indicated that they did not know, represents ample evidence that the teacher members are not only very conscious indeed of one of the union's primary goals but also that they support the union's view. Although attitudes may not correlate with behavior, one can hardly argue on the basis of these findings that the members of the JTU are not conscious of being union members or of their union's goals.

[19] For a thorough discussion of this problem see Chapter VI, pages 186-99, below.

Ambivalent Attitude of Teachers Toward the JTU

In spite of the foregoing, results of the writer's question-naire disclosed a marked ambivalence in the attitude of the teacher members toward the JTU. While overwhelmingly agreeing that the union is essential for the protection of their welfare, teachers at the same time overwhelmingly agreed that union policies do not reflect their opinions. On the one hand, when asked in question 25 whether they thought the JTU necessary for the protection of their liveli-hood, 63 percent responded "very necessary," 34 percent "necessary," and only 2 percent "not very necessary." Thus an incredible 97 percent thought the JTU either "very nec-essary" or "necessary." This virtually unanimous agreement among the teachers of the necessity of the JTU for the pro-tection of their welfare clearly indicates a high degree of awareness of the benefits that accrue to them as a result of their union membership and of its activities in their behalf. Furthermore, the younger the teacher the greater the belief in the necessity of the union. In the "very necessary" cate-gory were:

> 76 percent of the 20-29 year olds
> 63 percent of the 30-39 year olds
> 56 percent of the 40-49 year olds
> 50 percent of the 50-59 year olds

On the other hand, when asked in question 29 how strongly they thought the opinions of the average teacher were reflected in the union's action policies, 65 percent re-sponded "not very strongly," 28 percent "fairly strongly," and only one teacher "very strongly." Since the term "action policy" connotes primarily the political line of the JTU and only secondarily its non-political policies regarding the eco-nomic well-being of the teachers, this response suggests strong disapproval of the union's heavy emphasis on politi-cal matters that the teachers may not agree with and that they find not directly related to their immediate interests.

163

The contrast between the responses to these two questions is placed in sharp relief below:

RESPONSE TO QUESTION 25	RESPONSE TO QUESTION 29
Percentage of teachers who think JTU necessary for protection of their livelihood	*Percentage of teachers who think opinions of average teacher are reflected in the JTU's action policies*
63 percent—very necessary	.5 percent—very strongly
34 percent—necessary	28 percent—fairly strongly
2 percent—not very necessary	65 percent—not very strongly

Considered together, these findings reveal that while two-thirds of the teachers believe the JTU to be "very necessary" for their welfare, two-thirds also believe at the same time that their opinions are not taken into consideration by the leadership.

Two questions on the JTU survey reveal similar ambivalent tendencies in the teachers' attitude towards the union. When asked in question 5 how well they thought of the JTU's activities, a question that implied reference to its concrete achievements rather than its political posturing, 25 percent responded "very well," 57 percent "moderately well," and only 17 percent "not well" or "I don't know." Hence, 82 percent of the teachers indicated approval of the JTU's activities. In question 4, however, when asked how much confidence they had in the JTU, a question that implied faith in its leaders, only 8 percent responded that they had "complete confidence," while 57 percent answered "confidence by and large" or "on the whole" (*daitai*). Twenty-four percent indicated that they did not have confidence in the JTU while an additional 11 percent responded that they could not say whether or not they did. The higher percentage of those who approved of the JTU's activities compared with those who had confidence in the JTU suggests an ambivalence in attitude similar to the one discussed above. Before analyzing the reasons lying behind this ambivalent attitude of the teachers towards their union, we need to consider results of other questions that reveal the same kind of attitudinal split.

In line with the favorable attitude toward the JTU as indicated by strong support of the union in its efforts to improve their welfare, teachers have responded favorably to the Mutual Aid Society established by the JTU in April 1965. At the time the writer's questionnaire was administered, approximately half of the members throughout Japan had decided to participate. Although the system duplicates benefits received from the government, teachers apparently participate because of the low premiums, either ¥100 or ¥200 per month, whichever the teacher prefers. When asked in question 40 whether they thought the Mutual Aid Society was necessary for their livelihood, 26 percent responded "very necessary," 36 percent "necessary," 10 percent "not very necessary," and 19 percent that they did not know. Thus, 62 percent of the teachers thought the system either "very necessary" or "necessary," a substantial majority when it is remembered that the system at the time the questionnaire was distributed was only a few months old and that on a nationwide basis no more than 50 percent of the teachers had signed up. As the results of the questionnaire show, the attitude toward the Mutual Aid Society was favorable and, based upon the findings that a much higher percentage of 20-29 year olds (42 percent compared to the next highest percentage of 27 percent for the 40-49 year olds), it appeared that participation in the system would increase. This, in fact, occurred. By January 1971, 75 percent of all teachers had joined the society, a fact that strengthened the ties of the rank and file to the union.

By contrast and in line with the teacher members' unfavorable attitude toward the JTU, as revealed in their overwhelming belief that the union's action policies do not reflect the opinions of the average teacher, about two-thirds of the teachers thought that the JTU's action policies were created by either the top three men in the union (the chairman, the vice-chairman, and the secretary-general) or the Central Executive Committee (question 30). Only 9 percent thought that these policies were created by the Central Committee. A valid interpretation to be drawn from the results of both questions concerning policy decisions is that a very strong majority of the teachers feel that such decisions are not only made at an organizational level far removed from their influence but also that the content of these decisions does not normally reflect their desires. It must be quickly added, however, that this attitude probably does not exist with the same degree of intensity toward the *prefectural* unions. When asked in question 31 whether they thought their *prefectural* full-time union officers are elected in a democratic fashion, 68 percent responded "yes." Nevertheless, to return to the discussion of unfavorable attitudes toward the JTU, the teachers polled revealed that they have a low opinion of their leaders' capabilities. When asked in question 28 their opinion of their full-time union officers, a mere 5 percent responded "very capable," while only 27 percent responded "capable," followed by 45 percent who thought their officers merely "average," and 16 percent who thought them "unsatisfactory." Thus, while 61 percent disclosed a low opinion of their leaders' capabilities, only 32 percent had a high opinion.

How can this ambivalent attitude toward the JTU be explained? Why do teacher members strongly support the JTU, on the one hand, and soundly condemn it, on the other? Why do they indicate a willingness to participate in its activities at the local level while at the same time criticizing its activities at the national level, thus implying that a great gap exists between themselves and the national leaders? As interpreted by this researcher, one major reason for the ambivalent attitude results from the difference between the more immediate, pragmatic interests of the rank and file as compared to the more long-range, ideological interests of the national leaders. As revealed by the questionnaire and by numerous teachers in conversations with this writer on many occasions, teachers strongly support the JTU insofar as it works to improve their economic well-being, to protect them from administrative injustices, and to improve education. They recognize these aspects of the JTU's activities as absolutely essential to their own interests. They believe that their salaries have increased largely due to the efforts of the union, that the union has served as a watchdog against unfair personnel practices, and that the union has fought consistently against undesirable directions in educational policy. The majority of the teachers have been able to see the results of these union activities at the local level, within both their own school and their own prefecture. At the same time, however, the majority of the teachers, as interpreted by the results of the questionnaire, the JTU survey, and numerous interviews, have little enthusiasm for the kind of political activities engaged in by the JTU at the national level that have no direct bearing on their immediate interests and that are a direct result of the leadership's anti-status-quo ideological orientation. Quite plainly, the majority of the rank and file are much less ideologically oriented than are the national leaders and much more interested in immediate bread-and-butter issues. Thus, although it may be paradoxical, teachers simultaneously give both strong and weak support to the union. For instance, many teachers who may not agree with or approve of a particular policy of the JTU as determined by the national leaders— for example, the decision to oppose the normalization of relations between Japan and South Korea—will nevertheless go along with the policy to the extent of participating half-heartedly in the called-for demonstrations primarily because they feel a sense of obligation to the JTU, which has worked to increase their salaries and protect them from administrative injustices. It is a kind of quid pro quo arrangement. Thus, lying at the root of the teachers' ambivalent attitude toward the JTU is a weak interest in those policies formulated at the national level which are essentially ideo-

167

logical in nature and which, in the eyes of the majority, do not affect their immediate lives. They are caught by wanting the JTU and needing it even though they may not agree completely with its political policies.

A second major cause of the ambivalent attitude of the teacher members toward the JTU has its roots in the reality that teachers are employed by the government, by the local boards of education. This places them in the uncomfortable and awkward position of being in the middle between the government side and the union, since they are employees of the first and members of the second. Perhaps this sounds as though it ought to be a natural position for teachers, but for the Japanese elementary and lower secondary teachers it is not. There is still a strong reluctance to go against the traditional source of authority, the Ministry of Education, now partially represented by the local boards of education and also by the school principals. This reluctance is suggested by the teachers' response to a question on the JTU survey regarding their use of the standard instructional guides issued by the Ministry for each course. Let us put aside the legal question, about which there has been much dispute, of whether teachers are bound by law to follow the guides in their teaching; teachers were asked to what extent they used them. Ten percent responded that they "followed the guides closely," 76 percent that they "used them as a reference and added their own ideas," and only 16 percent that they "created their own courses without consulting the guides." This response indicates considerable reliance on the guides, which are products of the Ministry, even though in another question 32 percent of the teachers thought the Ministry's educational policies "bad," 57 percent "bad but not absolutely bad," and only 3 percent "good." The tendency to rely on the guides while at the same time believing the Ministry's policies undesirable exists not just because it is easier for teachers to follow the guides but because they are reluctant to go against Ministry authority. Even though teachers have come to believe that they have the

168

right and the duty to protect and to fight for their livelihood and working conditions,[20] they are still reluctant to act
in such a way as to antagonize their employer. In addition,
as the percentages above indicate, most teachers recognize
that some of the educational ideas that come down from the
Ministry are sound and ought not to be dismissed outright.
When the JTU takes a too hasty position of outright opposition to a policy merely because it has originated in the Ministry, many teachers are caught between loyalty to their employer on the one hand and to their union on the other, to
say nothing of loyalty to their pupils. Consequently, for this
second reason as well, the teachers' attitude toward the
JTU may best be described as ambivalent, although it
would be dangerous to underestimate their support for the
union.

Participation in Political Activities

In order to place ex-JTU officers near the center of political power in the Japanese political process, thereby maximizing the opportunities for exerting influence on the
making of public policy, the JTU makes a great effort to
elect to public office as many JTU candidates or candidates
sympathetic to JTU objectives as possible. (See Chapter VII
for a discussion of the JTU's electoral politics.) Consequently, in almost every election at the national, prefectural, or
local level the JTU either runs its own candidates or endorses candidates sympathetic to its interests. With a membership of more than 500,000, a very solid bloc of votes on
which to build, it is not surprising that the union urges its
teacher members to participate in a variety of ways in the

[20] See the results of a poll taken by the Ibaraki Prefectural Teachers' Union in 1964 in which 320 teachers were asked whether it is all
right to say that "teachers have the right and duty to protect their
own livelihood and to fight for better working conditions." The response was: 74 percent—Yes; 3 percent—No; 23 percent—I don't know.
Kyōshi no Kai (Teachers' Association), Kyōshi to iu Na no Shokugyō
(The Teaching Profession) (Tokyo: San-ichi, 1965), pp. 198-99.

169

campaigns to elect these candidates. The degree of willingness on the part of the teachers to do so indicates their willingness to participate in this particular, but very important, aspect of the union's activities and is a further reflection of their union consciousness.

As a general rule, teachers in most union chapters are requested to spend a portion of their time campaigning for union-sponsored candidates. Not all teachers do so, of course, but in some well-organized prefectural unions, such as the Iwate Teachers' Union, each teacher member is requested to send out campaign literature provided by the national or prefectural union to a list of individuals over whom he may have some personal influence, such as former students and parents of students he has taught or is teaching. In addition, each teacher is urged to make personal contact with at least five voters in order to discuss the merits of the union-backed candidates. In other ways as well, teacher members are urged to assist in the election of approved candidates. Thus the response to the question of whether the JTU should expend "more," "less," or "about the same" effort than at present in electing union candidates to public office reflects to some extent not only the teachers' attitude toward the concept of the union electing its own ex-officers to public office but also their attitude toward participating in this endeavor. In response to this question (number 24), 97 percent thought that the JTU should expend either "more" or "about the same" amount of effort in electing union candidates to public office. The response suggests a very high degree of awareness of and support by the teachers of this most important activity of the union.

In more detailed questioning, however, the teachers revealed that they have some reservations about the nature of their activities in working for the election of JTU candidates to public office. Question 23 pertained to a number of specific ways the JTU ought or ought not to involve its members in electing JTU candidates.[21] Results of this ques-

21 It ought to be remarked before beginning the discussion of the

tion revealed that support of the principle of electing JTU candidates to public office does not include willingness to participate in the form of "house-to-house campaigning." When asked whether the union should "encourage teachers to campaign for candidates by going from house to house," 70 percent of the teachers responded "no," and only 5 percent "yes." It is, of course, illegal in Japan for individuals to engage in house-to-house campaigning, and it may be the teachers' awareness of the illegality of this act that caused over two-thirds of them to express a negative opinion. It may also reflect the teachers' unwillingness to take the necessary time out of their busy daily lives to engage in this activity. On the findings of this questionnaire, it appears that the union would do better to confine the active support of the teacher members in campaigns to other types of activities.

If the teachers are unwilling to participate in the election of JTU candidates to public office by house-to-house campaigning, they are also reluctant to do so by giving money to special campaign funds over and above their regular dues. When asked whether the union should "collect money from each member to help union candidates," only 31 percent responded "yes," while 43 percent answered "no." Although the "noes" do not constitute a majority, their percentages in relation to the "yeses" suggest that most teachers are against special assessments for campaigns.

On the more positive side, 60 percent of the teachers thought that the JTU ought to inform union members which candidates are "friendly to labor." At the same time, however, the teachers were wary of permitting the JTU to exert too much pressure on them concerning which candidates

---

results of this particular question that for some reason inexplicable to the writer approximately 25 percent of the respondents, a disproportionately high percentage when compared to all the other questions, failed to answer this question. Thus the reader ought to be warned that the total percentages of the "yes" and "no" responses add up only to approximately 75 percent.

they should vote for. When asked whether the JTU ought to "advise members whom to vote for," 40 percent responded that the JTU should not do so, while 33 percent thought that it should. Again, the percentage differences are not great here, but they do suggest a sensitivity on the part of the teachers in protecting their independence of choice. These findings indicate that the teachers do not wish to be coerced into voting for any particular candidate, although they do wish to be informed by the union as to which candidates are friendly to union interests.

On the whole, the results of the writer's questionnaire and the JTU survey strongly indicate that the rank and file of the Japan Teachers' Union are more than willing to participate in most of the union's activities and that, far from being mere unaware lumps of clay in the organization, out of touch with the union's objectives, they possess a keen awareness of specific union goals, particularly those which affect their own livelihood and their own responsibilities as teachers. They revealed a willingness to attend union meetings, to participate in discussions, and to pay dues. They revealed their belief that the JTU ought to have the right to negotiate with the Ministry of Education at the national level, their belief that teachers ought to possess the right to strike, and their willingness to participate in illegal strikes if necessary. In addition, they virtually unanimously revealed their conviction that the union was necessary for the protection of their livelihood even though they disagreed with some of its policies. And, finally, they revealed their full support of the principle of electing JTU candidates to public office. These findings lead to the generalization that the majority of the members of the JTU have a strong degree of union consciousness and of willingness to engage in activities designed to benefit themselves and their union. This analysis suggests that there is greater support for certain kinds of union activities than the leadership, with its tendency to preoccupy itself with national and international political issues, is able to use effectively. Nevertheless, as

172

long as the leadership does not disaffect the rank and file more than it has, the JTU will continue to have enough support from its members to be able to exert considerable influence on the formulation and, more particularly, the implementation of educational policies.

CHAPTER VI

Claims and Demands
on the Educational Bureaucracy

AN ACTIVE interest group attempts to exert influence on a number of different areas within the governmental process. It urges political parties to endorse policies it favors; it works for the election of public officials and for the appointment of bureaucratic officials sympathetic to its interests; and it attempts to secure favorable decisions from the executive, legislative, and judicial branches of the government. Depending upon the nature of the governmental process in which the interest group finds itself, it may for reasons of efficacy choose to place greater emphasis on one area of government over another, but, in general, the desire of interest groups to have public policy-makers meet their claims and demands causes them to come into contact with the governmental process at a variety of points. One of the most important of these points is, of course, the bureaucracy. To the JTU at the national level that arm of the bureaucracy with which it has been most concerned and upon which it has attempted to exert its greatest influence has been the Ministry of Education, while at the prefectural and local levels it has been the prefectural and local boards of education.

Even though the Ministry of Education no longer has the absolute authority that the prewar Ministry possessed, it nevertheless is still the initiator of educational policies and is therefore logically a focal point for JTU pressure, while the postwar-created boards of education that are responsible for the implementation of Ministry policies and for negotiating with the teachers' unions are logical focal points of JTU pressure at the prefectural and local levels.[1] It must be quickly added, however, that because of the traditional reluctance of the Ministry to recognize the legitimacy of any teachers' organization that is *independent* of the Ministry, and because of the political divide between the Ministry, whose responsibility it is to implement LDP policies, and the JTU, which supports JSP policies, there has been little or no development in the institutionalization at the national level of the JTU's application of pressure on the Ministry. In Britain it is considered normal and proper for pressure groups to consult with ministries when a bill bearing on their interest is being drafted. In Japan, such procedure is woefully underdeveloped and, as far as the JTU and the Ministry of Education at the national level are concerned, non-existent. At the prefectural and local levels, however, the gap is not as wide and, in most of the prefectures, regularized channels of communication between the

[1] A full account of the changing relationship between the Ministry of Education and the Occupation-inspired prefectural and local boards of education since their establishment in 1958 would require separate treatment of book length. One of the fundamental changes, however, has been the shift from elective to appointive boards. Under the provisions of the Local Administration and Management Law passed by the Diet in 1956 over the heated opposition of the JTU, the members of the boards are no longer elected by the general public but are appointed by the head of the local government agency—the headman, mayor, or governor—with approval of the local assembly. Such a system opens the door for greater Ministry control over the boards through the application of Ministry pressure on the appointing officials. In addition, the same law increased Ministry control over the boards by reserving approval of the appointment of the prefectural superintendent to the Minister of Education. It also granted veto power to the Minister over the acts of prefectural and local boards, if he determined that a board had acted unjustly or unfairly. Ministry "control" over education was also increased by the granting of power to the Ministry to "positively advise, guide, and help prefectures." For a fuller explanation of this relationship, see Ronald S. Anderson, *Japan: Three Epochs of Modern Education* (Washington, D.C.: U.S. Department of Health, Education, and Welfare, 1959).

prefectural and local unions and the corresponding boards of education have been established.

Let us focus our attention on the national level first. Secretary-General Makieda made the point in February 1965 that since the end of the Occupation there have been no *regularly* scheduled formal contacts between the JTU and the Ministry.[2] Without regularly scheduled meetings between bureaucratic officials at the top and middle-ranking levels of the Ministry and their counterparts in the JTU, the JTU has been almost totally shut out from the possibility of influencing educational policies during the stage of their formulation within the Ministry. Influence of the JTU occurs through the JSP at a later stage, when Ministry-proposed bills are brought before the Diet. There have been occasional meetings between top officials in the Ministry and the top leaders of the JTU, but these have been extremely sporadic. Even the high level talks between the government and the heads of labor unions, including the JTU, which were initiated on the advice of the ILO Dreyer Commission after its fact-finding mission to Japan in early 1965, accomplished nothing and were soon abandoned. As for secret meetings, Makieda commented that they have been almost non-existent. This absence of personal contact was corroborated by officials within the Ministry's Local Affairs Section, which is responsible for gathering intelligence on the activities of the JTU. Several wistfully stated that they, as middle-ranking officials in the Ministry, would like to consult with their counterparts in the JTU but that such behavior was frowned upon very strongly by most high-ranking officials.[3] Given the vertical stratification of Japanese society, which greatly limits mobility of personnel across the boundaries of their own organizations, such horizontal contact would be rare even without the ideological

[2] Interview with Makieda Motofumi, February 13, 1965.

[3] Interviews with Sawada Michiya, Chief of the Local Affairs Section of the Ministry of Education, Tokyo, June 24, 1964, July 7, 1964, February 3, 1965, and April 8, 1965.

differences these two particular groups represent. Furthermore, the different social and educational backgrounds of the two groups of bureaucrats, in which most Ministry officials are graduates of universities while most JTU officials are graduates of normal schools, operates as a natural barrier to easy communication. At any rate, neither formal nor informal contacts have taken place with any degree of regularity. Revealing of the gap that exists in the personal relationships between the officials of the two bureaucracies is the fact that a Ministry bureaucrat at the national level would consider it almost unthinkable to go out drinking with a JTU bureaucrat. Since the political process in Japan is oiled to a considerable extent by *sake*, the limitation placed upon the JTU's efforts to influence policy-makers in the Ministry is immediately evident. This absence of personal contact on either a formal or an informal level cuts off communication and prevents the JTU from participating in or even knowing about prospective policies, to say nothing of daily administrative business.

Matsushita Keiichi, a well-known political scientist at Hōsei University, has described this process in which the government is allowed to operate through a bureaucracy cut off from pressure as a "reactionary system."[4] It is true, as Matsushita has implied, that bureaucratic officials of the JTU are cut off from presenting their views directly to the members of the various decision-making bodies in the Ministry of Education. But to say this is not to say that the JTU has had no influence whatsoever on these bodies. As will be made more evident in later sections of this chapter, the JTU is a "presence" in the educational world of Japan, and Ministry bureaucrats have learned through years of bitter experience that it is unwise to formulate policies that it knows will be fiercely resisted by the JTU. This does not mean that

---

[4] Matsushita Keiichi, "Rōdō Kumiai no Seiji Katsudō" (Political Activities of Labor Unions) in *Seiji Gaku Nempō, 1960: Nihon no Atsuryoku Dantai* (Annuals of the Japanese Political Science Association, 1960: Pressure Groups in Japan) (Tokyo: Iwanami, 1960), p. 105.

Ministry officials have resorted to policies that the JTU will not resist, but rather that it has modified certain policies as well as the timetable of their implementation in order to reduce the degree of JTU resistance, which has taken the form of a series of struggles against specific Ministry policies. Before proceeding with an analysis of the JTU's techniques of applying pressure in these struggles and their effectiveness against the educational bureaucracy—that is, the Ministry of Education at the national level and the boards of education at the prefectural and local levels—we must clarify the legal status and the legal rights of the JTU that have contributed so much to the nature of the relationship between the two sides and, consequently, to the pressure techniques adopted by the JTU.

LEGAL STATUS AND RIGHTS

In analyzing the legal status and rights of the JTU and their interpretation by the Ministry, we must remember that in prewar Japan no strong nationwide organization concerned with education existed in the society independent of the government. The single large teachers' organization, the Imperial Education Association, was merely a centrally directed arm of the Ministry of Education with no voice of its own. The few teachers' unions which sprang up from time to time, as has been discussed in Chapter II, were not protected by law and never attracted large numbers of teachers. Although the prewar Constitution permitted "Japanese subjects within limits of the law . . . liberty in regard to . . . association" (Article 29), independent teachers' associations were not encouraged and no provision guaranteed teachers as employees either the right to organize or to bargain collectively. In fact, labor law in prewar Japan did not exist in any meaningful sense at all. Those laws which were related to the labor movement, of which the few, small teachers' unions were a part, were intended to suppress it. That teachers' views ought to be heard in the

178

process of formulating educational policy or in determining salaries was anathema to an ideology and an administrative framework that placed education solely within the purview of the Ministry of Education responsible only to the Emperor. It was assumed that the Ministry of Education alone was responsible for the welfare of teachers.

For Education Ministry bureaucrats, therefore, coexistence on an equal footing with an independent teachers' organization was unthinkable. It was unthinkable for most teachers as well, however. They viewed themselves as rightfully belonging under the shelter and protection of the Ministerial umbrella and had a predilection to believe that Ministry policies must be correct. Consequently, the Ministry and the few teachers' organizations that existed in prewar Japan never developed any relationship other than the one governed by the values of paternalism. No slow, painful evolution of a relationship between two equal partners both concerned with educational problems ever occurred. No institutionalized channels for communicating the views of independent private teachers' organizations to governmental decision-making bodies were established. When, therefore, under radically new and liberal legislation, independent teachers' unions suddenly blossomed on a large scale after World War II, the Ministry and the unions had no experience to guide them in their effort to define their respective areas of interest and to build some kind of working relationship. For this reason, laws such as the Trade Union Law of 1945, which governed the relationship between the Ministry as the employer and the JTU as employee, began functioning before either side had a sophisticated understanding of their application. The twenty-five year postwar period may therefore be seen as the first stage in the process of developing some kind of working relationship between the Ministry and the JTU.

As discussed in Chapter III, the JTU, as a union subject to the provisions of the Trade Union Law, enjoyed the rights to organize, to bargain collectively, and to strike until

179

the latter two rights were taken away by a series of SCAP prohibitions beginning with General MacArthur's letter calling off the February 1, 1947 general strike. Although this directive referred only to the right to strike, later directives issued by SCAP in July 1948, as a result of widespread localized strikes the preceding March, banned unions comprised of public service workers from "carrying on collective bargaining." Thus, two years before the passage of the Local Public Service Law (LPSL) in 1950, which denied the rights of collective bargaining and of striking to unions of local public employees, these rights had been denied by "SCAP prohibitions and Cabinet enforcement orders" in spite of the existence of the Trade Union Law.[5]

Thus, the legal rights of the JTU to bargain collectively and to strike lasted in effect only a few short years. With the passage of the LPSL in 1950, the legal status of the JTU was redefined in such a way as to give prefectural unions the right to "negotiate," but not the right "to engage in collective bargaining," with prefectural boards of education, while the JTU at the national level was denied both the right to bargain collectively or to negotiate with the Ministry of Education. This redefinition of the JTU's legal status needs further explanation.

Under the LPSL, the JTU, as an organization comprised of *local* public servants, is no longer classified in the legal sense as a "trade union" but as a "personnel organization" (*shokuin dantai*), subject only to the provisions of the LPSL and no longer to those of the Trade Union Law. Prohibition of the JTU from negotiating with the Ministry of Education at the national level is tied up with this new classification and with the law's explanation of the right of local public employees to organize. The law, in harmony with Article 25 of Japan's postwar Constitution, which guarantees "the

[5] Law No. 261, December 13, 1950, *Chihō Kōmuin-hō* (Local Public Service Law). For SCAP's actions see Solomon B. Levine, *Industrial Relations in Postwar Japan* (Urbana: University of Illinois Press, 1958), p. 142.

180

right of workers to organize," gives elementary and secondary school teachers, who are local public servants, the right to join "an organization the object of which is to negotiate with the authorities of the local public body concerned with regard to the compensation, work hours and other working conditions" (Article 52, Paragraph 1). In addition, local teachers' organizations at the county, city, or village level are allowed to federate up to the level of the prefecture and to *negotiate* with the authorities. Beyond this level it is not unlawful for teachers' organizations to form nationwide confederations, but such nationwide teachers' confederations are *de facto* bodies only and are nowhere guaranteed by the LPSL or any other law the right to negotiate with national public bodies. Consequently, under the regulations of the LPSL the prefectural teachers' unions have the right to negotiate with prefectural boards of education, but the national JTU, a confederation of the prefectural unions, does not have the right by law either to bargain collectively or to negotiate with the Ministry of Education.

It is significant that the LPSL uses the term "negotiate" rather than the term "bargain collectively" when defining the nature of the contact that may take place between the prefectural unions and the prefectural boards. Such "negotiation" does not include the "right of collective agreement" —that is, it is not the result of collective bargaining—but only the right to conclude a "written agreement" (Article 55, Paragraph 1), which must, as the law states, "be carried out with sincerity" (Article 55, Paragraph 3). The exact effect of a "written agreement" is not fully explained in the law, but the Japanese government has stated that a "written agreement" is not the same thing as a "collective agreement" between labor and management of private industry within the meaning of the Trade Union Law.[6] This implies that a

[6] Statement by the Japanese government in a letter to the ILO Committee on Freedom of Association, October 2, 1961, referred to in "Analysis on the Legislation Governing Freedom of Association and the Exercise of Trade Union Rights in Japan," prepared by the

"written agreement" is less binding than a "collective agreement"; however, the exact legal binding force of a "written agreement" remains unclear.

The loss of the right of the JTU to bargain collectively or even to negotiate at the national level, together with the loss of its right to strike at any level, resulted in the demand by the JTU that these fundamental labor rights be restored. All of the JTU's annual action policy statements to date have demanded the recovery of these fundamental rights. Over the question of whether teachers *ought* to have the right to strike, of course, honest men in societies throughout the world differ. In Japan alone, different prefectural courts have come down on different sides of the question. More important than the conflicting legal opinions, however, is the atmosphere created by the general public's attitude, within which the JTU must function, toward the striking of teachers. Without question, there is a general consensus among the Japanese public that teachers ought not to participate in such activities, that such behavior has an unfavorable influence on children, and that in some way striking is not consistent with the image children should have of their teachers. Given this atmosphere, the government has not hesitated to punish either JTU leaders or the average teacher for having participated in what the government has interpreted as illegal strikes. As is shown in Table 8, by 1970 the government had meted out administrative punishments of various kinds to over 250,000 teachers, or half of the JTU's membership. As a result of this extensive punishment, in which more than half of those punished suffered some financial loss, the JTU's 1970 action policy reversed a standard policy of former years and abandoned the call for a nationwide strike. Consequently, although the JTU still demands the return of the right to strike, governmental action,

---

ILO Committee on Freedom of Association. The undated document was provided to the author by Takahashi Takeshi, Research Officer, ILO Tokyo Branch Office. The report was probably compiled in 1964.

Table 8

Number of Teachers Punished by the Government

	1957	1958	1959	1960	1961	1966	1967	1968	1969	1970
Criminal										
Indictments	4	73	56	0	37	5	0	0	0	1
Arrests	11	203	62	2	49	36	0	0	0	0
Interrogations	788	2,877	370	38	1,858	8,088	0	0	0	0
Number of Houses and Offices Searched	105	368	110	35	126	117	0	0	0	
Administrative										
Dismissals	0	9	104	10	27	5	2	24	906	0
Suspensions	11	130	151	0	154	367	215	192	41,387	81
Wage Decreases	34	516	193	4	808	514	5,439	12,951	72,375	12
Warnings	0	1,988	583	18	2,222	62,856	18,371	31,058	114,668	57
Total	45	2,643	1,035	32	3,211	63,742	24,027	45,125		150
	Saga struggle	Eff. Rat. struggle	Eff. Rat. struggle	Anti S.T. struggle	Achiev. Tests	Wage struggle	Wage struggle	Wage struggle	Wage struggle	No nation-wide strike

Source: Uno Hiroshi, "Komuin no Sutoraiki ni Taisuru Chōkai Shobun" (Disciplinary Punishment Against Strikers in the Public Service), *Jurisuto*, No. 472, February 15, 1971, p. 68.

unopposed by the general public, has succeeded, at least temporarily, in forcing the union to give up "striking" as a pressure technique. The price has been too high.

There is a little more sympathy among the general public and even among government officials, however, for restoration to the JTU of the right of collective bargaining, at least at the prefectural level. Collective bargaining agreements would have the binding power that present agreements reached through negotiations do not. Restoration of this right, however, which would require the granting of more power to the prefectural and local boards of education, does not appear to be a realistic foreseeable possibility. Resistance in the Ministry of Education is too strong. Faced with the improbability of these two basic rights being restored, the JTU's more realistic objective, while never abandoning its demands for restoration of these two basic rights, has been the establishment of the right of central negotiations (*chūō kōshō*). The establishment of negotiations—negotiations at the top level with leading officials of the Ministry—became one of the JTU's most insistent demands with the emergence of the moderate leadership in the late 1950's and early 1960's. This insistence was heightened by the political events in the spring and summer of 1960 and by the sudden cessation of the occasional talks between the Ministry and the JTU that had been permitted by Education Minister Matsuda Takechiyo during his incumbency from June 1959 to July 1960.

Throughout 1959 and 1960 the JTU had participated in a long series of nationwide left-wing united struggles against the revision or retention of the U.S.-Japan Security Treaty. By the spring of 1960 when the anti-Security Treaty riots had reached their fiercest stage, relations between the JTU and the Ministry had become sorely strained and talks had ceased. With the appointment of Araki Masuo as the new Education Minister by the Ikeda regime, which came into power one month after the riots had toppled the Kishi cabinet, relations deteriorated even further. Araki, a conservative politician from Fukuoka prefecture, where the JTU is notoriously radical and strong, announced his intention not to talk with leaders of the JTU and gave every indication that he wished to reduce the power of the union as much as possible.[7] With this blunt refusal to confer with JTU leaders, the call for central negotiations by the JTU increased even more in intensity. Thus, the establishment of central negotiations became one of the JTU's most widely heard demands and was to color the relationship between the two sides throughout the 1960's. But the demand for central negotiations ought to be viewed as merely one of a number of significant demands, even though the arguments garnered by the JTU to support the call for central negotiations involved all other major demands, since it was the JTU's belief that all of its aims would be better met if it enjoyed the right to negotiate with the Ministry at the national level.

In the following sections of this chapter, therefore, in which five of the JTU's most important demands on the educational bureaucracy are analyzed from the point of view of the issues involved, the techniques employed in presenting the demands, and the effectiveness of these techniques, the demand for central negotiations is treated separately. Discussion of other demands that appear under the section, "Central Negotiations," below, are treated only insofar as they relate to the JTU's arguments for the necessity of establishing central negotiations. The five demands, or struggles, chosen for analysis are: (1) establishment of central negotiations, (2) creation of adequate means to protect teachers' rights and to compensate for the loss of the right to strike, (3) abolition of the efficiency rating system of teachers, (4) modifications in the process of administering the nationwide achievement tests, and (5) full implementation of the recommendations of the National Person-

[7] Shigematsu Keiichi, "Ikeda Naikaku Kōitten Araki Masuo" (Strong Man Araki Masuo of the Ikeda Cabinet), *Nippon Zasshi*, April 1965, pp. 116-21.

nel Authority (NPA) for initiating the payment of salary increases in April rather than later in the year. There are, of course, a host of additional claims and demands that the JTU has made on the educational bureaucracy in the postwar period that could be analyzed. A number of them, such as the demand that the system of selecting members of boards of education not be changed from an elective to an appointive one, that moral education not be re-introduced into the curriculum, and that the authority of the Ministry to approve textbooks be rescinded—all demands that the JTU has lost—have been extremely important and have constituted great controversies between the Ministry and the union. These particular five demands have been selected for analysis, however, because, while somewhat less well known than others, they reveal not only the fundamental cleavage between the two sides but also the difference in the relationship between the JTU and the Ministry at the national level from the relationship between the prefectural and local unions and the corresponding boards of education at the lower levels. Analysis of the effectiveness of the techniques employed by the JTU in attempting to achieve these five demands will demonstrate the principle that the JTU has been most successful in influencing educational policies not at the time or place of their formulation—that is, at the national level—but at the time and place of their implementation—the prefectural and local levels.

CENTRAL NEGOTIATIONS

The demand for central negotiations with the Ministry of Education began to increase in intensity in August and September 1960. The chief means by which the JTU sought to persuade the Ministry to establish central negotiations was a series of direct letters from JTU Chairman Kobayashi to new Education Minister Araki. As a secondary and indirect means of bringing pressure to bear on the Ministry, the

JTU appealed to the International Labor Organization (ILO). In November 1960 it sent off the first of a number of lengthy reports to the ILO Committee on Freedom of Association and requested that body to investigate its complaints against the Japanese government.[8] In its effort to persuade the Ministry to permit central negotiations, therefore, it can be seen that the JTU relied principally on the

[8] The discussion in this section on the question of central negotiations is based on the following sources: (1) the letters from the JTU to the Ministry of Education, dated August 5 and 18, 1960, April 5, 1961, and September 16, 1963, and the replies from the Ministry to the JTU, dated August 15 and 29, 1960, April 10, 1961, and September 25, 1963 contained in Ministry of Education, *Kyōshokuin Dantai-ra Kankei Shiryō*; (2) two letters from Kobayashi Takeshi, Chairman of the JTU, and Ohta Kaoru, Chairman of the General Council of Trade Unions, to D. A. Morse, Director-General, Committee on Freedom of Association, International Labor Organization, Geneva, the first containing a lengthy report entitled *Complaints of the Japan Teachers' Union Against the Japanese Government*, dated November 9, 1960, and the second entitled *Answers from the Japan Teachers' Union to the Questions Raised by the Committee on Freedom of Association*, dated February 10, 1962; (3) two letters from Araki Masuo, Minister of Education, to the ILO Committee on Freedom of Association, the first containing a report entitled *Observations of the Japanese Government on the Complaints of the Japan Teachers' Union Against the Japanese Government*, dated January 13, 1961, and the second a report entitled *Observations of the Japanese Government upon Complaints of the Japan Teachers' Union Against the Japanese Government Relating to the 54th Report of the Committee on Freedom of Association*, dated October 10, 1961; (4) a letter from Miyanohara Sadamitsu, Chairman of the JTU, to Erik Dreyer, Chairman of the Fact-Finding and Conciliation Commission on Freedom of Association of the ILO, containing an untitled report concerning the limitations of the Personnel Commissions in compensating for the loss of the right to strike, dated June 25, 1964; (5) *Analysis of the Legislation Governing Freedom of Association and the Exercise of Trade Union Rights in Japan* prepared by the ILO Committee on Freedom of Association, undated; (6) and International Labour Organization, *Report of the Fact-Finding and Conciliation Commission on Freedom of Association concerning Persons Employed in the Public Sector in Japan*, Official Bulletin, Special Supplement, Vol. 49, No. 1, January 1966.

187

written word and the force of its arguments. These arguments, essentially four in number, as well as the counter-arguments advanced by the Ministry, need to be spelled out in some detail, for an understanding of why the JTU demanded central negotiations and an evaluation of the effectiveness of this particular demand. The JTU rested its first argument on the Constitution and the Fundamental Law of Education, pointing out that they embodied the principle that education belongs to the people (*kyōiku wa kokumin no mono de aru*), and that therefore no government in power at the time should use education for the purpose of executing its own policies. On the contrary, argued the JTU, the government and its administrative organs, such as the Ministry of Education, were obligated to listen to the voice of the people (*kokumin no koe*). By refusing to negotiate with the JTU, the Ministry was ignoring the voice of the people and enforcing a one-sided administration of education (*ippōteki na kyōiku gyōsei*), thereby trampling on the democratic principle that education belongs to the people.

To this line of reasoning, the Ministry replied that, under the parliamentary system, execution of the administration of education by the Education Minister in accordance with the laws legislated by the Diet, a body representative of the people, constituted democratic administration of education in accordance with the will of the people. Furthermore, since the JTU represented only one group of people in the nation it would be against the wishes of the people as a whole if the Ministry were to carry out the administration of education while negotiating only with the JTU. It ought to be pointed out here that a subtle implication of this argument on the part of the Ministry is that, because of the traditional hierarchical relationship between the Ministry and the teachers, the act of negotiating and reaching an agreement with the JTU would give the impression to the general public that the Ministry to some extent condoned the policies of the JTU. Clearly, this is something that the Ministry did not wish to do.

In its second argument, the JTU advanced the line of reasoning that in order to have meaningful influence on the determination of teachers' salaries, it was necessary for the JTU to negotiate with the Ministry at the national level rather than only with the boards of education at the prefectural level since wages in reality were determined at the national level.

The process by which the annual teachers' wage scale is adopted must be more fully understood in order to grasp the meaning of the JTU's second argument. As the system operates,[9] it is the responsibility of the National Personnel Authority (NPA) to study continuously the livelihood of teachers and each year to submit recommendations for their wages and bonuses to the Education Minister. On these recommendations, on the requests from the prefectural boards, and on the advice of the Finance Minister, the Education Minister then announces guidelines for the wages and bonuses of teachers throughout the country. These guidelines are intended merely as suggestions to the prefectural assemblies, which, by annually amending a Special Law Concerning Educational Personnel (*Kyōiku Kōmuin Tokureihō*), have the final authority in determining teachers' salaries in each prefecture. In actual practice, however, the wages and bonuses as set by the prefectural assemblies hardly differ from the guidelines suggested by the Ministry. The reason is clear: half of the necessary funds for teachers' salaries is provided for by the national government. Because of this financial dependence of the

[9] This discussion of the annual bureaucratic process by which teachers' salaries are determined is based on interviews with: Yamagata Kiyoshi, Head of the Research Department of the JTU, February 27, 1965; Sawada Michiya, Chief of the Local Affairs Section of the Ministry of Education, June 24, 1964; and Ogawa Jun-ichi, Chairman of the Iwate Teachers' Union, December 16, 1964.

189

prefectural governments on the national government, which is extremely reluctant to allocate funds to prefectural governments in excess of its guidelines, no amount of negotiating by the teachers' unions at the prefectural level can, in most cases, result in wages above the recommended national standard. Furthermore, most prefectures, themselves responsible for providing 50 percent of the funds for the wages and bonuses of teachers, do not have the economic capacity to go beyond the suggested guidelines. The result, argues the JTU, is that the right to negotiate over teachers' salaries at the prefectural level is largely meaningless.

The only meaningful negotiations at this level are those limited to "plus alpha," or those fringe benefits which are not included in the guidelines laid down by the national government but which may be included in the annual amendment to each prefecture's Special Law Concerning Educational Personnel. Only this "plus alpha"—the amount beyond wages and bonuses—is negotiable and if the prefectural union is able to win something, the necessary funds come out of the government's pocket, so to speak. There are a few exceptions to this general pattern. The wealthy prefectures of Osaka and Aichi, for example, have occasionally agreed, after negotiating with the teachers' unions, to allocate funds for wages slightly in excess of the national guidelines. In such cases the national government is obligated to match the increase voted by the prefectural assembly. The national government is against this practice, however, not only because it must part with more funds, but also because prefectural employees are then apt to receive slightly higher wages than national employees. Two conditions appear to be necessary for these exceptions to occur. First, the prefecture must be wealthy, and, second, it must be in a position to exercise considerable pressure upon the central government.

In the JTU's view, however, these few exceptions do not hide the fact that the prefectural teachers' unions have almost no direct influence upon the determination of teachers'

190

wages and bonuses. The JTU contends that wages and bonuses are determined *in fact* at the national level, where the JTU lacks the right to negotiate, and only *by law* at the prefectural level, where its right to negotiate is ineffective. Therefore, in order to have a meaningful voice in the determination of teachers' salaries, the JTU argues that it ought to be allowed to negotiate directly with the Ministry at the national level.

In countering this argument, the Ministry has merely stuck to the letter of the law and reiterated its point that since teachers are employed by prefectural boards of education and their wages determined by prefectural regulations, the Ministry itself stands outside the employer-employee relationship and is not, therefore, the proper body for the JTU to negotiate with. The Ministry has made it clear that JTU leaders who wish to negotiate over wages and working conditions ought to do so with the prefectural boards.

The third argument the JTU offered for the necessity of beginning central negotiations revolved around the thorny issue of the efficiency rating of teachers. By the summer of 1960 the JTU and the Ministry had experienced two years of violent confrontation over this question. The LPSL of 1950 required that local public employees be rated, but the Ministry had not attempted to implement a rating system for teachers until 1958. Article 40 of the LPSL states that "The appointing authorities shall periodically evaluate the work performance of personnel and shall take such appropriate action as the result of evaluation may call for." For teachers this meant that they would be rated by their principals. On the surface this may appear to be innocuous, but the JTU feared that the rating system would be used to weed out teachers whom the Ministry and the local boards of education thought politically undesirable. A study of the rating form drawn up by the Ministry reveals that there are a variety of ways of rating a politically undesirable teacher poorly, thus perhaps leading to his transfer to a remote

191

area, without the true reason appearing on the form in any way.[10]

The first part of the efficiency rating form requests such routine information about the teacher as his name, school, teaching subject, salary, age, sex, educational experience, medical history, special responsibilities in the school, employment experience, and the names of organizations to which he belongs. In the second part the principal is requested to rate the "teachers' efficiency" in considerable detail. Certain questions on the form do not refer only to a teacher's efficiency or ability, however, except by an extremely broad, prewar-type interpretation of what an efficient teacher ought to be. Many of the points on which the teacher is rated require wholly subjective evaluations of vague aspects of a teacher's character, which make it very easy for a principal who does not like a teacher to rate him "inferior," the lowest possible category.[11] But, more than this, many of the points on which the teachers are rated are so worded that only the prewar-type submissive, humble teacher would receive a high rating. For example, under a category labeled "sincerity," the fifth point asks whether the teacher is "methodical and reliable," the nuance being whether or not he carries out orders to the letter. Again, it is more than conceivable that a JTU activist would be rated "inferior" on this point. In still another category headed "intolerance and cooperation," point six inquires whether the teacher has the ability to make the "surrounding atmosphere harmonious or mild." Obviously, the independent thinker who disturbs the atmosphere with new ideas and his own opinions would be in danger of being rated low.

10 For a complete reprint of the efficiency rating form, see *Kimmu Kyōtei Mondai no Keii* (Complexities of the Problems Surrounding the Efficiency Rating System) (Tokyo: Todōfuken Kyōikuchō Kyōgi-kaihen, February 1960), pp. 105-28.

11 For each point under each category, the principal is supposed to rate the teacher from 5 to 1: 5 (excellent), 4 (fairly excellent), 3 (average), 2 (somewhat inferior), and 1 (inferior).

Thus, many questions on the form are so designed that an active JTU member who struggles to change existing educational policies could be rated low whether or not he is an effective classroom teacher. Consequently, the JTU declared that the rating system was political and that its purpose was to weaken the union. Although the JTU probably would have declared that any system of rating teachers, no matter what the form, was political, the actual form the Ministry of Education designed and sent out for use lent credence to the union's charges. As the above examples indicate, the form clearly reflects the Ministry's thinking on what constitutes a good teacher. Significantly, no emphasis is placed on originality or independence of thought; no place exists on the form for the rating of these qualities.

In addition to the tone of the questions, to which the JTU objects, many questions are so vague as to make it literally impossible for a principal to rate all the teachers in his school with any meaning. For example, in the category, "love for education," the principal is expected to rate each teacher from 5 to 1 (excellent to inferior) on each of the following points: 1. Does he love his pupils? 2. Does he have a correct understanding of his pupils? 3. Does he have a correct understanding of education? 4. Is he liked by students? When a principal has to sit down and rate about 50 teachers from 5 to 1 on more than 70 such vague qualities, the whole rating process becomes not only ludicrous but highly suspect. It is significant that the World Confederation of Organizations of the Teaching Profession (WCOTP), a "free-world" organization with a membership of 96 countries, meeting in Washington in 1959, passed a resolution declaring that the Japanese efficiency rating system of teachers was harmful both to education and to the teachers and sent a telegram to the Japanese Ministry of Education protesting its implementation. This discussion of the form used to rate teachers suggests that the JTU's charge that the Ministry intended to use the system to gain greater control of the teachers may not have been wide of the mark.

This fear, as well as the unsatisfactory results, discussed below, of the "absolute opposition" of the JTU to the implementation of the rating system led the union to appeal even more strongly to the Ministry for the setting up of central negotiations to solve the basic question of the rating of teachers. The rigid opposition of the JTU, in which it had called for the boycott of classrooms on September 15, 1958, led to the dismissal by prefectural boards of education of a sizeable number of prefectural union officers from their status as public service personnel. They were dismissed for having violated the LPSL, which denies public employees the right to strike. JTU statistics provided to the author show that in 1958 alone 52 full-time union officers were dismissed. Other sources reveal that between 1957 and 1961, the years covering the greatest turbulence over the rating system, 61 officers were dismissed, while, in addition, local boards of education took disciplinary action against 4,246 other union members, suspending 308, reducing the salaries of 873, and warning 3,065.[12] At the same time, in certain prefectures large numbers of teachers withdrew from the JTU. In Ehime, for example, union membership dropped from 7,673 in March 1958 to 4,259 in August 1960.[13] For all these reasons, but mainly because the rating system greatly affected the lives of teachers whom the JTU represented, the Miyanohara-led mainstream demanded that central negotiations be held.

To this third argument of the JTU, the Ministry turned a deaf ear and flatly refused to negotiate the question at all. Resting its argument again on a legal point, the Ministry argued that the efficiency rating system was not a proper subject for negotiation at either the prefectural or the national level because it was a system provided for by the

12 *Kyōiku Nenkan*, 1964.

13 "Separate Paper XIX" of the November 9, 1960 letter from Kobayashi and Ohta to D. A. Morse, p. 50.

LPSL as passed by the national Diet. It reasoned, therefore, that any revision of the law should be discussed in the Diet and not directly between the Ministry and the JTU. It was, of course, the JTU's position that prior to the changing of the law by the Diet, the JTU ought to have the opportunity to present its views to the Ministry. On this point, it is interesting to note that the press generally sided with the JTU. The *Yomiuri Shimbun*, for example, on August 15, 1960 argued in an editorial that the rating system should be discussed at the highest level. On August 30, 1961, an *Asahi Shimbun* editorial regretted that the Minister of Education was refusing to negotiate with the JTU and was thereby placing all of the responsibility and the troubles on the prefectural boards of education. A similar editorial appeared in the *Asahi Shimbun* on August 22, 1961.

The fourth and last major argument the JTU advanced in an effort to persuade the Ministry to agree to central negotiations centered on its ideological position as expressed in the Code of Ethics. The argument posited that because teachers in the prewar period had acquiesced in the training of children for war and had themselves learned the destruction of human happiness caused by war, their foremost desire in the postwar period, and therefore the fundamental objective of the JTU, was the preservation of peace. Consequently, the JTU wished to create a society that would also have as its fundamental objective the preservation of peace. But, more than this, the JTU argued that the destruction of human happiness can also be caused by a society that permits the existence of poverty, unemployment, and the suppression of fundamental human rights. Therefore, it was natural for teachers to unite to protect their employment conditions and their rights and to abolish any unjust administration of education by the authorities. These are, argued the JTU, "natural obligations" (*tōzen no sekimu*) of teachers in a democratic society and constitute the essence of the Code of Ethics. Therefore, the Code was not an obstacle in the path of negotiations, as the Ministry

195

had frequently charged, but in reality an explanation of why negotiations were necessary.

In its response to the JTU's argument, the Ministry asserted that the Code focused upon "the historical tasks that have been bestowed upon a people within a specific historical period," and was therefore based on the idea of achieving a social revolution by means of a class struggle. Furthermore, the Ministry accused the JTU of attempting to use the younger generation as a tool in overturning the existing social system based on the postwar Constitution. From the Ministry's point of view, this goal of the JTU, if achieved, would be destructive of democracy. The JTU would have to improve its character, argued the Ministry, before any negotiations could take place.

To a certain extent the Ministry's adamant refusal to negotiate with the JTU backfired. Araki's intransigent stand, symbolized by his repeated public denunciation of the JTU ("*Nikkyōso wa baka daroo*"), served in the long run to stimulate public sentiment against the Ministry's position. This became increasingly true throughout the first half of the 1960's as the union continued to ameliorate its tactics vis-à-vis the Ministry. At the same time, however, the firm stand of the Ministry contributed to the union's modification of its position. In June 1961, for example, the union's twenty-third annual convention amended the Code of Ethics and removed some of the more blatant Marxist terminology, which made the wording of the Code more palatable to the Ministry.

But the JTU also succeeded in influencing the Ministry, primarily through the ILO, which, after receiving many lengthy letters of complaint from the JTU and explanatory reports from the government, was permitted by the government to send a Fact-Finding Mission on Freedom of Association to Japan in January 1965. The Mission, led by Erik Dreyer, spent many hours meeting separately with the Ministry and JTU officials, as well as with other public labor union leaders, and recommended at the conclusion of the

196

series of meetings that the Prime Minister initiate "regular labor-management talks" between the government and unions of public employees.[14] The government, pressured by external (the ILO itself) and internal (the labor unions and the press) forces into ratification of the ILO Convention on Freedom of Association and Protection of the Right to Organize (No. 87), agreed to the idea of holding periodic high-level meetings with leaders of public workers' unions. These meetings, however, were infrequent and soon ceased. Nevertheless, as a result of an inter-party compromise that made the ratification of the ILO Convention possible, an Advisory Council, consisting of government, labor, and public members, was established. The Council's charge was to resolve a number of controversial points in the amendments to four national laws governing public workers, points that had been shelved to hasten the ratification of the ILO Convention. The government ratified the Convention on June 14, 1965 and the first Advisory Council began its deliberations shortly thereafter. By 1970, however, when the Third Advisory Council on the Public Service System was set up, little or no progress had been made by the first two Councils in bringing the labor and government sides closer together.

The problems between the two sides were legion and intricate but they stemmed from the propensity of the public unions to persist in combining their economic campaigns with political struggles, the latter having no demonstrable relation to the economic interests of the rank and file. Public unions, including the JTU, utilized the strike weapon, even though it was illegal and basically an economic weapon, in an attempt to force the government to adopt particular policies in political fields. Examples included using the strike technique in order to crush the Japan-South Korea talks, to prevent calls of U.S. nuclear-powered submarines, and to force withdrawal of U.S. troops from Vietnam. Of equal importance in preventing the two sides from resolv-

[14] *Japan Times*, January 24, 1965.

ing their differences, however, was the fundamental divergence of view regarding the right of public workers to strike. The government's view throughout the five years of the sporadic meetings of the First and Second Advisory Councils remained adamantly that of *absolute prohibition* of the right to strike in the public sector, while the public unions' view began with that of *total restoration* of the right to strike for public employees—later modified to the position that although the right to strike ought to be given to all public servants in principle, restriction of its use could be decided "for each category of public sector workers in a practical manner on the basis of the extent to which the cessation or disruption of the performance of their duties affect the people's life or interests."[15]

By the end of 1970 the problems of basic trade union rights of public servants remained unresolved. The First and Second Advisory Councils had made no substantial progress. The government came in for heavy criticism from the press. On October 18, 1970 the *Mainichi Shimbun* censured the government for its stubborn, anachronistic attitude, while the *Yomiuri Shimbun* on the same date urged the government to adopt early "the internationally established practice of modern labor-management relations in the public sector." The *Asahi Shimbun* of October 24 denounced the government's attitude toward the basic union rights of public servants as too stubborn and inflexible. It would appear that the government was determined to handle the relationship between itself and its employees in its own way in spite of external and internal pressures. Nevertheless, the Third Advisory Council continued to offer a forum for the exchange of views and the hope for eventual compromise and agreement. In this sense the JTU's demand for central negotiations, which was primarily responsible for the coming of the ILO Fact-Finding Commission to Japan and therefore the establishment of the subsequent Ad-

15 Japan, Prime Minister's Office, Second Advisory Council, *Report to the Prime Minister*, October 1970.

visory Councils, has had some measure of success, even though the demand for central negotiations itself has not yet been achieved.

PROTECTION OF TEACHERS' RIGHTS

In addition to its demand for central negotiations, which arose directly from the loss of its right to bargain collectively, a second major JTU demand to the educational bureaucracy has been the creation of an adequate system for the protection of teachers' rights, which arose from the loss of its right to strike. In an effort to convince the Japanese government and the Ministry of Education that the provisions in the LPSL for the protection of teachers' rights are inadequate, the JTU turned to the courts and, again, to the ILO. The restrictions placed upon the methods teachers may use in order to protect their rights and the system set up by the LPSL for the protection of their rights must be examined in order to understand the limitations of the system and the JTU's demand for improvement.

According to the LPSL, educational personnel, as local public servants, "must not resort to strike, slow-down, and other acts of dispute against their employer, who is the local people as represented by the agencies of the local public body" (Article 37, Paragraph 1). In addition, any teacher who has "conspired, instigated, incited the perpetration of, or attempted" acts of dispute is "liable to penal servitude for not more than three years or a fine of not more than one hundred thousand yen" (Article 61, Paragraphs 1 and 4). As compensation for the loss of the right to strike, the LPSL requires each prefecture to set up a personnel commission whose duties are to carry out continuing studies of wages, hours of work, and other working conditions and submit reports to the local assembly, the governor, or the prefectural board of education, to make recommendations to the appointing authorities on personnel administration, and "to render rulings or decisions on objections raised against the adverse actions toward the personnel" (Article 8). The JTU has maintained that since the LPSL gives the Personnel Commission the authority only "to recommend" and "to render rulings or decisions" that the local public bodies may or may not act upon, there are no procedures for the "conciliation, mediation, or arbitration" of disputes between prefectural teachers' unions and the local public authorities.[16] In the JTU's view the Personnel Commissions, therefore, have not provided adequate compensation for the loss of the right to strike.

The inability of the Personnel Commission to protect adequately the teachers' rights, which, in turn, has caused "illegal" action on the part of the teachers' unions, may be illustrated by the situation in Saga prefecture from 1953 to 1957. In Saga, according to its prefectural Wage Regulation, periodic increments of teachers' wages were to be implemented four times a year. This provision was observed until 1953 when repeated postponements of the increment began to occur and were suspended altogether for long periods at a time. The government has stated that because of a series of typhoons at the time and the heavy costs required to restore damaged areas, the prefectural authorities ran out of funds and could not pay the increments. The Saga Prefectural Personnel Commission from 1953 to 1957 made a series of recommendations to the prefectural authorities for the immediate implementation of the increment.[17] In spite of these strongly worded recommendations, however, the prefectural government failed to act. The JTU's interpretation of this is that a prefectural government is able to ignore the recommendations of the Personnel

[16] Letter from Miyanohara to Dreyer, June 25, 1964, p. 1.

[17] Letters to the Saga Prefectural Government from Koga Kaoru, Chairman, Personnel Commission, Saga prefecture, dated March 2, 1953, June 30, 1954, March 19, 1955, June 10, 1955, July 19, 1955, March 19, 1956, July 9, 1956, and November 20, 1956 contained in "Separate Paper VI" of the letter from Kobayashi and Ohta to D. A. Morse, November 9, 1960, pp. 15-25.

Commission when it so chooses, and that, therefore, the Personnel Commission is not adequate indemnity for the loss of the right to strike.

Several prefectural district courts have upheld the JTU's assertion that the recommendations of Personnel Commissions do not have binding power. In Iwate in 1954 when the prefectural government through by-laws twice postponed, in the face of the opposition of the Iwate Personnel Commission, the periodic increments for public service personnel for six months, the Iwate Teachers' Union (ITU) brought a suit before the District Court demanding deletion of the by-laws. The court ruled against the ITU on the grounds that "the wages of local public servants are to be fixed by the authorities unilaterally," and that "the opinion of the Personnel Commission has no binding power." The union maintains that this lack of power on the part of the Personnel Commissions has forced it, in its efforts to place pressure upon prefectural authorities, to resort to tactics that it considers legitimate but that the government considers a breach of the "no strike" law. The tactic that has been most widely used by the prefectural unions is "vacation with pay," in which a certain percentage of the teacher members in the schools of a particular prefecture are asked by the prefectural union leaders to take time off on a specified day or days. In connection with the postponement of increments in Saga prefecture, the Saga Teachers' Union (STU) was one of the first prefectural teachers' unions to use this tactic. Several steps led up to its use. The Saga Board of Education, in order to help solve the financial shortage, had proposed a reduction in the number of teachers. In its struggle against the curtailment of teachers, the STU used a wide variety of tactics, such as rallies before the prefectural government offices, three-day periods of abstaining from lunch, mailing of postcards, negotiation with the prefectural governor and the board of education, petitions to the Minister of Education in Tokyo, refusal to consult with students outside of class hours, manifestoes of a protest movement, publication of a "White Paper on Actual Conditions of Education in Saga Schools," signature campaigns and rallies of members of teachers' families. Finally, in February 1957 the STU directed 30 percent of all the members to take a "vacation with pay" on February 14 and 15 and 40 percent to do so on the 16th. The STU attempted to make this action legal by citing Article 39 of the Labor Standards Law,[18] which states that "the employer shall grant six days annual vacation with pay consecutively or separately to the workers who have been employed continuously for a year and were present over 80 percent of all of the working days." At the time, the teachers took the "vacation with pay" without the approval of their principals or local boards of education. After the teachers had carried out this tactic, the Saga Prefectural Board of Education responded that although a "paid leave of absence" is guaranteed by the Labor Standards Law, the collective exercise of that right by the STU was intended as a means of disputing to hinder the normal operation of education and was therefore against the purpose of the law. Such collective action, argued the Saga Board of Education, comes under the category of the acts of dispute that are prohibited by Article 32 of the LPSL. Consequently, the Saga Board of Education "exercised an administrative discipline" and suspended from public service status eleven of the members of the STU Central Executive Committee (CEC) for a period of one to six months. In addition to this administrative action, however, on April 24, 1957, the office of the union as well as the homes of those leaders were searched and the men were arrested. Four of the leaders were indicted on July 6 by the Saga District Prosecutor's Office for the alleged violation of Articles 32 and 61 of the LPSL, which prohibit teachers as local public servants from "conspiring, instigating, or inciting" the perpetration of "acts of dispute."

Five years later, in 1962, the Saga District Court ruled in favor of the STU, claiming that since the Personnel Com-

[18] Law No. 49, April 7, 1947, *Rōdō Kijun-hō* (Labor Standards Law).

mission does not provide adequate compensation for the loss of the right to strike, the action of the leaders of the STU CEC was justified.[19] In other words, the Court maintained that when the right to strike is denied, adequate compensatory measures must be available. Since the Personnel Commission is only an advisory body and since its decisions can become effective only when carried out by the authorities concerned in the local government, it does not provide adequate compensation for the loss of the right to strike.

Similar court decisions involving the leaders of other prefectural teachers' unions who directed and participated in "vacation with pay" struggle tactics have been handed down. On March 31, 1964, a decision of the Osaka District Court contained the following interpretation: "It is difficult to give a uniform judgment over which should be regarded as superior, the workers' right to strike, or the inhabitants' right to receive education, in case these are found incompatible. Even supposing that some steps are required to restrict the right of teachers to strike, it is impossible to find enough grounds to justify the negation of this right and the punishment of teachers in case they exercise this right and to justify the thesis that the inhabitants' right to education is above the teachers' right to strike."[20] The Osaka District Court, in agreement with the Saga District Court, also pointed out that "the various compensatory steps as provided by the LPSL cannot be regarded as sufficiently effective as compensation for the negation of the right to strike."[21]

In agreement with these court decisions, the JTU maintains that loss of the right to strike, without adequate compensatory measures, leaves the union members' rights unprotected. The JTU would, of course, like to eliminate Article 37 of the LPSL, thereby regaining its right to strike. Until this is accomplished, however, the JTU takes the posi-

[19] Letter from Miyanohara to Dreyer, June 25, 1964, p. 5.
[20] *Ibid.*   [21] *Ibid.*, p. 6.

tion that such struggle tactics as "vacation with pay" are legitimate means of exerting pressure and should not be misconstrued as a breach of the law. Support for this position was strengthened by two significant Supreme Court decisions, the first of October 26, 1966, which declared that punishment of *executives* of public workers' unions on *criminal* grounds for having participated in illegal strikes was unconstitutional, and the second of April 2, 1969, which made the same judgment in regard to the rank and file of public service unions. These two decisions declare that it is unconstitutional to interpret Article 37 of the LPSL as prohibiting all struggle activities of public servants who, even though denied the right to strike, still retain certain rights as laborers. What the Court has done is to strengthen the public unions vis-à-vis the government along the lines recommended by the ILO Fact-Finding Commission. No longer able to prosecute strikers on criminal grounds, the government's only recourse is to administer punishments. It is significant to point out that the ILO Fact-Finding Commission was extremely sympathetic to the JTU's assertion that the "vacation with pay" tactic was a legitimate means of exerting pressure since it recognized that effective compensatory means for the absence of the right to strike did not exist. In fact, the Committee recommended to the Japanese government that procedures for "conciliation, mediation, or arbitration of disputes between local public servants and local public bodies" be provided by law.[22]

Adequate means of protecting teachers' rights and of redressing their grievances becomes more important when the right to strike is denied. By calling attention to the weaknesses of the Prefectural Personnel Commissions, by appealing to the ILO, and by bringing cases to court, the JTU has exerted considerable pressure on the government and the Ministry of Education to improve the present system. The above review of the JTU's demands for central negotiations and for an improved mechanism for the pro-

[22] *Analysis of the Legislation Governing Freedom of Association*, p. 8.

tection of teachers' rights has shown that the JTU has not been powerless as an interest group vis-à-vis the government and the Ministry in spite of its unfavorable strategic position in the society and the absence of direct regular meetings with the officials of the Ministry of Education.

THE EFFICIENCY RATING SYSTEM

A third demand of the JTU on the educational bureaucracy, one that has been crucial to the development of the JTU as an interest group, has been the abolition of the efficiency rating of teachers. As discussed under the section "Central Negotiations," the JTU and the Ministry came to a violent confrontation over this question. The JTU initially adopted the policy of "absolute opposition by force" to the rating system and the effort to prevent its implementation constitutes the strongest, most widespread, and most significant struggle of the JTU's history. The union fiercely opposed the system, fearing that teachers would be rated on the basis of their political beliefs rather than on their ability as teachers. If this were to happen, teacher members, in order to curry favor with their principals might line up behind their political policies, thus weakening union strength. As part of its protest against the implementation of the system, the JTU charged, as it had frequently in the past, that the Ministry was reviving prewar-type nationalism and militarism. The Ministry, however, reiterated its irrevocable intention to have the boards of education implement the efficiency rating system in the fall of 1958, with the assertion that it was the right and the duty of an employer to rate the efficiency of his employees.

As explained earlier, the JTU's opposition to the enforcement of the rating system was legally untenable since the rating was required by the LPSL of 1950. Although the Ministry's position was based upon law, the articulate public, as revealed in letters to editors and in editorials,[23] ac-

[23] For a number of letters to editors, articles, public opinion sur-

cused the Ministry of high-handed treament of the JTU, while at the same time criticizing the JTU for its extreme stand. Many felt that the JTU should work towards amendment, not obstruction, of the existing law, just as many thought the Ministry should negotiate with the JTU.

Neither side wavered, however. The JTU, in an effort to dramatize its position, called for a nationwide boycott of classrooms not only by the teachers but by pupils as well. A nationwide rally was set for September 15. The JTU, attempting to muster maximum strength for its struggle, persuaded Sōhyō, the left-wing federation then comprised of 3,500,000 members of various unions, to support its scheduled boycott. Since Sōhyō's mainstream faction counted on the JTU's support for its own policy struggles, it joined forces with the JTU and ordered its members to keep their children home from school on that date. The public soundly criticized this tactic, which involved the use of children to gain what appeared to be limited union ends. In response to the proposed boycott, the Ministry declared on August 25, 1958, that it would mete out drastic punishment to those teachers who participated in the boycott. With both sides "eyeball to eyeball," a number of mediation attempts were tried. Neither an attempt by a group of distinguished university presidents nor an effort by the right wing of the JSP, which involved talks between Socialist Party Chairman Suzuki and Prime Minister Kishi, succeeded in bringing the

veys, and editorials revealing the public's reaction to the anti-efficiency rating struggle, see the following issues in 1958 of the *Daily Summary of the Japanese Press* (Tokyo: American Embassy, Translation Services Branch), August 30-September 2, pp. 2, 7; September 3, p. 4; September 4, pp. 1, 2, 3, 10; September 5, pp. 1, 4, 8, 10; September 6-8, pp. 4, 9, 12, 17; September 9, p. 1; September 10, p. 11; September 12, pp. 2, 5, 6; September 13-15, pp. 8, 9; September 16, pp. 1, 4, 13, 15; September 17, pp. 1, 2, 3; September 23-24, p. 4; September 25, p. 1; September 27-29, p. 5. See also *Summaries of Selected Japanese Magazines* (Tokyo: American Embassy, Translation Services Branch), August 11, 1958, pp. 26-30; Oya Soichi, "Japan Teachers' Union, a Lancer Corps of 500,000," *Nippon*, September, 1958.

two sides any closer.[24] Even if an agreement had been reached between Suzuki and Kishi, it is highly questionable whether the JSP could have carried it out since the party controlled neither Sōhyō nor the JTU. The Ministry was well aware, however, that a decisive victory over the JTU concerning the efficiency rating system would reduce the growing power of the JTU and constitute a giant step forward on the road towards a more centralized control of education. In an effort to make the boycott ineffective, therefore, the Ministry ordered all schools closed on September 15. The JTU, faced with such Ministry determination, dropped its policy of "absolute opposition by force" and switched to a policy of "non-cooperation." This change in policy, with its admission of the existence of the rating system, indicated the defeat of the JTU's former intransigent policy and the defeat of the JTU vis-à-vis the Ministry at the national level.

This defeat of the JTU at the national level, however, is misleading, for to conclude from it that the JTU had no further influence on the implementation of the rating system at the prefectural and local levels and in the individual schools would be erroneous. It is true that the JTU as an interest group had no influence whatsoever within the Ministry in drafting the rating form or in setting up the rating system. These decisions were made by the Ministry without consultation with JTU representatives. And it is also true that the JTU, in spite of its fierce struggle, was unsuccessful in preventing the rating system from being implemented in most schools. Thus, it might be concluded that the JTU was too weak to influence the Ministry or the prefectural and local boards of education to modify their views whatsoever. The JTU's continued "non-cooperation," however, soon resulted in the modification of the manner by which teachers were rated to such an extent that in most prefec-

[24] Numerous articles refer to this attempt. The best is "Socialist Party Urged to Act as Mediator in Teachers' Efficiency Rating Dispute," *Mainichi Shimbun* (editorial), September 5, 1958.

207

tures the whole rating system became totally meaningless. In other words, while the JTU may have been uninfluential at the national level in the formulation of the proposed rating system or in preventing it technically from being carried out, it was by no means impotent at the prefectural and local levels when it came to the actual filling out of the rating forms.

In Iwate prefecture, for example, the efficiency rating system was reduced to a meaningless operation by the policy of *naiyō shūsei* (modification of the contents) advanced by the Iwate Teachers' Union, which both the principals and the teachers supported. In harmony with this policy of *naiyō shūsei*, the ITU directed that the teachers fill out their own rating forms and supplied them with a "pattern of evaluation" that all teachers were requested to use. That is, a teacher was asked to rate himself on all questions throughout the form either 5 (excellent), or 4 (fairly excellent), but was not to rate himself 3, 2, or 1 on any point at all. The ITU even supplied sentences that were to be written on the form in the space where the principal was supposed to comment on the teachers. For example, the teacher was to write, "He is an extremely diligent teacher." Such a uniform system of rating teachers, of course, rendered the system harmless (*mugai*).[25] That the efficiency rating of teachers has become largely meaningless throughout the country has been confirmed by a number of Ministry officials who admit that the rating system, which was supposed to improve the quality of education, has not done so at all.[26]

[25] The discussion of the manner in which the efficiency rating system is carried out in Iwate is based upon interviews with: Fukushi Shunro and Ōsawa Toshinari, English teachers at the Iwate University Attached Junior High School, October 14, 1964; Ogawa Jun-ichi, Chairman of the Iwate Teachers' Union, December 16, 1964; Fujisawa Yosaburō, Superintendent of the Board of Education of Tonan Village, November 28, 1964; and Shioyama Seinosuke, Vice-Chairman of the Iwate Board of Education, December 22, 1964.

[26] Interviews with Sawada Michiya, Chief, Local Affairs Section,

Thus, concerning the rating system, it appears that the Ministry may have won the initial battle but lost the war. What the JTU objected to all along was the fact that it was not consulted at all on the question of whether teachers ought to be rated and, if so, how. That it was unsuccessful in preventing the implementation of the system, however, ought not to be misconstrued to mean that it has had no influence on how the rating of teachers has been carried out. This section illustrates the thesis that the JTU has been more successful in exerting pressure on educational policy at the prefectural and local levels than at the national level.

At the same time, however, the efficiency rating struggle was clearly a great turning point for the union. The policy of absolute opposition to governmental policies was rightly seen by the moderates as self-destructive. In order to preserve the JTU itself, to prevent further withdrawals, and to regain the confidence of the public, a more flexible approach had to be adopted. It was the very flexibility of the new approach that enabled the JTU to exert more effective pressure at the prefectural and local levels.

THE NATIONWIDE ACHIEVEMENT TESTS

A fourth demand of the JTU chosen for analysis concerns the Ministry-sponsored achievement tests. The issue came to a head in 1961 when the Ministry announced that the achievement tests would be administered in five subjects to all second- and third-grade middle school students. Prior to that year the Ministry had been administering achievement tests to students in selected schools only and in one or two subjects only. The purpose of instituting the tests on a nationwide basis, according to the Ministry, was to ascertain the level of education being achieved by students

---

Ministry of Education, June 24, 1964, and Beppu Tetsu, Chief, Local Affairs Section, Ministry of Education, November 4, 1970.

throughout the country in order to recommend various kinds of improvement. The Ministry wanted to discover the geographic areas in the country where students uniformly made a poor showing so that special efforts could be made in those areas. It stated that the results of the tests would be used solely for the purpose of improving the quality of education and of school facilities. In addition, the Ministry planned to publish statistical information based upon the test scores, such as the national mean score for each test at each grade level, and the ranking of each prefecture on each test.

The JTU announced its firm opposition, for a number of reasons, to the tests to be administered in 1961. First, it declared that the tests were based on the new middle school curriculum inaugurated by the Ministry in 1959. Since the JTU holds the position that the Ministry has only the right to *administer* education and not the right to decide on the *content* of education, it argued in the first place that the Ministry had had no right to introduce the new curriculum in 1959, and in the second place that it had no right to devise achievement tests that would lead to further curriculum revision. It felt that further revision would only accelerate undesirable changes. Secondly, the JTU feared that the results of the tests would not be used solely for improving the quality of education, but would be used against the teachers. The JTU feared, in other words, that teachers would be blamed for the low scores of pupils, particularly in remote areas where students were apt to be poor because of inadequate facilities. Thirdly, the JTU felt that such tests in themselves would produce unhealthy competition between teachers, between students, and between schools. It was afraid that such competition would be detrimental to education because it would lead to "teaching for tests" rather than "teaching for the good of the individual," and it argued that Japanese school children were already too "test-ridden."[27] It also feared that such competition would

[27] Interview with Numakunai Shimpei, November 13, 1964.

lead to base practices, such as teachers helping students on tests, the stealing of tests, and cheating among students. This appeared to be borne out several years later when a JSP assemblyman in Ehime prefecture reported that at the time of the taking of the nationwide achievement tests in 1963 the following incidents occurred: (a) in one school the principal and teachers first gave students tests of the preceding year and on the day of the examination placed high-scoring students at desks next to low-scoring students and encouraged the poor students to copy; and (b) in another school teachers opened the tests received from the Ministry prior to the test day, administered the test, and told all those who received below fifty percent to complain of sickness on the official test day and remain home. Only the good students were to compete. On the day of the test, however, almost all of the poor students showed up anyway. But the teachers did not allow them to take the test, forcing them instead to remain in the school playground.[28] Fourthly, the JTU argued that even if some kind of achievement tests were necessary, it was still not necessary to give them in every school, nor to give them in the same subject every year. The same purpose would be served, argued the JTU, if a certain percentage of schools were selected from each area and if the tests were administered once every two or three years. Lastly, the JTU argued that if the achievement tests were really for the purpose of collecting data on the ability of students in a particular course at a particular level, it saw no reason why the student's name need appear on his examination paper nor the test score on his academic record. The point here is that the JTU did not want students studying at schools with poor facilities to be discriminated against.

JTU resistance to the administering of the tests on October 26, 1961, was particularly strong in thirteen prefec-

[28] *Asahi Jānaru* (Asahi Journal), "Gaku-te Nihon-ichi Kyōsō no Mae to Ato" (The Before and After of the Nationwide Achievement Tests), July 19, 1964, Vol. 6, No. 29, pp. 87-94.

tures: Hokkaidō, Iwate, Akita, Yamagata, Gumma, Shizuoka, Kyoto, Shiga, Tottori, Kōchi, Ōita, Fukuoka, and Miyazaki.[29] Seventeen additional prefectures administered the tests in accordance with special compromises worked out between the prefectural teachers' unions and the boards of education. In Iwate prefecture the resistance of the union leaders and the teacher members was so strong that 90 percent of the middle schools throughout the prefecture were unable to administer the tests. Teachers gathered at the schools at 7:00 a.m. to prevent the tests from being given.[30] As a result of the activities of the ITU leaders in resisting the use of the tests, however, eight of the ITU CEC members lost their status as public service personnel.

The resistance by the ITU and by many of the other prefectural unions may have cost them a great deal, but, again, it must be pointed out that over time this resistance produced changes in the policy of the Ministry and the boards of education concerning the administration of the tests. By 1962 most prefectural boards had agreed to the JTU's basic demand that the names of the students not appear on the answer sheets nor the test scores on their academic records, while the JTU itself had softened its position to that of not opposing the use of the tests if the results were used solely to evaluate the academic level of education. While accepting the use of the tests in principle, however, the JTU did not drop its resistance to other aspects of the administration of the tests already mentioned and, in particular, continued to demand that JTU leaders and experts be consulted in the creation of the tests.

The dispute over the nationwide achievement tests again illustrates the principle that the JTU, while not able to influence substantially educational policies as they are formulated in the Ministry at the national level, has nevertheless exerted considerable influence on policies and their imple-

[29] *Iwate Nippō*, October 26, 1961.

[30] Interviews with Fukushi Shunro and Ōsawa Toshinari, October 14, 1964.

mentation at the prefectural level. This principle could be illustrated again and again. Similar results, for example, occurred in relation to a number of other crucial policies, such as the transfer and promotion of teachers and the reintroduction of moral education in the curriculum.

THE WAGE STRUGGLE

A final and extremely important struggle that the JTU waged in cooperation with Kankōrō, the public service workers' unions within Sōhyō, and that reached its peak between 1966 and 1970, was the wage struggle (*chingin tōsō*). The process by which teachers' salaries are determined has already been discussed in this chapter under the section, "Central Negotiations." It is, of course, the long-range policy of the JTU to abolish the present system of determining teachers' wages, which involves recommendations by the National Personnel Authority (NPA) to the government. Instead, the JTU leaders aim to determine wages of teachers through direct negotiations with the Minister of Education. More than this, their final objective is the restoration of the right of collective bargaining with the Ministry. Until this is achieved, however, the JTU's first objective is to persuade the government to accept the NPA recommendations as they stand each year, and, secondly, once the first objective is achieved, to persuade the NPA to recommend higher wages than it does.

Although teachers' wages, as well as those of all public servants, have advanced steadily since the low point of the immediate postwar period, the wage scale of governmental employees remains lower than that of the average worker in private business. The discrepancy grows greater with the length of service. A teacher in 1970 with twenty years of experience, for example, earned an average of ¥20,000 ($55.55) less per month than did the average private worker. Given this reality as well as the persistent rise in the cost of living, the JTU has, of course, never failed to demand sizable in-

213

creases in teachers' salaries. The focus of the 1966-1970 wage struggle, termed by Makieda as the most important problem of the public service workers' unions during the latter half of the 1960's, was slightly different, however.[31] The major problem concerning the wages of public servants was not that the government did not agree to pay the *amount* of salary increases as recommended by the NPA but that the government was delaying its implementation. Until 1964 salary increases each year were implemented by the government in October, whereas increases in wages in the private sector were implemented in April. The JTU argued that the half-year delay caused teachers to lose considerable sums of money, not just for any particular year in question, but for the rest of their lives, since the delay had a cumulative effect on their wage scale, retirement allowance, and pension. Thus, the primary objective of the 1966-1970 wage struggle was to persuade the government to implement the NPA recommendation that salary increases begin in April.

Gradually, year by year, the wage struggle achieved this goal. By 1971 implementation of salary increases for public servants took place in April. Changes in the month of implementation occurred as follows:[32] 1963—October, 1964-1966—September, 1967-1968—August, 1969—June, 1970—May, 1971—April. These changes have not been automatic, however, and have resulted largely from the pressure of the public unions, with the JTU playing a leading role. In 1969, for example, the JTU demanded that the implementation date of April, as recommended by the NPA, be fully met by the government. The government replied that advancement of the date was impossible. As a consequence, the JTU struck on October 8. When the government continued to maintain that advancement of the date was impossible, the JTU scheduled a second strike for December 18. One day before the strike, a compromise was reached by a Special Diet Countermeasure Committee, comprised of representa-

[31] Interview with Makieda Motofumi, December 4, 1970.
[32] Interview with Hara Takashi, January 7, 1971.

tives from the LDP, JSP, Komeitō, and DSP, to advance the date one month from June to May. The JTU, satisfied with the compromise, suspended the strike. Without pressure from the JTU and the other public unions, it is highly unlikely that advancement of the date of implementation of salary increases would have occurred as rapidly as it did.

A second major objective of the JTU's wage struggle has been to obtain overtime pay for teachers. Investigations by both the Ministry of Education and the JTU reveal that the average teacher works overtime every week. Both the Ministry and the NPA, on the one hand, and the JTU, on the other, have agreed in principle that teachers ought to be paid for overtime work. The stumbling-block, however, has concerned the means by which teachers ought to be compensated for such work. Controversy has raged over whether teachers, because of the unique nature of their work, should receive a special allowance based upon a percentage of their income (the position taken by the Ministry), or whether they ought to be paid on the basis of the actual number of hours they work overtime as ordinary laborers are (the position held by those within the JTU who adhere strictly to the concept that teachers are laborers). The JTU initially rejected the special allowance system on the grounds that it would obligate teachers to work overtime an unspecified number of hours, thus forcing them once again to become "holy teachers." Believing that a teacher's basic wage should be sufficient for a decent livelihood and that overtime pay should clearly be above and separate from the basic wage, JTU leaders were reluctant to accept an overtime system that in the future might come to be regarded as part of the basic wage. Gradually, however, although by mid-1971 the issue was still unresolved, the JTU was moving in the direction of accepting some kind of special allowance system. It appeared that acceptance of some such system was the only way teachers were going to be paid for overtime work at all. As the JTU CEC mainstream moved in this direction, however, anti-mainstream ele-

215

ments, wishing to maintain clearly the class distinction of teachers as laborers, became increasingly dissatisfied. In March 1971, for example, anti-mainstream teachers physically attacked meetings of the CEC, demanding that the Ministry's proposals be rejected. Unwilling to continue to refuse a system that will put more money into teachers' pockets, however, JTU leaders, in spite of some internal opposition, will probably agree in the near future to accept a special allowance for teachers as long as it is clearly understood to be separate from the basic wage.

The years of the wage struggle resulted in the administrative punishment of over 240,000 teachers. These punishments ranged from warnings to postponement of salary increases for three months, wage reductions for six months, and suspension of wages for nine months. By 1970 compensating teachers for these financial losses had cost the JTU ¥3,200,000,000 (almost $9,000,000). This was the primary reason the JTU instituted a "no strike" policy beginning in 1970. It is, of course, not accurate to conclude that the government meted out so many administrative punishments merely because teachers were participating in illegal strikes for economic gains. Although the government regards striking per se as illegal, it is difficult to know whether it would have meted out so many punishments if the JTU had limited its strike objectives to economic issues alone, instead of combining its various strikes for economic demands with political demands. It appears that the government applied sanctions on such an extensive scale from 1966 through 1969 in order to weaken the JTU and other public unions in an attempt to avert the possibility in 1970 of a repetition of the large-scale strikes and demonstrations that occurred in 1960 against the extension of the U.S.-Japan Security Treaty. Although other factors contributed to the relative mildness of left-wing activity in 1970, the government's prior widespread use of administrative punishments against the rank and file of the public unions no doubt contributed to this phenomenon. Be that as it may, the central demand of the wage struggle was finally achieved. In 1971 salary increases were being implemented in April and the JTU and the Ministry were well on their way towards an agreement concerning overtime pay. The wage struggle of the public service workers' unions, spearheaded by the JTU, contributed greatly to this favorable outcome, which indicates that in regard to certain demands the JTU, united with Sōhyō, has had considerable influence even at the national level.

CONCLUSION

The foregoing discussion of five of the JTU's claims and demands on the educational bureaucracy reveals that the union as an interest group has been far from impotent even though appearances suggest that it has lost a number of major battles with the Ministry of Education. In the light of prewar history, of course, whether or not the JTU has been totally successful in having its demands met is not as important as the fact that it has continued to exist and has continued to be strong enough to *make* its demands, frequently in a highly visible and noisy fashion. One must consider how far the reactionary tendency of the educational bureaucracy would have proceeded if the JTU had not existed. The foregoing analysis leads to the conclusion that the JTU has curtailed this tendency considerably: it has in several instances succeeded in moderating the policies of the Ministry at both the level of formulation and implementation, although it has had greater success at the level of implementation. The process of moderation, however, has worked both ways. Ministry firmness has contributed to the JTU's amelioration of its tactics and the modification of its attitudes towards the educational bureaucracy and the public. In this connection, the amendment to the Code of Ethics and the shift from an emphasis on politics to economics have already been mentioned. This moderation of the JTU's stance, has, in turn, resulted in the partial acceptance of the union by the educational bureaucracy, particu-

217

larly the prefectural and local boards of education. Much of the softening of tactics and modification of attitudes by the union may be attributed also to the emergence of the moderate Miyanohara faction as the mainstream, which wished to cut the losses in union membership that resulted from the union's earlier radical posture, although it is important to remember that most prefectural unions were never as radical in their dealings with their prefectural boards of education as the former radical mainstream was at the national level in its dealings with the Ministry. Many prefectural unions and boards of education have been quietly building working relationships for years. But the shift in attitude at the top from 1958 to 1962 greatly accelerated this process. Increasingly prefectural and local boards of education have come to recognize that the teachers' union has a legitimate role to play in solving educational problems. As the Vice-Chairman of the Iwate Board of Education remarked, "The board needs the teachers' union. There are frequently matters that the board may not be aware of and these should be brought to the attention of the board by the union."[33]

Acceptance of the union is, of course, greater at the prefectural and local levels than at the national level. Hopefully, increasing awareness of the legitimacy and usefulness of the JTU will gradually seep upwards. But the propensity of the Japanese educational bureaucracy to ignore the union whenever possible assures that the process will be a long and arduous one. Recognition of the *desirability* to children, teachers, education, and society in general of a teachers' organization *truly independent* of the Ministry of Education does not come easily to the minds of Japanese educational bureaucrats. If, however, the JTU continues to offer positive suggestions related to the welfare of teachers and the content and administration of education, rather than merely reacting negatively to Ministry

[33] Interview with Shioyama Seinosuke, December 22, 1964.

218

proposals, and if it continues to place major emphasis on economic and educational questions rather than purely political ones, acting in the process in a less antagonistic manner toward the bureaucracy and society, the image of the union as an ideology-ridden, disruptive organization will be slowly dispelled. Attitudinal changes will have to come from both sides in order to build up mutual trust. But if the present trend continues, the idea that the JTU is a healthy and useful countervailing power to the Ministry may gradually become accepted throughout Japanese society and the government, even by the Ministry itself, with the possibility in the future of increasing the effectiveness of the JTU's demands and struggles.

CHAPTER VII

Influence on Elections and Legislation

ALTHOUGH in the political processes of democratic governments both interest groups and parties seek to shape public policy, a distinction is normally made between them. Parties are primarily concerned with gaining direct control of governmental power by having their candidates win at elections, while interest groups are primarily concerned with gaining influence over governmental power by supporting candidates and legislative programs sympathetic to their interests. Interest groups in the United States, for example, do not as a rule attempt to elect their own leaders to public office; instead, they support candidates, in many cases regardless of their party affiliation, who will support the aims of the interest group. This distinction between interest groups and political parties is more sharply drawn in the United States than in Japan, however, where interest groups across the political spectrum run their own leaders as candidates for public office. These candidates run under the label of an existing party but there is a far greater identification of the candidate with a particular interest group than there is in the United States. This is particularly true of the JTU, which in the electoral process acts to a considerable extent as its own political party. The phenomenon has occurred because teachers' union leaders saw no alternative, other than direct political action, in the postwar years to achieving their ideological goals. The postwar teachers' union movement was therefore politically oriented from the start. Immediately after the war, even before the teachers' unions amalgamated into the JTU, leaders of these unions became candidates for election to the Diet. In the

April 20, 1947 election to the House of Councillors, for example, eight leaders of teachers' unions were elected.

As an interest group that proposes its own leaders for public office, the JTU resembles the National Union of Teachers (NUT) in Great Britain, which sponsors its own officers as candidates to the House of Commons. A major difference between the two, however, is that the NUT does not limit the sponsorship of candidates to any single political party or to any restricted segment of the political spectrum, but sponsors candidates in all three of the major political parties.[1] By contrast, the leaders of the national JTU, as discussed in Chapter IV, have firmly opposed the conservative parties, believing them to represent the continuation of the prewar ruling class, and have aligned themselves with the postwar labor movement and the left-wing political parties, including at times the Japan Communist Party. The JTU, as is true of all interest groups in Japan, has been attached predominantly to one party—in this case, the Japan Socialist Party.

In general terms, all observers of the postwar Japanese political scene have pointed out this close connection between particular interest groups on the one hand and particular political parties on the other. Interest groups tend to be party-attached. This phenomenon is perhaps most strikingly true of the relationship between leftist interest groups and political parties, where the interdependency between labor unions and Socialist parties results from the need of each for the other. From the point of view of the parties, Matsushita Keiichi has observed that the support of labor unions has been their sine qua non since the unions have contributed the bulk of the funds and a large number of candidates.[2] This conclusion is echoed by Alice H. Cook,

[1] For example, in the election of 1959, the NUT sponsored 9 candidates: 4 conservative, 4 labor, and 1 liberal. See Stephen Potter, *Organized Labour in British National Politics* (London: Faber and Faber, 1961), p. 248.

[2] Matsushita Keiichi, "Rōdō Kumiai no Seiji Katsudō" (Political

221

an American observer of Japanese trade unionism, who has affirmed that "the Socialist parties must rely almost entirely on the unions for their support."[3] From the point of view of the unions, the parties have provided the instruments through which unions have been able to participate in government, albeit as part of the opposition. Allan B. Cole et al. have concluded, for example, that, "since 1947, labor leaders have been the largest special interest group among SDP Diet members in both Houses."[4]

The JTU contributes mightily to this close relationship between leftist labor unions and the JSP through the participation of its candidates in the electoral process and of its elected representatives in the legislative process. In fact, it has consistently had a larger number of its leaders elected to both the House of Councillors and the House of Representatives than has any other single union in Japan. In the electoral process the JTU is naturally concerned first with nominating JTU candidates whenever and wherever possible; second, with securing their election; and, third, with supporting JSP candidates sympathetic to the JTU in those elections where it is not possible to nominate a JTU candidate. As a result of the 1952 Law Regulating Political Funds, which prevented organizations such as labor unions from contributing directly to political parties and which required the registration of all political organizations, the JTU created the Nihon Minshu Kyōiku Seiji Remmei or, in abbreviated form, Nisseiren (The Japan Political League for Democratic Education). As the political arm of the JTU, the Nisseiren is comprised of ex-JTU members who have

---

Activities of Labor Unions), *Nihon no Atsuryoku Dantai* (Pressure Groups in Japan), edited by the Japanese Political Science Association (Tokyo: Iwanami Publishing Co., 1960), pp. 86-112.

[3] Alice H. Cook, *Japanese Trade Unionism* (Ithaca: Cornell University Press, 1966), p. 159.

[4] Allan B. Cole, George O. Totten, and Cecil H. Uyehara, *Socialist Parties in Postwar Japan* (New Haven: Yale University Press, 1966), p. 316.

been elected to public office—to the national Diet or to prefectural, city, and village assemblies. Although membership also includes non-JTU affiliated scholars and "men of experience" who agree with the political aims of the Nisseiren, its policies are determined by the JTU CEC and most of its key leaders are ex-JTU officers. As the legal channel through which the JTU can receive money for campaign purposes and in turn distribute it to the candidates, the Nisseiren comes to life only during elections and does not have a separate existence in the Diet. Although JTU candidates are in reality selected by the JTU, the Nisseiren, as the legal agency that may recommend candidates to the voters, "approves" (kōnin) JTU candidates and "recommends" (suisen) sympathetic non-JTU candidates. Since teachers are not permitted to participate in political activities, a member of the JTU who wishes to become a candidate for elective office must resign from the teaching profession, thus automatically removing himself from the JTU. Legally he is no longer a union member, but for all practical purposes he is a JTU candidate.

In all election campaigns, whether for the House of Councillors, the House of Representatives, the prefectural governors and assemblies, or the city mayors, the JTU relies heavily on the "campaigning" of its teacher members. Although teachers, because of their status as public servants, are severely restricted by law from participating in campaign activities, prefectural unions circumvent the spirit of the law by one means or another. In Iwate, for example, an efficient and tightly knit organization exists within the union for carrying out election campaigns.[5] In each school an appointed JTU member is assigned the responsibility of directing the campaign activities of the teachers for each election. The standard practice in Iwate is for the responsible teacher to form a front committee called the Kyūryō Taisakuin or Salary Planning Committee, which has nothing to do with

[5] Interview with Fukushi Shunro and Ōsawa Toshinari, October 14, 1964.

223

its name. Its purpose is to organize the campaign activities of the teachers. Committee members request each union member to make up a list of the names of voters to be contacted during the campaign. Usually each list includes the names of the parents of the teacher's pupils, former pupils now of voting age, and five or six *sarariman*. It is physically impossible for each teacher to call on all of the names on his list, but the chairman of the Salary Planning Committee encourages each teacher to visit as many as possible. Strategy meetings are held to coordinate these activities and to decide which teachers and how many teachers should call on particular voters. Prefectural JTU headquarters supplies campaign literature to each Salary Planning Committee for distribution to the teachers, who, in turn, are expected to distribute it to the voters on their lists. Normally, this literature includes a postcard bearing a picture of the candidate, a brief summary of his achievements, and the recommendation of the Nisseiren as well as a flier containing somewhat more detailed information about the candidate. JTU leaders in Iwate estimate that about 70 percent of the teachers carry out these activities faithfully. The effect of such personal contact between teachers and voters conducted throughout the prefectures is impossible to measure, but probably, since teachers are usually respected by both parents and former students, it can sometimes be decisive. In addition, the fact that the teachers' union provides an organizational structure through which a JTU candidate and his campaign literature can reach almost all the voters throughout an entire election district gives him an advantage not enjoyed by candidates attached to unions concentrated in a single area. An analysis of two aspects of the relationship between the JTU and the JSP—the election to the Diet of the JTU leaders as JSP candidates and the influence of the elected JTU-JSP representatives on educational policies as enacted in the Diet—will illuminate not only how the JTU exerts influence in the electoral and legislative processes but also the degree of its effectiveness.

ELECTIONS

For the size of its membership, the JTU has been remarkably successful in electing its own officers to the national Diet. With a membership of approximately 550,000, the JTU from 1959 through 1971 has had an average of 27 representatives in the Diet at any point in time, or from 11 to 18 in the House of Representatives and from 10 to 15 in the House of Councillors. Since 1959 the total number of JTU Diet members has been as follows:

	H. of C.	H. of R.	Total
As of August 1959	15	13	28
As of August 1962	10	18	28
As of August 1965	11	16	27
As of August 1968	12	17	29
As of August 1971	12	11	23

Roughly, the JTU has had 1 representative per 18,000 members in the Diet as a whole, 1 per 43,000 in the House of Councillors and 1 per 31,000 in the House of Representatives. Compared with other trade unions, the number of leaders the JTU has been able to elect to the Diet is impressive. As Table 9 shows, from 1958 through 1969 the

Table 9

JSP, Kankōrō, and JTU Representatives in the Diet

	House of Representatives				
	1958	1960	1963	1967	1969
	29th Diet	37th Diet	45th Diet	55th Diet	63rd Diet
JSP	167	145	144	141	90
Kankōrō	24	34	38	45	31
JTU	13	18	16	17	11

Sources: Appropriate years of *Shugiin Yoran* (Directory of the House of Representatives); Interview with Hara Takashi, Trade Union Section of the Ministry of Labor, December 17, 1970.

JTU representatives in the lower house comprised from one-half to one-third of all Kankōrō (Japan Council of Government Workers' Unions) representatives, who themselves made up from one-sixth to one-third of the JSP Diet members. Interestingly, as JSP strength declined over these years, Kankōrō's strength proportionate to the JSP increased. The JTU's strength, however, from 1958 to 1969 decreased relative to Kankōrō's strength but increased relative to the strength of the JSP as a whole. In spite of the decline in the JSP, the JTU's ability to elect its own officers to the Diet remains strong.

Perhaps the most convenient way to analyze the election of JTU candidates to the Diet on the JSP ticket is to divide the discussion into three parts corresponding to the three different kinds of elections which are involved: the election of candidates to the House of Councillors who represent the national constituency, to the same House who represent prefectural constituencies, and to the House of Representatives who represent electoral districts within the prefectures. By looking at the JTU candidates and the executive positions they have held in the JTU's organizational structure prior to being selected to run in each of these elections, we may analyze the role the JTU has played in relation to the JSP in the nomination and election of JTU candidates. Such an analysis will go a long way toward explaining the relationship between the JTU and the JSP and the role the JTU has been able to play in the electoral process in the effort to further its interests.

Election of National Candidates to the House of Councillors

As we turn first to the candidates for election to the House of Councillors in the national constituency, we must remember that 100 of the 250 members of the House of Councillors represent the national constituency, while the remaining 150 represent prefectural constituencies. Since 125, or half, of the 250 members are elected every three years for six-year terms, 50 candidates are elected by the national constituency and 75 by the prefectural constituencies in any single election. Each voter votes twice, once for a national candidate and once for a prefectural candidate. Any organization such as the JTU that has a horizontal sweep throughout the entire country has an obvious advantage in both types of elections to the House of Councillors.

Generalizations about the background and degree of success of the national candidates to the House of Councillors may be made by analyzing the six elections to the upper house from 1956 through 1971. As shown in Table 10, the JTU ran a total of 18 races in the national constituency with a total of 14 candidates (4 ran twice), winning 14 times and losing 4 times. Eleven of the 14 were top executive officers of the JTU at the national level just prior to their Diet candidacy, while, of the remaining 3, 2 were chairmen of their prefectural unions in Kyushu, and 1 a member of the Matsuoka City Council. Interestingly, through 1971 all of the 4 chairmen of the JTU since its founding successively resigned from the chairmanship and successfully ran as national candidates to the House of Councillors.[6] In addition, since 1953 2 vice-chairmen of the JTU and 2 chairmen of the Women's Department have followed this pattern. JTU candidates for election to the House of Councillors in the national constituency have been, therefore, with few exceptions, high executive officers of the JTU at the national level. Since such top leaders during their incumbency as national officers become known beyond the confines of the single prefecture from which they rise to national leadership, they are obvious choices for candidacy in the national constitu-

[6] Araki Shōzaburō, Chairman of the JTU from 1947 to 1950, was elected to the House of Councillors in the national constituency in the election of June 4, 1950; Oka Saburō, Chairman from 1950 to 1953, in the April 24, 1953 election; Kobayashi Takeshi, Chairman from 1953 to 1962, in the July 1, 1962 election; and Miyanohara Sadamitsu, Chairman from 1962 to 1971, in the June 27, 1971 election.

Table 10

Nationwide JTU Candidates to the House of Councillors in the Elections of 1956, 1959, 1962, 1965, 1968, and 1971

Election	JTU Candidates	Party	Total Vote	Ranking	Result	Cut-Off Vote
7/56	Takada Naoko	JSP	461,594	3	Won	240,712
	Ogasawara Fusao	JSP	311,671	24	Won	
	Araki Shōzaburō	JSP	285,591	34	Won	
	Yajima Mitsuyoshi	JSP	283,511	36	Won	
		Total	1,142,367			
6/59	Oka Saburō	JSP	389,301	28	Won	266,150
	Chiba Chiyose	JSP	295,554	45	Won	
	Toyose Teiichi	JSP	279,330	49	Won	
	Ueda Otoichi	JSP	199,115	75	Lost	
		Total	1,163,300			
7/62	Kobayashi Takeshi	JSP	574,809	15	Won	376,901
	Katayama Iwao	JSP	355,844	56	Lost	
	Nagaki Masamitsu	JSP	339,377	59	Lost	
		Total	1,270,014			
7/65	Suzuki Riki	JSP	502,200	32	Won	439,909
	Chiba Chiyose	JSP	480,667	41	Won	
	Toyose Teiichi	JSP	408,324	57	Lost	
		Total	1,391,191			
7/68	Kobayashi Takeshi	JSP	698,065	22	Won	477,493
	Yasunaga Hideo	JSP	511,587	47	Won	
		Total	1,209,652			
6/71	Suzuki Riki	JSP	478,723	47	Won	443,854
	Miyanohara Sadamitsu	JSP	470,491	48	Won	
		Total	949,214			

Source: Compiled from the *Mainichi Shimbun* of the following dates: July 7-9, 1956; June 1-3, 1959; June 30 to July 2, 1962;

ency. Although the pattern vacates the top union position, thus facilitating turnover in office, and guarantees the election of a JTU official to the upper house, it nevertheless suggests that the top leaders of the JTU have placed membership in the national Diet rather than leadership of the JTU as their ultimate goal.

That the candidates for election to the House of Councillors in the national constituency have been such highly placed officers of the JTU suggests that the JTU is able to act virtually independently of the JSP in selecting these candidates, even though it is within the interests of the JSP to concur. In addition, the size of the national JTU electorate, which probably consists primarily of teachers' union members and their families (roughly 1,100,000), and only marginally of external voters (from 1956 to 1971 the total JTU vote for national candidates in any single election did not exceed 1,391,191), makes it possible for national JTU candidates to be elected largely on the basis of the union's own voting strength. This fact, which frees the JTU from party influence in the selection of these candidates, permits the executives of the JTU to appoint the JTU candidates themselves. The JSP later endorses these candidates but it has no influence over their selection or over the number who will run. In these matters, the JTU acts independently simply because it is capable of doing so.

If JTU leaders are able to select their own candidates for election to the House of Councillors in the national constituency, they are also able to determine the election strategy to be pursued. They have been able to gain the election of as many as four candidates in a single election, as occurred in July 1956. What was the strategy that proved so successful? First, prior to that election the JTU leaders calculated that about 250,000 votes would be needed to insure the election of a single candidate in the national constituency. That is, they calculated that candidates who received fewer than 250,000 votes would not place among the top fifty and therefore not be elected.

Their calculation proved to be close to accurate as the candidate (not a JTU man) who placed fiftieth received 240,712 votes.[7] Since the leaders conservatively estimated that the JTU could muster approximately 1,000,000 votes throughout the country from its membership and sympathetic voters, their strategy was to select 4 candidates and to divide the country into 4 geographical campaign areas in such a way that the JTU vote would be about 250,000 in each. By limiting the campaign literature and the actual campaigning of each candidate to an assigned area, the strategists hoped to reduce to a minimum the number of unnecessary votes beyond 250,000 needed for a candidate to be elected. Although they underestimated the total voting strength of the JTU somewhat, the votes for the 4 candidates split evenly enough for all of them to be elected, placing 3rd, 24th, 34th, and 36th, as indicated in Table 10.

A similar strategy has been followed in each of the succeeding elections of nationwide candidates to the House of Councillors. With the steady decrease in the total number of all nationwide *candidates*, however, along with the corresponding increase in the total number of votes required to elect each candidate, coupled with the decline since 1965 in the total number of votes for JTU candidates, the number of candidates the JTU has been able to elect to the House of Councillors in the national constituency has declined.[8] In the 1959 election, the JTU succeeded in electing only 3 of its 4 candidates and by 1962 was forced to run only 3 candidates and to divide the country into only 3 campaign areas. In spite of dividing the country into 3 larger areas, however, the JTU was able to elect only 1 candidate in the national constituency to the House of Councillors' 1962 elec-

[7] *Asahi Nenkan*, 1956.

[8] The number of nationwide candidates to the House of Councillors declined from 145 in 1953 to 106 in 1965. The last place national candidate received the following number of votes in each House of Councillors' election since 1953: 1953—159,762, 1956—240,712, 1959—266,150, 1962—376,901, 1965—439,909, 1968—477,493, 1971—443,854.

230

tion. It revived somewhat in 1965 by electing 2 candidates and has been able to elect 2 candidates in each election since. The reduction from 4 to 2 in the number of JTU candidates elected to the House of Councillors in the national constituency has not been only the result of a decrease in the JTU's voting strength, however. In fact, the candidate who placed third among the 3 JTU candidates in 1965 and who lost the election received 408,324 votes, almost double the number of votes necessary to elect a candidate in 1956, nine years before. In 1956 when the lowest number of votes needed to be elected was 240,712, the JTU was able to elect 4 candidates with a total vote of 1,142,367. In 1965, however, when the cut-off point had increased to 480,667, the JTU was able to elect only 2 candidates, in spite of a larger total vote of 1,391,191.

In the 1962 and 1965 elections, however, part of the JTU's inability to elect all 3 candidates was its failure to receive an approximately equal number of votes for each candidate. In 1962, for example, candidate Kobayashi, widely known because of his chairmanship of the JTU for nine years, proved to be too popular, placing 15th and receiving approximately 200,000 more votes than necessary to win, while the JTU candidate who placed 56th lost by only 21,000 votes, and the candidate who placed 59th lost by less than 40,000 votes.[9] If the JTU's strategy had been slightly better and part of Kobayashi's campaign area given to the other 2 candidates, all 3 might have succeeded in being elected. Similarly, in the 1965 election, since the 2 JTU candidates who won received 100,000 votes in excess of the number required for both of them to place within the top 50, and the 3rd candidate lost by only 30,000 votes, he, too, could have been elected if the votes had been more evenly distributed. By 1968, however, with no dramatic increase in the JTU's voting strength in sight, it became obvious that the union could elect no more than 2 candidates to the House of

[9] *Asahi Nenkan*, 1962.

231

Councillors in the national constituency. Realistically, therefore, in the elections of 1968 and 1971 the JTU put up no more than 2 candidates. In both elections it succeeded in electing candidates but the total number of votes dropped sharply in 1971. Garnering 260,338 votes less than in the preceding election, the 2 JTU candidates in 1971 placed 47th and 48th, respectively, dangerously close to the 50th cut-off point. If this sharp decline continues, the JTU will not be able to elect more than 1 candidate to the House of Councillors in the national constituency in any single election in the future.

The foregoing analysis of the JTU's role in electing its own national candidates to the House of Councillors, in spite of its ability to elect fewer candidates than it once did, strongly indicates that the union itself, and not the JSP, selects the candidates and elects them. It also suggests that these candidates win elections primarily because of their identity with the JTU rather than with the JSP. Teachers vote for these candidates first and foremost because of their status as union leaders who, once elected, will be able to promote the interests of the teachers in the Diet. That they are JSP candidates is of secondary importance.

Election of Prefectural Candidates
to the House of Councillors

In each House of Councillors' election in which every three years half of the members are elected, 75 prefectural candidates are elected. Each of the 46 prefectures in Japan is entitled to from 2 to 8 seats in the House of Councillors with the more populous prefectures having the greater number of seats. Table 11 gives a statistical picture of the JTU prefectural candidates to the House of Councillors in the 5 elections from 1953 through 1971. The degree of autonomy with which the JTU is able to select its own prefectural candidates to the House of Councillors varies depending upon the union's electoral strength in each prefecture. In those prefectures where it appears that the JTU vote will be large enough to secure the election of a JTU candidate, prefectural JTU leaders, similar to the procedure followed by national JTU leaders in the selection of national candidates, select their candidates independently of the JSP. Since union leaders believe they have the necessary votes to win, they need not consult with JSP leaders or leaders of other trade unions. Because of this ability to act independently in the election of nationwide candidates and some prefectural candidates to the House of Councillors, the JTU's *proportional* strength is greater in the House of Councillors than in the House of Representatives.

In those prefectures where the union appears strong enough to elect JTU prefectural candidates to the House of Councillors, the union's election strategy is normally uncomplicated. This is essentially because even though in any single House of Councillors' election most prefectures elect more than one candidate, no prefectural teachers' union has been strong enough to split its vote and elect more than one candidate, although three have tried. Consequently, the election strategy normally consists of persuading all union members in the prefecture and as many sympathetic parents and workers as possible to vote for the JTU candidate. It should be remembered also that a candidate who is running for the second or third time has undoubtedly built up his support base (*jiban*) beyond that of the teachers' union and become more widely known throughout the prefecture, an obvious advantage. The stark facts that the 3 elected candidates in 1962 were all incumbents, that 4 of the 5 elected in 1965 were incumbents, that 4 of the 6 elected in 1971 were incumbents, and that all of them received a greater number of votes than the total number of JTU members in their prefectures dramatize this point.

In those prefectures where the JTU does not have the strength to elect its own candidate to the House of Councillors without the help of the votes of other trade union members, the JTU leaders are forced to bargain with the leaders of other unions in an attempt to gain their backing. Al-

233

Table 11

JTU Prefectural Candidates to the House of Councillors in the
Elections of 1956, 1959, 1962, 1965, 1968, and 1971.

Election	JTU Candidates	Party	Prefecture	Result
7/56	Suzuki Hisashi	JSP	Akita	Won
	Itō Akimichi	JSP	Gumma	Won
	Sōma Masuji	JSP	Tochigi	Won
	Matsunaga Chūji	JSP	Shizuoka	Won
	Naruse Banji	JSP	Aichi	Won
6/59	Akiyama Chōzō	JSP	Okayama	Won
	Yonoda Isao	JSP	Hokkaidō	Won
	Kase Kan	JSP	Chiba	Won
	Morita Mikio	JSP	Aomori	Lost
	Sugihara Kazuo	JSP	Toyama	Lost
	Hamada Shintarō	JSP	Tokushima	Lost
	Kōzōno Tamotsu	JSP	Miyazaki	Lost
	Yuyama Isamu	JSP	Ehime	Lost
7/62	Suzuki Hisashi	JSP	Akita	Won
	Itō Akimichi	JSP	Gumma	Won
	Naruse Banji	JSP	Aichi	Won
	Matsunaga Chūji	JSP	Shizuoka	Lost
	Morita Mikio	JSP	Aomori	Lost
	Sugihara Kazuo	JSP	Toyama	Lost
	Hamada Shintarō	JSP	Tokushima	Lost
	Yamashita Masako	JSP	Wakayama	Lost
	Tajiri Kazuo	JSP	Ōita	Lost
	Ishikawa Shozō	JCP	Ōita	Lost
	Matsubara Kazuo	JCP	Mie	Lost
7/65	Kawamura Seiichi	JSP	Hokkaidō	Won
	Kase Kan	JSP	Chiba	Won
	Ono Akira	JSP	Fukuoka	Won
	Oka Saburō	JSP	Kanagawa	Won
	Matsunaga Chūji	JSP	Chizuoka	Won
	Akiyama Chōzō	JSP	Okayama	Won
	Sugihara Kazuo	JSP	Toyama	Lost
	Komiya Ichitarō	JSP	Fukuoka	Lost
7/68	Sugihara Kazuo	JSP	Toyama	Won
	Naruse Banji	JSP	Aichi	Won
	Morita Mikio	JSP	Aomori	Lost
	Ōba Sōzō	JSP	Yamagata	Lost
	Wada Keikyū	JSP	Fukushima	Lost
	Murakami Rokuzō	JSP	Wakayama	Lost
	Ninomiya Takeo	JSP	Ōita	Lost

Table 11—*continued*,

Election	JTU Candidates	Party	Prefecture	Result
6/71	Kawamura Seiichi	JSP	Hokkaidō	Won
	Kataoka Katsuji	JSP	Kanagawa	Won
	Kase Kan	JSP	Chiba	Won
	Matsunaga Chūji	JSP	Shizuoka	Won
	Kōtani Mamoru	JSP	Hyōgo	Won
	Ono Akira	JSP	Fukuoka	Won
	Akiyama Chōzō	JSP	Okayama	Won
	Ogawa Jin-ichi	JSP	Iwate	Lost
	Hase Shun-ichi	JSP	Toyama	Lost
	Satō Yoshimi	JSP	Yamagata	Lost

Source: Compiled from the *Mainichi Shimbun* of the following dates: July 7-9, 1956, June 1-3, 1959; June 30 to July 2, 1962; July 4-7, 1965, July 7-9, 1968; and June 27-29, 1971.

though it might seem logical from the viewpoint of the national JTU, a prefectural teachers' union never makes a deal with another trade union in which both agree to support a JTU candidate in another prefecture. Cooperation between the trade unions does not extend that far. Selection of the prefectural candidates to the House of Councillors depends, instead, upon which trade union is the strongest within the prefecture and which candidate, therefore, can start off with the largest number of votes. If the JTU hopeful appears to have the largest initial support and is therefore the most likely candidate to win, the JTU leaders, primarily to get their own man elected, and the JSP leaders, primarily for the good of the party as a whole, attempt to persuade the other trade unions not to put up their own candidate. If the JTU and the party are successful in this, the other unions will normally back the JTU candidate. Conversely, if a candidate from another trade union appears to have the greatest support but still not enough to win, the JSP leaders try to persuade the other trade unions, including the JTU, not to put up their own candidate but to back the most likely winner. The JSP is not always successful in persuading unions not to put up candidates; as a result the JSP vote is sometimes split so widely that either no JSP candidate is elected or a fewer number are elected than otherwise might have been possible.

From what level within the union's organizational structure have the JTU prefectural candidates to the House of Councillors come? To consider only the successful candidates, there were altogether 15 JTU leaders who were elected as prefectural candidates to the upper house in the 6 elections from 1956 to 1971, although 9 were elected twice and 3 were elected three times. Of these 15, 13 were former chairmen of their prefectural unions. Obviously, the most advantageous position from which to become elected as a JTU candidate to the House of Councillors in the prefectural constituency is that of chairman of a prefectural union, particularly a populous one that sends 3 or more Councillors to the Diet in any single election. The prefectural unions in Hokkaidō, Chiba, Kanagawa, Aichi, Shizuoka, Okayama, and Fukuoka have consistently been able to garner sufficient votes to elect and re-elect their prefectural leader. Why these particular prefectures and not others? The explanation lies not only in the size of the JTU vote itself—a crucial factor in Hokkaidō, for example—but also in the relative size of the JSP vote in general in such large industrial prefectures as Kanagawa and Fukuoka. In addition, the strength of a candidate's personal organization and following and the advantages of incumbency play their roles. In the light of the overall decline of JSP strength in the House of Councillors in both the national and prefectural constituencies since 1956, the ability of the JTU to elect its candidates to the upper house, which has given it from 10 to 15 Councillors at any one point in time over the past fifteen years and which in 1971 gave it 12, has remained remarkably strong.

Election of Candidates to the
House of Representatives

If the JTU can act with a large degree of autonomy in selecting candidates to the House of Councillors, it has less freedom of action in selecting candidates to the House of Representatives. Instead, in the elections to the lower house that must occur at least once every four years, the JTU must cooperate or bargain not only with the JSP but also with other trade unions that have voting strength and candidates to offer. Given Japan's "medium-district system," in which the country is divided into 123 electoral districts, each sending from 3 to 5 members to the House of Representatives, the votes of only the teacher members in any single election district, in spite of the horizontal sweep of the JTU, are normally too few to elect a JTU candidate. He needs additional votes. By the same token, other trade union candidates as well normally cannot be elected solely by the votes of their own union members. Consequently, "cooperation" among the trade unions through the Prefectural Council of Trade Unions becomes mandatory. In essence, selection of the JSP candidate or candidates to the House of Representatives in any single election district is fought out not only among the trade union leaders but also between them and JSP aspirants not directly associated with trade unions, to say nothing of national JSP leaders. Many factors come into play in the process of selecting a candidate, particularly, of course, the proved or possible voting strength of each potential candidate. Prior to the selection of JSP candidates for each election to the House of Representatives, incumbents have already demonstrated their ability to win and have an existing pyramidical hierarchical *jiban* from the Diet down through the prefecture to the election district, making their candidacy automatic.

In the process of selecting new candidates, however, JSP leaders meet with the Prefectural Council of Trade Unions, consisting of Sōhyō-affiliated unions, and attempt to persuade the union leaders to choose not only those candidates who are most likely to win but also the proper number of candidates that will result in the election of the largest number of JSP members. A battle always takes place between the JSP and the Prefectural Council of Trade Unions because the party leaders want to select candidates who will maximize the number of elected JSP members, whereas the leaders of each union want to select candidates who will maximize the number of elected members of their particular union. In a district where only one JSP candidate has any likelihood of being elected, the party leaders, in order to concentrate the JSP vote on one individual, strongly desire that only one candidate run. Sometimes, however, two powerful unions, each seeking the election of its own candidate, cannot agree on a single candidate and thus each runs its own candidate on the JSP ticket; because of the resulting split in the JSP vote, this increases the possibility that neither will be elected. The JSP frowns on this practice but it is not always powerful enough to prevent it. In an election district where there is the likelihood of electing two JSP candidates, party leaders try to persuade union leaders to choose candidates who will split the Socialist vote fairly evenly. If one of the candidates receives many more votes than he needs to win he will deprive the other candidate of the necessary votes to win. Again, however, the efforts of the party leaders are largely to no avail since, in the case of the JTU at least, the potential candidate is almost always the prefectural chairman of his union, with personal ambitions to be elected to the Diet. If he happens to be too popular in the election district where he hopes to run, he is not about to step aside and allow a less popular JTU candidate to run for the sake of maximizing the party's total number of elected candidates. The attempted solution, not always successful, to the problem of being "too popular," which plagues Japanese elections to the House of Representatives, is for the candidate to calculate his voting strength and limit his campaigning to those groups and areas within the election district, just sufficiently to assure victory but not a landslide. In any case, JTU leaders fight for the selection of candidates primarily on the basis of what is good for the union and only secondarily on the basis of what is good for the party.

238

Tables 12 through 16 list the JTU candidates to the five House of Representatives elections of 1958, 1960, 1963, 1967, and 1969. In those campaigns for district candidates to the House of Representatives in which a JTU candidate has been selected to run, the JTU provides campaign literature for distribution not only to its own members but also to all the members of trade unions within the election district that have agreed to support the JTU candidate. The reverse is true as well and the JTU normally campaigns for a JSP-recommended candidate in much the same way it does for its own candidates.

As was the case with the JTU prefectural candidates to the House of Councillors, most of the candidates elected to the House of Representatives were former chairmen of their prefectural unions. Specifically, of the 26 candidates elected from 1958 to 1969 (3 were elected all five times, 5 elected four times, 4 elected three times, 7 twice, and 7 once) 15 were former chairmen of their prefectural unions, 5 former secretary-generals, 2 former vice-chairmen, 3 former members of their prefectural union's CEC, and 1 a former branch secretary-general.

One of the striking facts that emerges from the foregoing analysis of the JTU's participation in elections to both houses of the Diet is that the overwhelming majority of successful candidates were former chairmen of their prefectural unions. From 1953 through 1970 well over half of all of the prefectural chairmen of the JTU ran as candidates to either the House of Councillors or the House of Representatives and 23 succeeded in being elected.[10] As briefly discussed in the section on "Leadership" in Chapter V, however, prefectural leadership in the JTU no longer serves as a relatively easy stepping stone for election to the Diet.

[10] Chairmen of the following prefectural teachers' unions were elected to the Diet during this period: Hokkaidō, Akita, Iwate, Yamagata, Fukushima, Niigata, Toyama, Kumamoto, Gumma, Hyōgo, Ehime, Ōita, Tokyo, Chiba, Tochigi, Kanazawa, Shizuoka, Aichi, and Fukuoka.

Table 12

JTU Candidates to the May 22, 1958 House of Representatives Election

	Seats in Elect. Dist.	JSP Cand.	JTU Cand.	JSP Cand. Other Than JTU Elect.	JTU Cand. Elect.				Rank Among Elect.	Times Elect.
Hokkaidō (1)	5	2	1	1	1	Yokoji Setsuo	JSP	Won	1	3
Iwate (1)	4	3	1	0	1	Yamanaka Gorō	JSP	Won	1	1
Yamagata (1)	4	1	1	0	1	Nishimura Rikiya	JSP	Won	2	3
Fukushima (2)	5	2	1	1	1	Kubota Toya	JSP	Won	2	1
Niigata (1)	3	2	1	0	1	Sakurai Masuo	JSP	Won	1	2
Toyama (1)	3	1	1	0	1	Minabe Yoshizō	JSP	Won	1	2
Hyōgo (4)	4	2	1	0	1	Ōnishi Masamichi	JSP	Won	3	2
Wakayama (2)	3	1	1	0	1	Tsujihara Hiroichi	JSP	Won	2	3
Okayama (2)	5	2	1	1	1	Yamazaki Motoo	JSP	Won	3	3
Hiroshima (1)	3	2	1	0	1	Ōhara Tōru	JSP	Won	2	1
Yamaguchi (2)	5	2	1	1	1	Ukeda Shinkichi	JSP	Won	3	5
Kumamoto (2)	5	2	1	0	1	Kawamura Tsuguyoshi	JSP	Won	3	2
Ōita (2)	3	2	1	0	1	Komatsu Kan	JSP	Won	3	2
Chiba (2)	4	2	1	1	0	Sakurai Shigenao	JSP	Lost	3	1
Yamanashi (1)	5	2	1	1	0	Kobayashi Shin-ichi	JSP	Lost		
Aichi (2)	4	2	1	1	0	Katō Seiji	JSP	Lost		
Osaka (1)	4	3	1	1	0	Nohara Satoshi	JSP	Lost		
Kōchi (1)	5	3	1	1	0	Takahashi Takeyuki	JSP	Lost		
Fukuoka (3)	5	2	1	1	0	Hida Kentarō	JSP	Lost		
Kagoshima (1)	4	2	1	1	0	Kawasaki Kanji	JSP	Lost		
Kagoshima (Amami Islands)	1	1	1	0	0	Izumi Yoshirō	JSP	Lost		

Total Elected: 13
Total Defeated: 7
Total Candidates: 20

Source: Compiled from the *Mainichi Shimbun*, May 24, 1958.

JTU Candidates to the November 20, 1960 House of Representatives Election

	Seats in Elect. Dist.	JSP Cand. Elect.	JTU Cand. Elect.	JSP Cand. Other Than JTU Elect.	JTU Cand. Elect.				Rank Among Elect.	Times Elect.
Hokkaidō (1)	5	3	1	1	1	Yokoji Setsuo	JSP	Won	1	4
Iwate (1)	4	1	1	0	1	Yamanaka Gorō	JSP	Won	1	2
Yamagata (1)	4	2	1	0	1	Nishimura Rikiya	JSP	Won	2	4
Fukushima (2)	5	1	1	0	1	Noguchi Tadao	JSP	Won	1	2
Gumma (3)	4	2	1	1	1	Yamaguchi Tsuruo	JSP	Won	4	1
Toyama (1)	3	1	1	0	1	Minabe Yoshizō	JSP	Won	3	3
Yamanashi (1)	5	3	1	0	1	Kobayashi Shin-ichi	JSP	Won	4	3
Aichi (2)	4	1	1	0	1	Katō Seiji	JSP	Won	1	3
Wakayama (2)	3	1	1	0	1	Tsujihara Hiroichi	JSP	Won	3	4
Osaka (1)	4	1	1	0	1	Nohara Satoshi	JSP	Won	2	1
Hyōgo (4)	4	1	1	0	1	Miki Yoshio	JSP	Won	1	1
Okayama (2)	5	2	1	0	1	Yamazaki Motoo	JSP	Won	3	4
Hiroshima (1)	3	1	1	0	1	Ōhara Tōru	JSP	Won	2	2
Ehime (1)	3	1	1	0	1	Yuyama Isamu	JSP	Won	3	1
Kumamoto (2)	5	1	1	0	1	Kawamura Tsuguyoshi	JSP	Won	3	3
Ōita (1)	4	1	1	0	1	Ninomiya Takeo	JSP	Won	3	1
Ōita (2)	3	1	1	0	1	Komatsu Kan	JSP	Won	3	3
Kagoshima (2)	3	1	1	0	1	Murayama Kiichi	JSP	Won	2	1
Fukuoka (3)	5	2	1	0	0	Hida Kentarō	JSP	Lost	7	
Miyazaki (1)	3	2	1	1	0	Tajiri Mitsugu	JSP	Lost	4	
Kagoshima (1)	4	2	1	0	0	Kawasaki Kanji	JSP	Lost	5	
Niigata (1)	3	2	1	1	0	Sakurai Masuo	JSP	Lost	4	

Total Elected: 18
Total Defeated: 4
Total Candidates: 22

Source: Compiled from *Asahi Shimbun*, November 22, 1960.

Table 14

JTU Candidates to the November 21, 1963 House of Representatives Election

	Seats in Elect. Dist.	JSP Cand.	JTU Cand.	JSP Cand. Other Than JTU Elect.	JTU Cand. Elect.				Rank Among Elect.	Times Elect.
Hokkaidō (1)	5	3	1	1	1	Yokoji Setsuo	JSP	Won	1	5
Iwate (1)	4	2	2	0	1	Yamanaka Gorō	JSP	Won	1	3
Fukuishima (2)	5	2	1	0	1	Noguchi Tadao	JSP	Won	1	3
Tokyo (7)	5	3	1	2	1	Hasegawa Shōzō	JSP	Won	5	1
Aichi (2)	4	3	1	0	1	Katō Seiji	JSP	Won	1	2
Wakayama (2)	3	1	1	0	1	Tsujihara Hiroichi	JSP	Won	3	5
Osaka (1)	4	2	1	0	1	Nohara Satoshi	JSP	Won	3	4
Hyōgo (4)	4	1	1	0	1	Miki Yoshio	JSP	Won	2	2
Okayama (2)	5	2	1	1	1	Yamazaki Motō	JSP	Won	4	5
Hiroshima (1)	3	1	1	0	1	Ōhara Tōru	JSP	Won	3	3
Ehime (1)	3	1	1	0	1	Yuyama Isamu	JSP	Won	3	2
Ōita (1)	4	1	1	0	1	Ninomiya Takeo	JSP	Won	4	2
Ōita (2)	3	1	1	0	1	Komatsu Kan	JSP	Won	3	4
Kumamoto (2)	5	1	1	0	1	Kawamura Tsuguyoshi	JSP	Won	4	4
Kagoshima (1)	4	2	1	1	1	Kawasaki Kanji	JSP	Won	4	1
Iwate (1)	4	2	2	1	0	Ogasawara Fusao	JSP	Lost		
Yamagata (1)	4	2	1	1	0	Nishimura Rikiya	JSP	Lost		
Gumma (3)	4	2	1	1	0	Yamaguchi Tsuruo	JSP	Lost		
Tokyo (3)	3	2	1	1	0	Takada Naoko	JSP	Lost		
Yamanashi (1)	5	2	1	1	0	Kobayashi Shin-ichi	JSP	Lost		
Niigata (1)	3	2	1	1	0	Sakurai Masuo	JSP	Lost		
Hyōgo (5)	3	1	1	0	0	Ōnishi Tadashi	JSP	Lost		
Nagasaki (2)	4	2	1	1	0	Eguchi Taisuke	JSP	Lost		

Total Elected: 16
Total Defeated: 8
Total Candidates: 24

JTU Candidates to the January 29, 1967 House of Representatives Election

	Seats in Elect. Dist.	JSP Cand.	JTU Cand.	JSP Cand. Other Than JTU Elect.	JTU Cand. Elect.				Rank Among Elect.	Times Elect.
Hokkaidō (1)	5	3	1	1	1	Yokoji Setsuo	JSP	Won	1	6
Iwate (1)	4	2	1	1	1	Yamanaka Gorō	JSP	Won	4	4
Fukushima (2)	5	2	2	0	1	Noguchi Tadao	JSP	Won	5	4
Fukushima (2)	5	2	2	0	1	Karahashi Azuma	JSP	Won	3	1
Gumma (3)	4	1	1	0	1	Yamaguchi Tsuruo	JSP	Won	4	2
Tokyo (7)	5	3	1	1	1	Hasegawa Shōzō	JSP	Won	3	2
Yamanashi	5	2	1	1	1	Kobayashi Shin-ichi	JSP	Won	1	4
Shizuoko (3)	4	1	1	0	1	Saitō Masao	JSP	Won	3	1
Aichi (2)	4	1	1	0	1	Katō Seiji	JSP	Won	1	3
Hyōgo (4)	4	1	1	0	1	Miki Yoshio	JSP	Won	1	3
Hyogo (5)	3	1	1	0	1	Iga Sadamori	JSP	Won	3	1
Okayama (2)	5	2	1	1	1	Yamazaki Motoo	JSP	Won	5	6
Hiroshima (1)	3	1	1	0	1	Ōhara Tōru	JSP	Won	2	4
Kumamoto (2)	5	2	1	1	1	Kawamura Tsuguyoshi	JSP	Won	5	5
Ōita (2)	3	1	1	0	1	Komatsu Kan	JSP	Won	2	4
Kagoshima (1)	4	2	1	1	1	Kawasaki Kanji	JSP	Won	3	2
Kagoshima (2)	3	1	1	0	1	Murayama Kiichi	JSP	Won	2	2
Yamagata (1)	4	2	0	1	0	Nishimura Rikiya	JSP	Won		
Ishikawa (1)	3	2	1	0	0	Kitai Soteji	JSP	Lost		
Gifu (1)	5	3	1	1	0	Takahashi Shigenobu	JSP	Lost		
Mie (2)	4	2	1	1	0	Yamaguchi Shigeo	JSP	Lost		
Osaka (2)	5	2	1	1	0	Hiragaki Miyoji	JSP	Lost		
Osaka (6)	3	1	1	0	0	Nohara Satoshi	JSP	Lost		
Wakayama (2)	3	1	1	0	0	Tsujihara Kōichi	JSP	Lost		
Nagasaki (2)	4	2	1	1	0	Eguchi Taisuke	JSP	Lost		
Ōita (1)	4	2	1	0	0	Ninomiya Takeo	JSP	Lost		

Total Elected: 17
Total Defeated: 9
Total Candidates: 26

Source: Compiled from Mainichi Shimbun, January 31, 1967.

Table 16

JTU Candidates to the December 27, 1969 House of Representatives Election

	Seats in Elect. Dist.	JSP Cand.	JTU Cand.	JSP Cand. Other Than JTU Elect.	JTU Cand. Elect.			Rank Among Elect.	Times Elect.
Iwate (1)	4	2	1	1	1	Yamanaka Gorō	JSP Won	4	5
Gumma (3)	4	1	1	0	1	Yamaguchi Tsuruo	JSP Won	3	3
Niigata (4)	3	1	1	0	1	Kijima Kihei	JSP Won	1	1
Yamanashi	5	2	1	1	1	Kobayashi Shin-ichi	JSP Won	3	4
Shizuoka (3)	4	1	1	0	1	Saitō Massao	JSP Won	2	2
Aichi (2)	4	1	1	0	1	Katō Seiji	JSP Won	4	4
Hyōgo (4)	4	2	1	0	1	Miki Yoshio	JSP Won	4	4
Wakayama (2)	3	1	1	0	1	Tsujihara Hiroichi	JSP Won	2	6
Hiroshima (1)	3	1	1	0	1	Ōhara Tōru	JSP Won	3	5
Kumamoto (2)	5	1	1	0	1	Kawamura Tsuguyoshi	JSP Won	4	5
Kagoshima (1)	4	2	1	0	1	Kawasaki Kanji	JSP Won	4	3
Yamagata (1)	4	2	1	1	0	Ōba Sōzō	JSP Lost		
Fukushima (2)	5	2	2	0	0	Noguchi Tadao	JSP Lost		
Fukushima (2)	5	2	2	0	0	Karahashi Azuma	JSP Lost		
Tokyo (7)	5	2	1	0	0	Hasegawa Shōzō	JSP Lost		
Gifu (1)	5	2	1	1	0	Takahashi Shigenobu	JSP Lost		
Hyōgo (5)	3	1	1	0	0	Iga Sadamori	JSP Lost		
Okayama (2)	5	2	1	1	0	Yamazaki Motoo	JSP Lost		
Kumamoto (1)	5	2	1	0	0	Fujisaki Hisao	JSP Lost		
Ōita (1)	4	2	1	0	0	Ninomiya Takeo	JSP Lost		
Kagoshima (2)	3	1	1	0	0	Murayama Kiichi	JSP Lost		

Total Elected: 11
Total Defeated: 10
Total Candidates: 21

Source: Compiled from *Mainichi Shimbun*, December 29, 1969.

The fact that only 1 of the 11 successful candidates elected to the House of Representatives in December 1969 was a first-time candidate indicates how few the new faces have become. In the election of 1960 there had been 6 elected first-time candidates. By the 1969 election, however, only 1 was elected for the first time, while 1 was elected for the sixth time, 3 for the fifth time, 3 for the fourth time, 2 for the third time, and 1 for the second time. Since the average age of these men was only fifty-two, their youth plus their ability to solidify their power while in office suggests that they will not be easily dislodged. For existing prefectural chairmen, therefore, there is little or no possibility of becoming elected to the House of Representatives unless the present incumbent dies or steps down. Since a defeated candidate usually runs again in the succeeding election, even defeat does not ensure candidacy for the prefectural chairman who is waiting in the wings. For prefectural union officers who have not yet become chairmen, the prospect of being elected to the House of Representatives is even more remote. This situation is true for election to the House of Councillors in the prefectural constituency as well. It is clear, therefore, that the tendency toward long terms for the incumbents in the Diet along with the reduction in the total number of JTU candidates successfully elected has narrowed sharply the openings for new younger hopefuls as compared with the union's earlier years.

That such a large number of JTU prefectural chairmen, as well as vice-chairmen and secretary-generals, have opted for election to the Diet rather than remain full-time professional union leaders has a number of implications. First, it suggests that such leaders, whether or not they strongly wanted to become Diet representatives, had a good chance of running successfully because of initial support of the teacher members. Second, it suggests that in the past the step from prefectural leader to national union leader and/or the Diet had a kind of inevitability about it. It was the expected route for at least the more forceful leaders from prefectures with strong union organizations. Third, it suggests that the prestige of being a Diet representative has been virtually irresistible. Lastly, it suggests that top JTU leaders have placed a higher priority upon functioning in the political process as elected politicians than as professional union officers. Given the ability of the JTU to get its candidates elected and the reliance of the JSP on the JTU (as well as on other unions, of course) for supplying candidates for election to the Diet, JTU candidates will undoubtedly continue to run and be elected even though the room at the top for new candidates has diminished.

A second striking fact that emerges from the foregoing analysis of the JTU's role in the electoral process is the considerable degree of autonomy it exercises in its relationship to the JSP. It is evident that JTU leaders in the selection of candidates place the interests of the union first and the party second. Very often, of course, party leaders agree that the candidate selected by the union is also the best candidate for the good of the party. In addition, since the JSP by and large does not maintain a separate organizational structure below the prefectural level, it relies upon unions, which have the votes and the necessary funds, to supply the candidates. This dependency is the essential weakness of the party vis-à-vis a union such as the JTU. In reality the JTU, by selecting, financing, and electing its own candidates to the Diet, functions to a great extent as its own political party. It would be more accurate to say that as a special interest group, one of the primary ways it attempts to exert influence on public policy is by electing its own representatives to public office. In this, it has been extremely successful. To what extent JTU candidates, once they take their seats in the Diet as JSP members, are able to influence the formulation of public policy is another story, however.

LEGISLATION

The ability of the JTU as an interest group to participate directly in the formulation of educational policies at the national level has been seriously curtailed by the polarization of postwar Japanese politics. The JTU has given its support exclusively to the political parties on the left, which, except for a brief period shortly after the war, have not been able to gain control of the reins of the government. In the formulation by the ruling LDP, the Cabinet, and the Ministry of Education of the long series of postwar educational policies that the JTU has so violently opposed, the JTU has not enjoyed direct access to the members of these bodies during the policy-making stage. No permanent institutionalized channels have been set up between the JTU and the LDP, between the JTU and the Cabinet, or between the JTU and the Ministry of Education, which would have enabled the union to participate directly in the formulative stages of educational policies. This is not to say, however, that the JTU has had no influence on public policy-making regarding education, but it emphasizes that its influence at the top level has been more indirect than direct. Because the Diet functions primarily as a policy-enacting body rather than a policy-making body, even the JTU's influence in the Diet may be considered indirect, although on a few occasions its influence has been very strong. Largely because JTU leaders have not enjoyed access to the key points in the policy-formulating process, JTU representatives in the Diet function to the extent that they are able as lobbyists for the teachers' union. The JTU has made its voice heard in the Diet primarily through the standing education committees in both houses, which, with the exception of occasional clashes on the Diet floor and demonstrations before the Diet building, have constituted the chief forum for the parliamentary debates between the LDP and the JTU.

JTU Diet representatives have not only pressed for appointment to the standing education committees but also have made full use of the public hearings held by these committees to bring to light what they have considered unfair administrative practices on the part of the Ministry of Education and the boards of education. They have also, of course, made full use of their right to interpellate government leaders on the Diet floor. More than this, in order to operate as effectively as possible in the Diet, the JTU has increased its strength to the maximum possible by persuading the JSP to adopt its educational policies. The JSP is, of course, stronger than the JTU in the Diet; however, the JTU can augment its strength in the Diet by having the JSP adopt its policies.

Influence on the Japan Socialist Party's
Educational Policies

Concerning educational questions, the influence of the JTU on the JSP is so strong as to make the party's educational policies virtually synonymous with those of the JTU. Both Makieda Motofumi, Secretary-General of the JTU in 1965, and Fujimaki Shimpei, Deputy Director of the Secretariat of the Policy Research Board of the JSP in 1963, have affirmed that the Education Bureau of the JSP, which is responsible for party educational policy, is dominated by JTU leaders.[11] This dominance is reflected in the fact that the head of the party's Education Bureau is invariably a JTU Dietman as are approximately eighty percent of its members. In addition, when the Bureau meets annually to determine educational policies to be submitted to the party convention for adoption, non-Diet leaders of the JTU, normally including the chairman, the secretary-general, and appropriate department heads, attend. As a result, the educational policies adopted by the JSP are almost identical to those of the JTU. Differences that sometimes occur between the party and the union are those which are apt to arise from the party's tendency to be concerned with long-range objectives as compared with the union's tendency to be concerned with more immediate interests. An example of this, offered by Makieda, is: "The JSP requests the abolition of

[11] Interviews with Makieda Motofumi, February 13, 1965; and Fujimaki Shimpei, Deputy Director of the Secretariat of the Policy Research Board of the JSP, June 14, 1963.

the Ministry of Education, to be replaced by a National Board of Education. Of course, the JTU also desires this goal, but since the Ministry does exist in reality, the JTU has to be more concerned with the practical ways of dealing with the existing situation."[12] In spite of such differences in outlook, the JSP has unfailingly adopted the educational policies of the JTU intact.

Influence on the Diet's Standing Education Committees

Membership on each of the standing education committees is, by law, allotted to the parties in proportion to the number of seats they hold in each house. Given the fact that throughout the twenty-five-year period of this study, the JSP, except for the sharp decline in December 1969, has held roughly one-third of the seats in each house, its membership on each standing education committee has reflected this proportion. As indicated in Table 17, figures of party affiliation of the members of each committee from 1959 through 1970 reveal that of the 30 members on the House of Representatives' Standing Education Committee an average of 9 were JSP members, and that of the 20 members on the same committee in the House of Councillors an average of 6 were JSP members. When the committees are appointed, JTU leaders are asked by JSP leaders how many JTU Dietmen they want to have on each committee; as a result the JTU Diet members on each committee sometimes comprise more than two-thirds of the total number of JSP members. Of particular note is that as JSP strength in the standing committees has declined, JTU strength relative to the total JSP strength has increased. Furthermore, JTU strength on the committees has at times been increased by JTU JCP Dietmen, such as by the JCP Representative, Iwama Masao, who in the years covered in Table 17 sat on the House of Councillors' Standing Education Committee from 1959 through 1961.

[12] Interview with Makieda Motofumi, February 13, 1965.

Table 17

Party Affiliation of the Members of the Diet's
Standing Education Committees

| Year | House | Total Number Members | LDP | JSP | | DSP | JCP | | Others |
				Total	JTU		Total	JTU	
1959	HR	30	19	11	5	0	0	0	0
	HC	20	11	6	5	0	1	1	2
1961	HR	30	19	10	5	1	0	0	0
	HC	20	11	6	4	0	1	1	2
1963	HR	30	20	9	4	1	0	0	0
	HC	20	12	5	4	1	0	0	2
1965	HR	29	18	10	4	1	0	0	0
	HC	20	11	6	3	0	0	0	3
1967	HR	30	17	9	8	2	0	0	2
	HC	20	11	6	4	0	0	0	3
1970	HR	30	18	6	5	1	1	0	4
	HC	20	11	5	5	1	1	0	2

Source: Kokkai Nenkan, 1959-1970.

These figures reveal the dominant role JTU Dietmen have played among the JSP Dietmen on each of the Standing Education Committees. It must be re-emphasized, nevertheless, that the committees as a whole have been controlled, of course, by the majority of LDP members. In spite of dominant LDP power, however, the public hearings held by the committees have offered the JTU forums for publicizing its views on educational policies. At a public hearing held by the House of Councillors' Standing Education Committee on May 16, 1961, for example, union-member witnesses summoned by the committee accused the Ehime Board of Education and specific principals and vice-principals of placing pressure on teachers to withdraw from the union.[13] According to the JTU witnesses, one means of pres-

[13] As reported by the JTU in a letter to the ILO, referred to in the ILO's *Official Bulletin*, Vol. 46, No. 1, Supplement, January 1963, 66th Report, Case No. 179, pp. 35-67.

sure was the establishment of an Education Research Conference in Ehime, ostensibly organized by teachers to represent their interests vis-à-vis educational authorities, but, in fact, organized by the educational authorities themselves and subsidized by them in an effort to weaken the union. JTU witnesses at the hearing maintained that no teacher was permitted to join the Education Research Conference if he were a member of the union. They therefore made the point that JTU members were being discriminated against and that, even worse, teachers who were not members of the conference were not receiving fair treatment at the time of appointment. One of the witnesses at the hearing, the Assistant Principal of the Hisari Lower Secondary School, stated that when two new teachers fresh from college were assigned to his school and went to the office of the board of education to pick up their seals of appointment, these were handed over only after they had signed papers making them members of the conference.

At the same public hearing of the upper house's standing education committee, other alleged discriminatory practices against members of the JTU came to light. A woman teacher named Nishi Nagako testified that the vice-principal of her school visited her mother, gravely ill, when she herself was not at home and proceeded to ask her mother to use her influence to persuade the daughter to leave the union, making the point that if the daughter did not do so, she would be transferred to another school. The conversation was witnessed by a younger sister, a fact verified by the Human Rights Protection Bureau, which became involved in the case as a result of the death of the mother the day following the conversation with the vice-principal. Numerous other examples of educational authorities pressuring teachers to resign from the union were brought to light at the same hearing. As these few examples indicate, the standing education committees, with their large contingent of JTU Dietmen, have served as one means through which the JTU has

251

been able to question educational authorities and bring unfair administrative practices to the attention of the public.

Of course, both adoption by the JSP of the JTU's educational policies and the role played by the JTU Dietmen in the education committees do not spell legislative victory. Literally dozens of bills originated by the JTU and proposed in the Diet by the JSP have died in the LDP-controlled Standing Education Committees of the Diet. Although in most cases the LDP listens to, but does not accept, the views of the JTU and the JSP, a few bills containing the essence of a particular JTU policy or demand have nevertheless been passed by the Diet. This has been accomplished by creating, over a long period of time, such a broad-based demand for a particular measure that in the end the LDP has had no choice but to submit its own bill embodying the JTU's demand. Somewhat ironically, at such times the JSP and the JTU find themselves supporting an LDP proposal. But this strategy of building up a large-scale demand for a particular policy has been adopted not only because of the weak position of the JTU and the JSP in the Diet but also because of the refusal of the Ministry of Education to take any serious notice of the proposals of the JTU in the first place. Perhaps the most outstanding example of a bill passed as a result of a long-term, broad-based strategy was the Law Guaranteeing the Hiring of Substitute Teachers for Women Teachers Absent for Childbirth (Law 200) of 1961.[14] The JTU had fought for this bill ever since 1947 when, through collective bargaining with the Ministry of Education, it had won the right of women teachers to take sixteen weeks leave with pay for childbirth.

The JTU has also been the prime mover in preventing the passage of certain bills it thought highly undesirable. A famous example was its successful prevention of the passage of the School Textbook Bill of 1956. The LDP and the Ministry of Education, in order to gain greater authority over the

[14] Law No. 200, February 9, 1961, *Joshi Kyōiku Shokuin no Shussan ni Saishite no Hojo Kyōiku Shokuin no Kakuho ni Kansuru Hōritsu.*

writing and publishing of textbooks, fought for its passage. As discussed in Chapter III, the bill aimed squarely at reducing and eventually eliminating the extensive influence the JTU had at the time over the distribution, supply, and choice of textbooks. However, because of the fierce resistance of the JTU and its ability to gain the support of the academic community—the President of Tokyo University and nine other presidents of leading educational institutions issued a joint statement severely attacking the bill—the Textbook Bill did not pass the Diet. As a result, although certain restrictive administrative measures have been put into effect since 1956, the process by which textbooks are compiled, published, and distributed is not as rigidly controlled by the Ministry today as it would have been if the Textbook Bill had passed.

These examples reveal the moderating influence of the JTU and the fact that it has not been wholly impotent in the Diet. Working within the legislative process, the JTU has, of course, advocated numerous bills that by 1970 had reached various stages in the law-making process. In that year, for example, bills concerning the following two areas were under consideration in the Diet: first, a bill providing for the posting of guards in all elementary and secondary schools in order to allow teachers to concentrate their energies more directly on educational matters by relieving them from the necessity of acting as school guards, a task that requires teachers to sleep in the schools on a rotation basis to guard against fire and theft; and, second, a bill providing for an overtime work allowance.

In addition, a number of bills proposed by the JTU had been introduced into the standing education committees but had not been reported out: for example, bills to lower the teacher-pupil ratio; to increase the number of senior high schools under construction in order to prepare for the expected sudden rise in the number of students at that level; to increase public funds for kindergartens; to upgrade the level of teachers in schools for the blind, deaf, and handicapped by enabling them to acquire teaching licenses equivalent in rank to those held by teachers in regular public schools; to upgrade education and teachers' salaries in remote areas and coal-mining districts; to amend the Japan Scholarship Society Law relieving kindergarten teachers and school nurses of the obligation to repay loans; and to expand part-time high school education courses and correspondence courses for working youths.[15] These proposals indicate a number of the constructive attempts the JTU has made in the Diet on behalf of education and teachers in Japan.

Factional Affiliation

Just as JSP Dietmen belong to a number of fluctuating factions spread across the left-right spectrum of the party, so too do JTU JSP Dietmen. They are not all members of the same faction within the JSP. Nevertheless, throughout the postwar period the majority of the JTU representatives in the Diet have been members of factions comprising the party's left wing, although by 1968, partly as a result of shifts in the position of factions themselves and partly as a result of shifts to different factions by individuals, the majority of JTU Dietmen were in centrist or right-wing factions.

More specifically, until mid-1967, half of the JTU Dietmen in both houses were members of the Wada faction, one of the largest left Socialist factions in the JSP, which nevertheless in 1960 modified its position to support the more moderate structural reformers.[16] This movement was in accord with the de-radicalization of the JTU that took place throughout the decade of the 1960's. By 1970 half of the

[15] JTU, Department of Organization, *Nikkyōso: Watakushitachi no Undō to Sono Soshiki* (The Japan Teachers' Union: Our Movement and Organization), Tokyo: JTU, 1963, pp. 27-29.

[16] For a discussion of the Wada faction see Allan B. Cole, George O. Totten, and Cecil H. Uyehara, *Socialist Parties in Postwar Japan* (New Haven: Yale University Press, 1966), pp. 282-86.

JTU Dietmen were members of the faction led by centrist Katsumata Seiichi, Wada's successor (Table 18). As members of the Katsumata faction, JTU Dietmen played significant roles as mediators in working out compromises among the four major factions that formed a precarious coalition to lead the party in October 1967. The significant point here is that the JTU Dietmen are no longer a force pulling the JSP to the left but rather have become a force for maintaining party unity and for carrying out party reform.

In determining the effectiveness of JTU Dietmen in influencing the formulation of educational policy, we find that factional affiliation does not appear to be an important variable. There is no significant difference between the JTU and the various factions regarding educational policy since, as discussed above, the JSP adopts the JTU's policies. Therefore, no matter what faction a JTU Dietman belongs to, it would be unlikely that the leader of his faction would demand that he take a position on an educational matter contrary to that of the JTU. At the same time, however, as clearly brought out in the first part of this chapter, JTU Dietmen are responsible to constituencies beyond that of merely teachers. In addition, they receive campaign funds not only from the JTU itself, however circuitously channeled through the party structure, but also from the faction to which they belong. These two facts merely indicate that JTU Dietmen, while serving the interest of the union and its members, must also be aware of the advantages of factional loyalty. The relationship between the two may best be viewed as complementary rather than contradictory, both contributing to the Dietman's ability to be re-elected and to play as effective a role as possible in the Diet.

As participants in the functions of the Diet, the JTU Dietmen's influence in the Diet is, of course, circumscribed by their membership in a minority party. In addition, their influence as individuals on the JSP in the Diet is not as great as the influence of the non-Diet JTU leaders. JTU Dietmen perform the investigative and legislative functions their po-

255

Table 18

Factional Affiliation of JTU Members in the Diet
(as of March 1970)

House of Representatives

Katsumata Faction *Constituency*

Katō Seiji	Aichi 2
Kawamura Tsuguyoshi	Kumamoto 2
Tsujihara Hiroichi	Wakayama 2
Kawasaki Kanji	Kagoshima 1
Saitō Masaō	Shizuoka 3

Sasaki Faction

| Kobayashi Shin-ichi | Yamanashi |

Kōno Faction

| Miki Yoshio | Hyōgo 4 |

Eda Faction

| Ōhara Tōru | Hiroshima 1 |
| Yamaguchi Tsuruo | Gumma 3 |

Others

| Yamanaka Gorō | Iwate 1 |
| Kijima Kihei | Niigata 4 |

House of Councillors

Tōkakai

Akiyama Chōzō	Okayama
Kase Kan	Chiba
Kobayashi Takeshi	National
Chiba Chiyose	National
Matsunaga Chūji	Shizuoka
Ono Akira	Fukuoka
Kawamura Seiichi	Hokkaidō
Yasunaga Hideo	National

Sasaki Faction

| Naruse Banji | Aichi |
| Suzuki Riki | National |

Others

| Oka Saburō | Kanagawa |
| Sugihara Kazuo | Toyama |

Source: *Mainichi Shimbun*, March 6, 1970.

sition enables them to, but real influence comes from the union outside the Diet. To the teachers these limitations are not as important as the mere fact that there are former teachers' union leaders in the Diet. This has given them and their union prestige in their own eyes, has contributed to their political socialization in Japanese society as a whole, and has given them a sense that at the top of the governmental structure there are representatives acting in their interests, even though they may not always be able to prevent the passage of undesirable measures or push through desired ones.

This brief analysis of the JTU in the electoral and legislative processes at the national level points to the conclusion that although the union, largely because of its own independent strength, has been extremely successful in electing its own leaders to the Diet, it has had far less success in having its policies translated into law by the Diet. Electoral success has not, of course, spelled legislative victories, although the "presence" of the JTU in the Standing Education Committees and in the Diet as a whole has contributed to its ability to question the policies and administrative practices of the government and to keep its views before the legislative body. More important, on specific occasions, through the application of indirect and united influence, the JTU's view has prevailed and prevented the passage of proposed undesirable governmental legislation. As the JTU achieves greater acceptance by the government in the future, its members in the Diet may be able to be more influential than in the past.

CHAPTER VIII

Conclusion

THE PURPOSE of this broad cross-sectional case study has been to describe and analyze the influence of the Japan Teachers' Union on its own members and on the formulation and implementation of educational policies. At a higher level, the objective has been to evaluate the significance of the very existence of this large, active, independent, non-governmentally-controlled teachers' union to Japanese politics and society. As this study has shown, the JTU is a complex organism to deal with as an interest group because it is one thing at the national level and forty-six different things at the prefectural level. In one prefecture, Tochigi, union membership is now only one percent of educational personnel; in others, it has been reputedly as high as ninety-nine percent. Some prefectural teachers' unions, such as Shimane and Tokushima, have never had a union leader elected to the Prefectural Assembly, the House of Councillors, or the House of Representatives, while others, such as Hokkaidō, have succeeded in electing at one time as many as eight of their members to the Prefectural Assembly, and one to each of the houses in the Diet. The mainstream leadership of some prefectural unions, such as Akita, has been dominated by those who support the Communist Party, while in others the mainstream leadership has supported the left wing of the JSP, and in still others the right wing of the JSP. Furthermore, union leadership in certain prefectures has been enlightened and ready to compromise with local boards of education, while in others it has remained doctrinaire and inflexible. By and large, at the national level meaningful negotiations have not taken place between the JTU and the Ministry of Education, whereas at the prefectural level negotiations between the unions and boards of education have come to take place almost as a matter of course in most prefectures. In spite of the complexities, however, conclusions may be drawn from the foregoing study concerning the influence of the JTU on its own members and on the formulation and implementation of educational policies; finally, an evaluation may be made concerning the significance of the JTU to Japanese politics and society.

INFLUENCE ON THE TEACHER MEMBERS

In regard to the influence of the JTU on Japanese teachers, the study has demonstrated, particularly in the analysis of the questionnaire concerning teacher attitudes, that the JTU has gone a long way toward changing the understanding the elementary and lower secondary teachers have of their role in education. In the prewar period teachers thought of themselves as participating in a sacred occupation, one in which they understood they were not to make demands as individuals or as groups for improvement in education or in their own welfare. By contrast, in the postwar period, as a consequence of the very existence of the JTU and its activities, teachers have come to understand not only that they have a right to demand a better livelihood but also that they have a right to demand that their views be considered in the process of formulating and implementing educational policies. That teachers strongly believe they have a right to demand a better livelihood was clearly revealed by the findings of the writer's questionnaire discussed in Chapter V in which ninety-seven percent of those polled thought the JTU either "very necessary" or "necessary" for the protection of their livelihood. This great shift in the attitude of the elementary and lower secondary teachers reflects one of the JTU's strongest influences on teachers.

That teachers now believe that their views ought to be considered in the formulation and implementation of educational policies was clearly evidenced by their willingness to attend union meetings and willingness to participate in illegal strikes if necessary, their belief that the JTU should have the right to negotiate with the Ministry of Education at the national level, and their strong support in electing their union leaders to public office. These attitudes indicate not only that teachers are aware of their union's goals, but also that they now perceive their role as educators differently. The long postwar struggle between the JTU and the Ministry of Education has contributed greatly to an increased awareness by teachers of their responsibility as professionals. The argument here is not that the prewar teachers were unaware of their professional status, but rather that the postwar elementary and lower secondary teachers' conception of their responsibility as professionals has enlarged. This was an important by-product of the many years of struggle between the union and the Ministry. Even though the society as a whole and teachers in particular recognize the legitimate role the Ministry and the boards of education have to play in the formulation and implementation of educational policies, the years of questioning and resisting by the JTU of many policies of the educational bureaucracy—questioning and resisting that occurred to one degree or another by teachers in almost every school throughout Japan—have inevitably led to greater awareness by teachers of educational problems and an increased desire to express their own views and to exercise personal judgment. Certainly the defeat in war, the Occupation reforms in education, and the exposure to democratic ideas operating in the society as a whole have contributed enormously to this change in the teachers' image of themselves. At the same time, however, it would be difficult to overestimate the role played by the arguments, the activities, and the struggles of the JTU—struggles that involved all teachers throughout Japan—in producing this

260

enhanced self-image. Without question the JTU has influenced teachers to be more conscious of and to demand more consideration of their views as professionals.

The writer does not wish to be misunderstood here. In his judgment Japanese elementary and lower secondary school teachers have come a long way, but they are still too dependent on both the Ministry and the union and, in addition, they are still too hamstrung by both. Good teachers are fashioned by giving teachers the freedom and the responsibility to create their own courses and their own teaching methods. The Ministry's tight control over curriculum results in teachers who too often resign themselves to teaching solely according to Ministry guidelines. In relation to the union, teachers are still too often cowed by union activists into supporting decisions they actually oppose. Greater trust in teachers on the part of both the Ministry and the union would help to create more effective teachers.

The JTU has had significance to teachers in other areas as well, particularly in the area of protecting them from unfair administrative practices. Certain prefectural unions, for example, have reached working relationships with the prefectural boards of education to prevent the sudden, arbitrary transfer of teachers to remote areas. In these prefectures the boards have agreed to discuss personnel matters with union leaders prior to making final decisions. Such power and participation on the part of the prefectural unions has cut down on the number of transfers of teachers to remote areas without sound educational reasons. In fact, in such prefectures where remote schools must, of course, be staffed, an equitable rotation system has been worked out as a result of union demands. In addition, as we have seen in Chapter VI, the JTU has been able to fight for the protection of the rights of teachers by bringing to the courts a large number of cases of what it has considered the improper and unjust dismissal of a number of full-time officers from their public service status. The sustained efforts the JTU has made to inform teachers of their rights as teachers has bolstered their image of themselves and of their role in the teaching profession. Thus, to the elementary and lower secondary teachers, the significance of the JTU has been incalculable. Their representatives now sit in the Diet, their lawyers now defend them in the courts in cases of possible unfair administrative treatment, their union leaders now negotiate on their behalf with prefectural and local boards of education, and in every school they themselves constitute an organization designed to protect their interests. None of these things existed in the prewar period. More than this, teachers now exercise a greater degree of individual judgment than they did before the war in planning the content of their courses and in devising new teaching techniques. Although the JTU is by no means solely responsible for these developments, its influence in moving Japanese teachers in these directions cannot be denied.

INFLUENCE ON THE FORMULATION AND IMPLEMENTATION OF EDUCATIONAL POLICIES

In regard to the influence the JTU has had on the formulation and implementation of educational policies, this study has demonstrated that the union has had a moderating influence on policies determined by the government and administered by the educational bureaucracy. We have seen that the JTU has had greater influence at the lower level of policy implementation than at the higher level of policy formulation. This phenomenon has occurred because of the ideological and structural gap between the JTU and the government at the national level which has made the gaining of direct access to points in the decision-making process at the top virtually impossible. At the prefectural and local levels, however, where the ideological and structural gap narrows considerably, the JTU has been able to exercise strong influence through direct access to the boards of education and the principals. In spite of the wide gap at the top, we have nevertheless seen that on specific occasions the JTU has been able to exercise considerable influence on the formulation of policy through united action with the JSP and Sōhyō. It has also exercised influence through demonstrations and strikes. Perhaps even more important has been the influence on policy-makers of the JTU's very existence. Even though no JTU leaders have participated directly in the policy-making process within the LDP and the Ministry of Education, the hidden, unspoken influence of the JTU in the minds of the policy formulators and the fear of the union's possible, if not predictable, reaction to specific policies has clearly had a restraining influence on the kinds of policies formulated and the methods of their implementation. One hint of this was the decision not to implement the efficiency rating system until 1958 even though it was authorized by law in 1950. Nevertheless, the main conclusion of this study is that the JTU's greatest influence has occurred at the prefectural and lower levels, where policies formulated by the Ministry at the top have undergone change in the process of implementation.

The moderating influence of the JTU at the level of implementation was seen to be particularly strong in regard to the administration of the efficiency rating system, which through union action was rendered largely meaningless, and the nationwide achievement tests, in which as a result of union action the administrative decision was made not to enter test scores on students' permanent academic records. Although the study did not analyze other crucial policy decisions—such as, for example, the introduction into the curriculum of moral education courses beginning in 1956—the JTU's moderating influence upon these policies has been equally strong. The determination by teachers not to use the moral education hour for that purpose or the decision to teach their own interpretation of the Ministry's suggested course has been encouraged and condoned by the union. In addition, the moderating influence of the JTU in regard to educational policies has been manifested at the school level by the fact that teachers themselves, although strongly influenced by Ministry policies and guidelines, no longer consider them holy writ. The prevailing mood among teachers is that such policies and guidelines, particularly those concerning the content of courses, should be studied carefully but need not be accepted *in toto*. They may be either accepted, modified, or rejected, depending upon the teachers' evaluation of their merit. Good points are to be used, unacceptable ones ignored. Perhaps no other statement in this book reveals the influence the JTU has had on education in Japan more than the foregoing.

The JTU's position regarding a host of other educational problems not discussed here may have considerable influence in the future, particularly in light of the more positive and creative approach JTU leaders are beginning to take in regard to educational policies and the more time and attention they are giving to fundamental educational problems. The JTU, for example, is placing great stress on raising the level of compulsory education from nine to twelve years and on retaining the comprehensive high school. It argues against the Ministry's decision to divide the high school curriculum into two separate tracks: one for non-university-preparing students and one for students planning to enter a university. The JTU advocates the American-inspired single system on the grounds that the division of students into two not only perpetuates an elite class, thereby inhibiting the growth of an egalitarian society, but also tends to discriminate against students in rural areas, where only the non-university option is apt to be offered. Significantly, the JTU does not shut its eyes to the differences in ability of students since it is not opposed to the division of students within a single system into ability groupings as long as students can be switched easily from one group to another on the basis of their changing performances and desires. How much influence the union will have on such matters in the future remains to be seen, but union pressure cannot be denied.

264

Regarding certain policies the JTU's influence has been not merely moderating but decisive. The pregnancy leave, the hiring of substitute teachers, and the successful prevention in 1956 of the passage in the Diet of the government-proposed Textbook Bill are prime examples. In addition, as brought out in Chapter VI, the influence of the JTU, along with that of the ILO Committee on Freedom of Association, has been very strong in persuading the government to work towards establishing adequate compensatory measures for the loss of the union's right to bargain collectively and to strike.

In the author's judgment, therefore, because JTU leaders at the top have adopted a non-subservient, non-obedient, anti-traditional posture, buttressed by a Marxist-oriented view of Japanese society, the net result of the existence and activities of the JTU on educational policy in postwar Japan has been positive. In fact, the existence of the JTU as an independent teachers' union has been indispensable to the democratization of Japanese education, a process that is by no means complete but that the JTU through its activities as a strong countervailing power to the heretofore absolute Ministry of Education has greatly assisted. Much credit must be given here to the government and the Ministry for this phenomenon. By maintaining a firm stand against the extreme radicalism of the JTU at the top and by taking firm action in selected prefectures, the Ministry has actually helped the more moderate leaders within the union to gain power. As a result, the JTU's educational policies themselves have become more moderate and more positive. The intransigence of both sides, which both sides increasingly came to see as detrimental to education itself, led in the long run to the inching of each side toward the other, and to a greater acceptance of each side by the other. In addition, the victory of the more moderate leaders, partially caused by the government's firm stand, led to the narrowing of the gap between the union's radical ideological leadership at the top and the more practical rank and file. This

265

gap, though now narrowed, has persisted partly because of the ability of radical leadership cliques who founded certain prefectural unions to maintain themselves in office, and partly because national leaders were forced to go along to a certain extent with the policies of a few strong radical anti-mainstream prefectural unions to prevent them from forming splinter unions. Nevertheless, the overall trend at the prefectural level since 1958 has been towards a decline in the strength of the radicals and a rise in the strength of the moderates. In spite of signs in the late 1960's and early 1970's of an increase in radical activity at the local level, actual control remained overwhelmingly in the hands of the moderates. If this trend continues, the JTU's strategic position in Japanese politics and society will improve in the future, thus increasing its moderating and positive influence on the formulation and implementation of educational policies.

SIGNIFICANCE TO JAPANESE POLITICS AND SOCIETY

As an opposition-aligned interest group that, among other methods, has attempted to influence the formulation and implementation of educational policies by electing its leaders to public office, the JTU has not only had some measure of success but has also had a measure of influence on Japanese politics in general. As has been repeatedly stated, the JTU has acted as one of the many significant groups in Japanese politics that have comprised the support for the Socialist opposition throughout the postwar period. As a beneficiary of the legitimation of the left wing in Japanese politics immediately after the war, the JTU has been a major actor on the stage of left-wing politics. Indisputably, the JTU, through the election of a substantial number of its leaders, has contributed to the ability of the JSP to hold approximately one-third of the seats in the Diet. In this sense, the JTU has contributed significantly to the strength of the political opposition in postwar Japanese politics. At the same time, however, the efficiency of the JTU's organization at the prefectural and local levels, which has made nominations and elections of JTU leaders possible, has both helped and hindered the JSP. From one point of view, the JTU has contributed significantly to the JSP's success, but from another point of view the JTU, along with other trade unions, by operating as the party's organizational apparatus at the prefectural and local levels, has hindered the JSP from extending its own party organization beyond that of labor groups. Thus, the JTU has contributed to the inability of the JSP to grow beyond the one-third limit.

If the JTU has both added to and detracted from the strength of the JSP, however, its mere continued existence as a political interest group within the total spectrum of Japanese politics has helped to institutionalize pluralism in Japanese politics to a far greater degree than existed in the prewar period. The JTU has certainly been resisted by the government, but it has by no means been annihilated or even suppressed to the degree it would have been under the prewar monolithic structure. In this sense, the JTU is a manifestation of the greater degree of democracy operative in Japanese politics.

As a noisy participant in opposition politics, the JTU has contributed to the strength of the peace movement in Japan, helping to keep alive pacifistic sentiment among the people and the desire to retain unamended Article ix of the Constitution, the famous "no war" article. At the same time, the JTU, because it has a stake in preserving the fundamental rights guaranteed by the Constitution to individuals and groups, has incessantly emphasized people's rights at all its union meetings and thus has contributed through the teaching of its members in the classrooms to a greater awareness of these rights on the part of the Japanese public, especially the youth. JTU leaders raise their voices vigorously when they believe the fundamental rights of the JTU as a union or the rights of teachers as individuals have been infringed.

267

To what extent the JTU's emphasis on rights, coupled with its participation in obstructionist tactics in the Diet against the ruling party and its anti-governmental demonstrations in the streets, has contributed to the readiness in recent years of certain elements of Japanese youth to resort to non-democratic, disruptive, and violent behavior in order to achieve their objectives is difficult to say. Unrest among youth is a worldwide phenomenon and may at root be apolitical rather than political; i.e., it may spring from feelings against the technocratic state, regardless of the state's particular ideology. The Japanese youth movement still appears to be politically oriented, however, and the writer cannot escape the conclusion that the JTU, particularly in the 1950's, certainly contributed to the idea that established authority could best be opposed through disruptive tactics. In this sense, the JTU shares, along with other such groups in Japanese society, the responsibility for having contributed to the lack of respect for the Diet among opposition groups and the readiness of such groups to take to the streets. Nevertheless, such behavior by certain elements of Japanese youth has many causes and, moreover, is not unrelated to the worldwide disaffection of the young.

With the exception of the activity of fringe groups on both the far left and the far right, there were signs by the early 1970's that Japanese politics were becoming less polarized and less rigidly ideological. Gradually, over the decade of the 1970's the JTU will undoubtedly move in the direction of freeing itself from strict adherence to Marxist-Leninist principles, but the process will require the continuation of vigorous leadership if the union is to stay intact, and the top leaders are not to be isolated from the more rapid rightward movement of Japan's left wing as a whole. No doubt JTU leaders will move more slowly than leaders of other left-wing groups because of their long association with the left Socialists, their tendency to be strongly influenced by left-wing intellectuals in the academic world, and their fear of losing the support of several important prefectures (e.g., Fukuoka) controlled by the anti-mainstream. Thus in 1970 the JTU continued to oppose the unification of labor on a non-class-conscious basis. Nevertheless, the future belongs to the moderates. Independent prefectural teachers' unions make little sense since they hold no real power. By the same token, the possibility of some right-wing LDP-supporting teachers' organization gaining strength is nil. Such groups nurtured by the Ministry of Education have gained no strength over the last decade. In addition, the members of the JTU, the teachers of Japan, will continue to pull the JTU to the right and force it to be more vitally concerned with their own immediate problems, whether related to their welfare or to the content and administration of education.

The greatest significance of the JTU to the society as a whole is that it has constituted the largest single organized interest group in the field of education outside the educational bureaucracy itself. In this role the JTU has functioned as the most significant countervailing power in the field of education to the government and the Ministry of Education. That teachers feel that there ought to be a countervailing power to the government and the Ministry has been demonstrated in this study by the finding that they support the activities of the JTU whether or not they are in agreement with particular issues at particular times, precisely because they believe that the power of the Ministry ought to be offset by another interested group in the society. In a larger sense, the existence of the JTU as a countervailing power has made possible the exposure to the general public of a wide range of disparate views regarding educational policies, views that policy-makers have not been able to ignore. In this sense, perhaps the most significant contribution of the JTU to Japanese society is that through its struggles it has brought the question of education to center stage in Japanese domestic life. With an aroused public, it seems unlikely that any government will be able to secure the same degree of authority over education exercised before the war. The point here is not whether the public has strongly supported the union or whether certain patterns of recentralization have been reestablished. The important fact is that the public has come to play a greater role in education than it did before the war. Parents, whether in agreement or disagreement with the JTU's position on any given issue, have become more actively concerned as a result of the battles between the two sides. In this sense, the JTU, whose struggles have dramatized educational problems, has contributed an immense service to the cause of Japanese education. Fires of concern have everywhere been kindled. There is no better assurance for the future preservation and growth of liberal education in Japan than an alert, articulate public.

Teachers support the union because it represents for them the most effective way of improving their welfare, of protecting their interests, and of criticizing and keeping watch on governmental educational policies. In this role, the JTU remains a large, dynamic interest group. Paradoxically, signs that the union is placing greater and greater stress on education and economics rather than on politics suggest that in the future its voice may be heeded more than ever before. In addition, if the leadership continues to moderate substantially union policies, bringing them more in line with the views of the rank and file, it should be strengthened internally. Particularly, the more the union helps its members to become free, creative, and responsible teachers in the classrooms, the more support it will receive. The schools that blanket Japan need imaginative teachers as free as possible from both governmental and union dictates. With such moderations in policy, some already long underway, the union's strategic position in the society should be enhanced as well. If this continues to happen, the JTU's ability to influence teachers, education, and politics will increase, not only at the prefectural and lower levels, where its real influence to date has been strongest, but at the national level as well.

270

Appendices and Bibliography

The Collective Bargaining Contract Between the Council of All-Japan Teachers' Unions and the Ministry of Education
Ministry of Education
Hatsu Gaku No. 127, 19 March 1947

THE Ministry of Education, hereinafter referred to as A, and Zen Nihon Kyōin Kumiai Kyōgi Kai (The Council of All-Japan Teachers' Unions), hereinafter referred to as B, hereby make an agreement for collective bargaining based upon the spirit of the Labor Union Law, as follows:

CHAPTER I. PRINCIPLES

Article I

> A shall recognize B as an agent for collective bargaining. A shall be responsible for the security of the living of the members of B. A and B shall cooperate and be responsible for the enhancement of democratic education.

Article II

> A shall not make any discrimination based on sex distinction against the members of B.

CHAPTER II. MATTERS CONCERNING PAY

Article III

> A shall undertake to establish a pay system that will secure for the members of B and their families the standards of wholesome and cultured living. In deciding fundamental principles of pay, the representatives of both parties shall participate.

Article IV

A shall confer with B to establish a retirement bonus system without imposing a burden on members of B.

CHAPTER III. MATTERS CONCERNING WORKING HOURS AND BUSINESS AFFAIRS

Article V

The working hours of teachers shall be as follows:
1. There shall be 42 working hours a week.
2. The standard daily teaching time shall be 4 hours.
3. As to other working hours, A and B shall decide by mutual agreement within the limits of preceding rules.

Article VI

Twenty free study days shall be granted every year.

CHAPTER IV. MATTERS CONCERNING FREE DAYS AND VACATIONS

Article VII

Sundays, holidays, and Labor Day shall be free days. Employees shall be paid for free days.

Article VIII

Twenty free days each year shall be granted in consideration of service.

Article IX

Three physiological free days in a month and 16 weeks off duty before and after childbirth shall be granted. Absence due to pregnancy shall be recognized as free days upon presentation of medical certification. For one year after childbirth, nursing hours shall be granted.

CHAPTER V. MATTERS CONCERNING SICKNESS AND MEDICAL
TREATMENT

Article X

> Three years with full pay shall be allowed for the treatment of tuberculosis.

CHAPTER VI. MATTERS CONCERNING PERSONNEL AFFAIRS

Article XI

> The fundamental standards relative to personnel affairs, including appointment, discharge, transfer, rewards and punishments, shall be considered by the Personnel Affairs Committee composed of members of A and B.

> The constitution and operation of the Personnel Affairs Committee shall be set in accordance with those of the Council of Business Affairs.

Article XII

> A shall not discharge any of the union members:
> 1. For participation in the union movement.
> 2. During the period necessary for medical treatment of injuries or sickness contracted while on duty, and for 90 days thereafter.
> 3. During a resting period before and after childbirth, and 90 days thereafter.

CHAPTER VII. MATTERS CONCERNING THE UNION MOVEMENT

Article XIII

> A shall allow members of B to engage fully in union affairs while occupying their regular posts. The number of such members shall be decided at a conference of A and B.

Article XIV

> A shall permit members of B to engage in union movement activities. A trip on union business shall be

275

treated as an official trip after the principal has been informed, but no travelling expenses shall be granted.

Article XV

A shall allow B the use of buildings or facilities under its control for union activities.

Article XVI

If a dispute, or the threat of one, should arise, A will not take any step against the union by applying the Administrative Order.

Article XVII

A, when engaged in a dispute with B, will not negotiate with a union or its members who have seceded.

CHAPTER VIII. MATTERS CONCERNING THE COUNCIL OF BUSINESS AFFAIRS

Article XVIII

A and B shall set up a Council of Business Affairs, based on the aims of this contract. As to the constitution of the Council and the application of its rules, another agreement will be made between the two contracting parties.

Article XIX

The Council of Business Affairs, based on this contract, will concern itself with the following affairs:
1. Matters concerning pay, injury compensation, personnel, and positions.
2. Matters concerning working hours, free days, and vacations.
3. Matters concerning the educational budget.
4. Matters concerning the handling of business affairs.
5. Matters concerning welfare.

6. Matters concerning education and culture.

7. Other matters recognized by the Council as necessary.

Article XX

Both parties shall be responsible for the bona fide enforcement of the decisions of the Council of Business Affairs. Any of the preceding items shall be included in a written agreement, if both parties deem it necessary to do so.

CHAPTER IX. MATTERS CONCERNING THE STANDARDS OF PREFECTURAL COLLECTIVE BARGAINING

Article XXI

A, considering it proper for the prefectural chapters of B to enter into collective bargaining agreements with the prefectural governments, shall encourage the realization of the following:

1. Matters concerning vacations.

2. Matters concerning the number of union officials.

3. Matters concerning personnel affairs.

CHAPTER X. OTHER AFFAIRS

Article XXII

A shall not interfere with the political interests of the members of B.

Article XXIII

A shall recognize the freedom of a member of B to hold another public office, insofar as it does not conflict with his regular duties. A shall provide facilities necessary to execute duties of office.

Article XXIV

The duration of this agreement shall be for six months. A and B may change the effective duration of this agreement before the end of the prescribed period by mutual agreement, if they find that general economic conditions or some other unavoidable situation makes it necessary. If no announcement be made by either of the parties concerned of the invalidation of this agreement one month before its expiration, it will be effective for six more months. If the intention to invalidate the agreement is announced, the agreement will remain effective until the new one comes into being.

UNDERSTANDING

1. A and B shall make efforts to realize as soon as possible the following:
   (1) The uniting of all the teachers' unions in the country into one single union, so that it will be the only agent for collective bargaining with A.
   (2) The including of all the teachers, in principle, as members of the union mentioned in the preceding clause.
2. If a union affiliated with B is the only one in a metropolis or prefecture, it will be authorized to make agreements on the basis of the above understanding.

3 March 1947

Provisionally signed by

Seiichirō TAKAHASHI, Minister of Education
Masao IWAMA, Chairman of the Campaign Committee of the Council of All-Japan Teachers' Unions
Yoshihei HIMURO, Superintendent of the Central Labor Committee

Source: A mimeographed copy of the official English translation of this Contract was given to the author by Sawada Michiya, Chief of the Local Affairs Section of the Ministry of Education.

278

A Code of Ethics
for Teachers (1952)

UNTIL the present time the teachers of Japan, under the pressures of a half-feudalistic ultranationalistic system, have been forced into a logic of subservience. Because the Japanese social system today has reached a point where reconstruction from a completely different point of view is necessary, we must cut our ties with past conventions and embrace a new ethic.

A code of ethics is not merely a set of universal and eternal rules, but rather a set of changing principles which must be grasped through a fight to accomplish the historical tasks which have been bestowed upon a people within a specific historical period. Today, however, the workings of our society are causing poverty and unemployment to become more and more universal and are forcing even the independence of the country onto dangerous ground.

The threat of a modern destructive war is distorting our recognition of these historical tasks and deflecting our will to overcome them. In such a state of affairs our earnest desire to seek a peaceful society in which human rights are respected, industrial production is increased, and the exploitation of man by man is no longer permitted cannot be attained without a high degree of autonomous growth toward maturity on the part of the laboring class. Needless to say, teachers are laborers. The more the difficulty of the situation increases, the more the teachers of Japan, along with all laborers, must increase their unity, protect the youth of the country, and face these historical tasks with courage and intelligence. Based on a recognition of the

279

above facts, we hereby establish the following code of ethics:

I. Teachers Shall Work with the Youth of the Country in Fulfilling the Tasks of Society

Upon our shoulders have been laid the historical tasks of protecting peace, insuring the independence of the country, and realizing a society free from exploitation, poverty, and unemployment. Believing in democracy, we are unswerving in our desire to fulfill these tasks.

The youth of the country must be raised and educated to become capable workers who will give themselves, each according to his own abilities, to the accomplishment of these tasks. There is no other road by which the youth of Japan can attain freedom and happiness.

Teachers shall live and work with the youth and shall be the organizers of and counselors in a schooling designed to meet this necessity. Each teacher shall make an intensive critical examination of himself and shall study and make efforts to prepare himself for his new role in education.

II. Teachers Shall Fight for Equal Opportunity in Education

Equal opportunity in education and respect for the dignity of the individual, as guaranteed by the Constitution, are today still dead letters. The youth of today are severely restricted in their educational opportunities because of the social and economic limitations placed upon the individual. It may be said in particular that no serious consideration has been given to educating either the multitudes of working young people or mentally and physically handicapped children. Children are not being guaranteed equality of conditions for life and growth either within or without the schools. We have reached a point where eighteenth-century individualism no longer opens the way to the development of the individual. Today social procedures must be followed in order to create equal opportunities in education.

Teachers shall of themselves be keenly aware of this necessity and shall in all quarters fight for equality in education.

III. Teachers Shall Protect Peace

Peace is the ideal of mankind; war destroys all the hopes of mankind. Without peace the historical tasks facing Japanese society cannot be accomplished. The desire of the people for peace becomes strongest when individual rights are respected and when the people are able to hold hopes for an improvement in social conditions and have strong faith in progress. Discontent and loss of hope on the part of the people may serve to impel a country down the road to war.

Teachers shall be advocators of the brotherhood of man, leaders in the reconstruction of life attitudes, and pioneers in respecting human rights, and as such they shall stand as the most courageous defenders of peace against all those who advocate war.

IV. Teachers Shall Act on Behalf of Scientific Truth

Progress takes place within a society when the members of that society, acting on behalf of scientific truth, seek a rational approach to historical tasks. Actions that ignore the fruits of science serve to suppress that in man which makes him seek progress. Teachers shall respect the progress-seeking element in man, shall carry out scientific explorations on nature and society, and shall create a rational environment conducive to the growth and development of young people.

To these ends teachers shall share their experiences and shall work closely with scholars and specialists in all fields.

V. Teachers Shall Allow No Infringements on Freedom in Education

Our freedom of research in education as well as of action is often suppressed by improper forces. Academic freedom

281

as well as freedom of speech, thought, and assembly, although guaranteed in the Constitution, are nevertheless actually being restricted severely. Infringements on freedom in education serve to obstruct healthy learning by young people, to hinder intellectual activity, and furthermore to endanger the proper development of the nation. Teachers, being deeply aware of this, shall fight against all improper pressures in education.

VI. TEACHERS SHALL SEEK AFTER PROPER GOVERNMENT

Successive governments, under the pretext of making education politically neutral, have long deprived the teachers of Japan of their freedoms and have forced them to serve in whatever way the government has desired. After the war, having been given the freedom to participate in political activities, teachers banded together and fought for proper government, but now such political freedom is again being taken from them. Government is not something to serve the interests of any one group; it belongs to all the people. It is the means for us to attain our desires in a peaceful manner.

Teachers, together with all working men, shall participate in political activities and shall pool their resources in seeking proper government.

VII. TEACHERS SHALL FIGHT SIDE BY SIDE WITH PARENTS AGAINST CORRUPTION IN SOCIETY AND SHALL CREATE A NEW CULTURE

In our towns and villages our young people are surrounded day and night by corruption of all kinds that is exerting a degenerative influence on their wholesome minds. Unwholesome amusements are suggested in movies, plays, and even in the tales told by the neighborhood children's storytellers; degenerative tendencies are to be found in newspapers, radio programs, and in books and magazines; the type of atmosphere surrounding bicycle and race tracks and urban amusement districts tends to weaken the soul of the nation. All these exert a particularly strong and poisonous influence on the youth of the country.

Teachers shall combine their efforts with parents in protecting youth from the corrupting influences of society, shall live and work with youth in a proper manner, and shall create a new culture of the working man.

VIII. TEACHERS ARE LABORERS

Teachers are laborers whose workshops are the schools. Teachers, in the knowledge that labor is the foundation of everything in society, shall be proud of the fact that they themselves are laborers. At the present stage of history, the realization of a new society of mankind that respects fundamental human rights, not only in words but in deed as well, and that utilizes resources, technology, and science for the welfare of all men is possible only through the power of the working masses, whose nucleus is the laboring class. Teachers shall be aware of their position as laborers, shall live forcefully believing in the historical progress of man, and shall consider all stagnation and reaction as their enemies.

IX. TEACHERS SHALL DEFEND THEIR RIGHT TO MAINTAIN A MINIMUM STANDARD OF LIVING

Having been forced thus far to live in noble poverty under the proud name of educator, teachers have been ashamed to voice their demands for even the minimum material benefits necessary for their existence. To demand just recompense for their own labors would have been unthinkable to teachers of the past. Because of this situation, teachers have lost all desire and zeal for imparting to their students a proper education, and their lives have come to be ruled by exhaustion, indolence, and opportunism.

Teachers shall consider it their right and duty to protect their own right to maintain a minimum standard of living and to fight for optimum conditions under which to live and labor.

283

X. TEACHERS SHALL UNITE

The obligations that history has given to the teachers can be fulfilled only if teachers unite. The strength of the teacher is exhibited through organization and unity; organization and unity give constant courage and strength to the activities of the teachers. Moreover, there is no other way today in which the teacher can establish himself as an individual except through unity of action. The teachers of Japan, through the labor movement, shall unite with the teachers of the world and shall join hands with all laborers.

Unity is the highest ethic of the teacher.

Source: Quoted in *Journal of Social and Political Ideas in Japan*, Vol. I, No. 3, December 1963, Appendix IV, pp. 129-31.

The Fundamental Law
of Education 1947 (Law No. 25)

HAVING established the Constitution of Japan, we have shown our resolution to contribute to the peace of the world and welfare of humanity by building a democratic and cultural state. The realization of this ideal shall depend fundamentally on the power of education. We shall esteem individual dignity and endeavour to bring up a people who love truth and peace, while education, which aims at the creation of culture that is both universal and rich in individuality, shall be spread far and wide. We hereby enact this Law, in accordance with the spirit of the Constitution of Japan, with a view to clarifying the aim of education and establishing the foundation of education for a new Japan.

ARTICLE I. AIM OF EDUCATION

Education shall aim at the full development of personality, striving for the rearing of the people, sound in mind and body, who shall love truth and justice, esteem individual value, respect labor, and have a deep sense of responsibility, and be imbued with an independent spirit, as builders of a peaceful state and society.

ARTICLE II. EDUCATIONAL PRINCIPLE

The aim of education shall be realized on all occasions and in all places. In order to achieve the aim, we shall endeavour to contribute to the creation and development of culture by mutual esteem and cooperation, respecting academic freedom, having a regard for the practical matters of everyday life, and cultivating a spontaneous spirit.

285

Article III. Equal Opportunity in Education

The people shall all be given equal opportunities of receiving education according to their ability, and they shall not be subject to educational discrimination on account of race, creed, sex, social status, economic position, or family origin. The state and local public bodies shall take measures to give financial assistance to those who have, in spite of their ability, difficulty in receiving education for economic reasons.

Article IV. Compulsory Education

The people shall be obligated to have boys and girls under their protection receive nine years of general education. No tuition fee shall be charged for compulsory education in schools established by the state and local public bodies.

Article V. Coeducation

Men and women shall esteem and cooperate with each other. Coeducation, therefore, shall be recognized in education.

Article VI. School Education

The schools prescribed by law shall be of a public nature, and, besides the state and local public bodies, only the juridical persons prescribed by law shall be entitled to establish such schools. Teachers of the schools prescribed by law shall be servants of the whole community. They shall be conscious of their mission and endeavour to discharge their duties. For this purpose, the status of teachers shall be respected, and their fair and appropriate treatment shall be secured.

Article VII. Social Education

The state and local public bodies shall encourage home education and education carried out in places of work or elsewhere in society. The state and local public bodies shall endeavour to attain the aim of education by the establishment of such institutions as libraries, museums, civic halls, etc., by the utilization of school institutions, and by other appropriate methods.

ARTICLE VIII. POLITICAL EDUCATION

The political knowledge necessary for intelligent citizenship shall be valued in education. The schools prescribed by law shall refrain from political education or other political activities for or against any specific political party.

ARTICLE IX. RELIGIOUS EDUCATION

The attitude of religious tolerance and the position of religion in social life shall be valued in education. The schools established by the state and local public bodies shall refrain from religious education or other activities for a specific religion.

ARTICLE X. SCHOOL ADMINISTRATION

Education shall not be subject to improper control, but it shall be directly responsible to the whole people. School administration shall, on the basis of this realization, aim at the adjustment and establishment of the various conditions required for the pursuit of the aim of education.

ARTICLE XI. ADDITIONAL RULE

In case of necessity, appropriate laws shall be enacted to carry the foregoing stipulations into effect.

Source: Quoted in *Journal of Social and Political Ideas in Japan*, Vol. I, No. 3, December 1963, Appendix II, pp. 122-24.

Questionnaire for Japan Teachers' Union Members

　私はニューヨーク市のコロンビア大学、大学院生で、博士論文として日本教職員組合について研究するため来日しました。私は日本政府及び合衆国政府のどちらにも関係していない、独立の研究員です。

　論文の課題は、戦後日本の小中学校教育に日教組があたえた影響という事です。このために私は、日教組の組織と組合の目的を遂行するための方法を研究しなければなりません。しかし、組合員の皆様のご意見をうかがわなければ、日教組についての正しい理解が得られません。

　ですから、できるだけ正確に下記の質問にお答えくださつて、私の研究にお力添えいただきたいと思います。

　このアンケートの結果は政府はもとより日教組の関係者にも絶体お見せしません。過去に、東北大学で英語を教しえていた時から日本の教育問題に強い関心を持っていましたし、また、合衆国で高校教師としての経験もあり、教師に対しての深い尊敬と教師の問題についての共感を持つています。

　お時間をとり申し訳ありませんが、お答えいただければ、たいへん、うれしく思います。

　このアンケート用紙のどこにもお名前を記入していただかなくて結構です。

　　　　　　　よろしくお願い申しあげます。

　　　　　　　　　　ドナルド　R．サーストン

1. 解答月日　　＿＿＿＿月＿＿＿＿日
2. 勤務校名　　＿＿＿＿＿＿＿＿＿＿
3. 年令　　　　＿＿＿＿＿
4. 才出身地（都道府県）＿＿＿＿＿＿
5. 性別　　男　女　（〇で囲んでください）
6. 教師としての勤務年数（累計）＿＿＿＿年
7. 日教組組合員としての年数　　＿＿＿＿年
8. 現在ある学年主任をしていますか。　はい　いいえ
　　　　　　　　　　　　　　（〇で囲んでください）
9. 現在ある教科主任をしていますか。　はい　いいえ
　　　　　　　　　　　　　　（〇で囲んでください）
10. 現在、日教組の分会長（分闘長）またはある科目の研究分科会の委員（教研推進委員）などをしていますか。
　　　　　　　はい　いいえ　（〇で囲んでください）

11. 学歴（あなたが履修された戦前の中学校または高等女
学校以上の学校名を記入してください）

（該当欄に✓のしるしをつけ　　（該当欄に校名と都道府県名を記入
てください）　　　　　　　　してください）

校名　　　　都道府県名

a. 戦前の中学校または　　＿＿＿＿＿＿＿＿＿＿＿＿
高等女学校

b. 戦前の師範学校　　　＿＿＿＿＿＿＿＿＿＿＿＿

c. 戦前の専門学校　　　＿＿＿＿＿＿＿＿＿＿＿＿

d. 戦前の高等師範学校　＿＿＿＿＿＿＿＿＿＿＿＿

e. 戦前の高等学校　　　＿＿＿＿＿＿＿＿＿＿＿＿

f. 戦前の大学　　　　　＿＿＿＿＿＿＿＿＿＿＿＿

g. 戦後の二年制大学　　＿＿＿＿＿＿＿＿＿＿＿＿

h. 戦後の四年制大学　　＿＿＿＿＿＿＿＿＿＿＿＿

i. その他（説明してく　＿＿＿＿＿＿＿＿＿＿＿＿
ださい

12. 昨年一年間（昭和39年１月から12月）に学校で開かれ
た組合の会合に約何回ぐらい出席しましたか。

約＿＿＿＿＿＿＿＿回

13. 上記の会合回数についてどう思いますか。
（該当欄に✓のしるしをつけてください）

a. ＿＿＿＿＿＿多すぎる。

b. ＿＿＿＿＿＿適当。

c. ＿＿＿＿＿＿少なすぎる。

14. 上記の会合をどう考えますか。
（該当欄に✓のしるしをつけてください）

a. ＿＿＿＿＿＿何をおいても組合会合に出席した
い。

b. ＿＿＿＿＿＿大ていは会合に出席する。

c. ＿＿＿＿＿＿出席したいと思うときもありそうで
ないときもある。

d. ＿＿＿＿＿＿大ていは会合に出席しない。

15. 上記の会合での発言について。
   （該当欄に✓のしるしをつけてください）

   a. ＿＿＿＿＿＿＿しばしば発言する。

   b. ＿＿＿＿＿＿＿時々 発言する。

   c. ＿＿＿＿＿＿＿たまに発言する。

   d. ＿＿＿＿＿＿＿発言しない。

16. 上記の会合での同僚の発言について。
   （該当欄にのしるしをつけてください）

   a. ＿＿＿＿＿＿＿ほとんど全員が発言する。
   b. 約半数が発言する。

   c. ＿＿＿＿＿＿＿少数しか発言しない。

17. 学校長も組合員であるべきだと思いますか。
   はい　いいえ　（〇で囲んでください）

18. 教頭も組合員であるべきだと思いますか。
   はい　いいえ　（〇で囲んでください）

19. 月刊雑誌「教育評論」について。
   （該当欄に✓のしるしをつけてください）

   a. ＿＿＿＿＿＿＿毎月読む。

   b. ＿＿＿＿＿＿＿時々読む。

   c. ＿＿＿＿＿＿＿たまに読む。

   d. ＿＿＿＿＿＿＿読まない。

   e. ＿＿＿＿＿＿＿その雑誌について知らない。

20. 組合費について。（該当欄に✓のしるしをつけてください）

   a. ＿＿＿＿＿＿＿高すぎる。

   b. ＿＿＿＿＿＿＿適当。

   c. ＿＿＿＿＿＿＿低すぎる。

21. 公務員として教師は「スト」権を持つべきだと思いま
   すか。（該当欄に✓のしるしをつけてください）

   a. ＿＿＿＿＿＿＿はい。

   b. ＿＿＿＿＿＿＿いいえ。

   c ＿＿＿＿＿＿＿わからない。

22. 現在、教師の「スト」は違法ですが必要なら「スト」に参加しますか。

    a. _____はい。

    b. _____いいえ。

    c. _____わからない。

23. 日教組が次のような方法で政治活動をすべきだと思いますか。(該当欄を○で囲んでください)

    a. 組合員にどの公職選挙立候補者が組合に友好的であるかを示唆する。   はい　いいえ

    b. 組合員にだれに投票すべきかを助言する。   はい　いいえ

    c. 組合員を公職選挙に立候補させる。はい　いいえ

    d. 組合から出た立候補者に対しての選挙用寄付金を組合員から集める。   はい　いいえ

    e. 組合推せん立候補者のために教師に戸別訪問させる。   はい　いいえ

24. 日教組は組合選出立候補者のために、どのくらい努力をすべきだと思いますか。
(設当欄に✓のしるしをつけてください)

    a. _____現状よりもっと。

    b. _____現状ぐらい。

    c. _____現状よりすくなく。

25. 教師の生活を守るために日教組が必要だと思いますか。(該当欄に✓のしるしをつけてください)

    a. _____たいへん必要だと思う。

    b. _____必要だと思う。

    c. _____あまり必要だと思わない。

    d. _____わからない。

26. 日教組の交渉権について。
（該当欄に✓のしるしをつけてください）
a. _____ 中央交渉権をもつべきである。
b. _____ 都道府県またはそれ以下のレベルで
のみ交渉すべきである。
c. _____ わからない。

27. 組合の在籍専従職員の員数について。
（該当欄に✓のしるしをつけてください）
a. _____ 多すぎる。
b. _____ 適当。
c. _____ 少なすぎる。
d. _____ わからない。

28. 上記専従の指導者としての活動状況についてどう思い
ますか。（該当欄に✓のしるしをつけてください）
a. _____ たいへんよい。
b. _____ よい。
c. _____ 普通。
d. _____ 不満足。

29. 一般教師の意見がどの程度　日教組の方針に反映して
いると思います。（該当欄に✓のしるしをつけてください）
a. _____ たいへん強く。
b. _____ 割合強く。
c. _____ あまり強くない。

30. だれが日教組の年度運動方針案を作製すると思います
か。（該当欄に✓のしるしをつけてください）
a. _____ 中央執行委員長、同副委員長及び書
記長。
b. _____ 中央執行委員会。
c. _____ 中央委員会。
d. _____ わからない。

31. 都道府県の専従は民主的に選出されていると思います
か。はい　いいえ　（〇で囲んでください）

32. 現在、組合専従になりたいと思いますか。
はい　いいえ　（○で囲んでください）

（裏につづく）

33. あなたが現在、組合専従になる可能性があると思いますか。（該当欄に✓のしるしをつけてください）

a. ＿＿＿＿＿＿＿＿可能性が大。

b. ＿＿＿＿＿＿＿＿可能性がかなりある。

c. ＿＿＿＿＿＿＿＿可能性がすくない。

d. ＿＿＿＿＿＿＿＿可能性が皆無。

e. ＿＿＿＿＿＿＿＿わからない。

34. 組合主催の教育研究会に出席したことがありますか。（全国、都道府県及び各支部の研究会をふくむ）
はい　いいえ　（○で囲んでください）
「はい」の場合、昨年一年間（昭和39年1月から12月）に約何回出席しましたか。　　　約＿＿＿＿＿回

35. 上記の教育研究会が授業上の諸問題解決にどれ程役に立つていると思いますか。
（該当欄に✓のしるしをつけてください）

a. ＿＿＿＿＿＿＿＿たいへん役に立っている。

b. ＿＿＿＿＿＿＿＿かなり役に立っている。

c. ＿＿＿＿＿＿＿＿あまり役に立っていない。

36. 文部省または教育委員会主催の教育研究会に出席したことがありますか（全国、都道府県及び地方で開かれたものをふくむ）
はい　いいえ　（○で囲んでください）
「はい」の場合、昨年一年間に約何回出席しましたか。
約＿＿＿＿＿回

37. 上記の教育研究会が授業上の諸問題解決にどれ程役に
    立っていると思いますか。
    （該当欄に✓のしるしをつけてください）

    a. ＿＿＿＿＿＿＿たいへん役に立っているか。

    b. ＿＿＿＿＿＿＿かなり役に立っている。

    c. ＿＿＿＿＿＿＿あまり役に立っていない。

38. あなたは今まで個人的に教育委員会等によつて日教組
    からの脱退をもとめられた経験がありますか。
    か。　はい　いいえ　（〇で囲んでください）

39. あなたは、日本教職員共済会（日教済）加入しています
    はい　いいえ　（〇で囲んでください）

40. 上記の日教済は教師の生活のために必要だと思います
    か。（該当欄に✓のしるしをつけてください）

    a. ＿＿＿＿＿＿＿たいへん必要だと思う。

    b. ＿＿＿＿＿＿＿必要だと思う。

    c. ＿＿＿＿＿＿＿あまり必要だと思わない。

    d. ＿＿＿＿＿＿＿わからない。

Questionnaire for Japan Teachers' Union Members (*English Translation*)

I am a graduate student at Columbia University in New York City and have come to Japan to carry out research for my doctoral dissertation. I have no connection with either the United States or Japanese government but am an independent researcher.

The subject of the dissertation concerns the influence of the Japan Teachers' Union on elementary and lower secondary education in Japan. Consequently, I must study such matters as the organizational structure of the JTU and the policies it advocates for achieving its objectives. In order to gain an accurate understanding of the union, however, I must ascertain the opinions of its members as well.

Therefore, if you would be kind enough to answer the following questions as accurately as possible, you would greatly assist my research.

Having previously taught English at Tohoku University, I have a keen interest in the educational problems of Japan. In addition, my experience as a high school teacher in America has given me a deep respect for the problems of teachers.

I apologize for taking your time, but I will be very grateful if you will answer the questions.

You need not write your name anywhere on the questionnaire.

Thank you for your kindness.

DONALD R. THURSTON

NOTE: *The following questionnaire was completed by 222 teachers. For the interest of the reader, the actual number of teachers who responded to each question has been inserted. The numbers do not always add up to 222 simply because certain teachers left certain questions unanswered. Where appropriate the average number has been inserted.*

1. Date questionnaire is being answered:_____ Month
   _____ Day
2. Name of School _____
3. Age ___36___ (average)
   20-29:   26 teachers
   30-39:   126 teachers
   40-49:   51 teachers
   50-59:   18 teachers
4. Birthplace _____
5. Sex: Male ___143___ Female ___79___ (Circle appropriate word)
6. Number of years you have been teaching: ___16___ years. (average)
7. Number of years you have been a JTU member:__13__ years. (average)
8. Are you *now* in charge of a particular grade level?
   Yes _43_____ No _177_____ (Circle appropriate word)
9. Are you *now* in charge of a particular subject?
   Yes_79_____ No _137____ (Circle appropriate word)
10. Are you *now* your school's union representative or a representative of any union-sponsored educational study group?
    Yes_79____ No _189____ (Circle appropriate word)
11. Educational History   Name of School   Prefecture
    a. Prewar Middle School or
       High School for Women_____7_____
    b. Prewar Normal School_____15_____

    c. Prewar Technical School _____84_____

    d. Prewar Normal School
        for High School Teaching_____22_____

    e. Prewar High School_____11_____

    f. Prewar University _____14_____

    g. Postwar Two-Year College_____58_____

    h. Postwar Four-Year University____5_____

    i. Other (Explain) _____

12. About how many *school* union meetings have you attended in the past calendar year? About __9____ meetings. (average)

13. Do you think there are too many school union meetings, too few, or about the right number? (check most appropriate answer)

    a. _____6__ Too many

    b. ____162__ About the right number

    c. _____47__ Too few

14. What do you think about the above meetings?

    a. _____18__ Would rather go to a union meeting than to almost anything else

    b. ____156__ Usually prefer to go to a union meeting

    c. _____46__ Sometimes prefer union meeting; sometimes prefer to do other things

    d. _____0__ Usually prefer to do something else

15. How often do you speak up at union meetings?

    a. _____30__ Often

    b. _____57__ Occasionally

    c. _____97__ Seldom

    d. _____35__ Never

16. How many of your fellow teachers in your school speak up at union meetings?

    a. _____26__ Most of them

    b. _____78__ About half of them

    c. ____109__ Very few of them

17. Do you think principals should be union members?

    Yes __130____ No __63____ (Circle appropriate word)

18. Do you think vice-principals should be union members?
     Yes __160__ No __34__ (Circle appropriate word)
19. How often do you read *Kyōiku Hyōron?* (JTU publication)
     a. ____8____ Every month
     b. ____46____ Occasionally
     c. ____63____. Seldom
     d. ____90____ Never
     e. ____13____ I don't know the magazine
20. Do you think union dues are too high, too low, or about right?
     a. ____121____ Too high
     b. ____98____ About right
     c. ____0____ Too low
21. Do you think that teachers, who are public service workers, should have the right to strike?
     a. ____128____ Yes
     b. ____54____ No
     c. ____36____ I don't know
22. Although it is illegal for teachers to strike at present, will you participate in a strike if it is necessary?
     a. ____121____ Yes
     b. ____59____ No
     c. ____39____ I don't know
23. Should the union participate in political activities in any of the following ways? (Circle "yes" or "no" for each activity)
     a. Tell members which candidates are friendly to labor
                 Yes ____134____ No ____43____
     b. Advise members whom to vote for
                 Yes ____74____ No ____90____
     c. Try to get its own members elected to public office
                 Yes ____123____ No ____43____
     d. Collect money from each member to help union candidates
                 Yes ____70____ No ____95____

299

    e. Encourage teachers to campaign for candidates by going from house to house

                          Yes   10   No   156

24. How much effort should the JTU expend in getting union candidates elected to public office?

    a.   74 More than at present

    b.   128 About the same as at present

    c.   7 Less than at present

25. Do you think the JTU is necessary for the protection of the teachers' livelihood?

    a.   139 Very necessary

    b.   77 Necessary

    c.   5 Not very necessary

    d.   1 I don't know

26. Concerning negotiations between the union and the government side:

    a.   193 The union should have the right to negotiate at the national level

    b.   8 The union should negotiate only at the prefectural level and below

    c.   15 I don't know

27. Does the union have too many full-time union officers, too few, or about the right number?

    a.   13 Too many

    b.   126 About the right number

    c.   37 Too few

    d.   41 I don't know

28. What do you think of your full-time union leaders?

    a.   11 Very capable

    b.   61 Capable

    c.   100 Average

    d.   36 Unsatisfactory

29. How strongly do you think the opinions of the average teacher are reflected in the union's action policies?

    a.   1 Very strongly

    b.   62 Fairly strongly

    c.   145 Not very strongly

30. Who do you think creates the teachers' union's action policies?
    a. ___11___ The top three men in the CEC (Chairman, Vice-Chairman, Secretary)
    b. ___132___ The Central Executive Committee
    c. ___21___ The Central Committee
    d. ___43___ I don't know

31. Do you think that your prefectural full-time officers are elected in a democratic way?
    Yes ___152·___ No ___38___ (Circle appropriate word)

32. Do you want to become a full-time union officer now or in the future?
    Yes ___5___ No ___207___ (Circle appropriate word)

33. What chance do you think you would have for becoming a full-time union officer?
    a. ___0___ Great possibility
    b. ___2___ Fair possibility
    c. ___48___ Small possibility
    d. ___140___ No possibility
    e. ___26___ I don't know

34. Have you ever participated in a union-sponsored educational study meeting at either the local, prefectural, or national level?
    Yes ___140___ No ___69___ (Circle appropriate word)
    If your answer is "yes," about how many times did you participate in these meetings in the last calendar year?
    ___1.75___ times (average)

35. How useful have these meetings been in helping you to improve your classroom teaching ability?
    a. ___22___ Extremely useful
    b. ___91___ Fairly useful
    c. ___68___ Not very useful

36. Have you ever participated in a Ministry of Education or Board of Education sponsored educational study meeting at either the local, prefectural, or national level?
    Yes ___171___ No ___29___ (Circle appropriate word)

If your answer is "yes," about how many times did you participate in these meetings in the last calendar year? ___2.45_ times (average)

37. How useful were these meetings in helping you to improve your classroom teaching ability?
    a. ___9___ Extremely useful
    b. _113_ Fairly useful
    c. _75_ Not very useful

38. Have you ever personally experienced any request from the side of the Board of Education to withdraw from the union?
    Yes __4___ No _211___ (Circle appropriate word)

39. Are you a member of Nikkyōso's Mutual Aid Association?
    Yes _134___ No __72___ (Circle appropriate word)

40. Do you think the Mutual Aid Association is necessary for the livelihood of the teachers?
    a. ___58___ Very necessary
    b. ___80___ Necessary
    c. .__22___ Not very necessary
    d. ___43___ I don't know

Bibliography

OFFICIAL DOCUMENTS AND PUBLICATIONS

Japan. Education Reform Council. *Educational Reform in Japan: The Present Status and the Problems Involved.* Tokyo, 1950.

——— Ministry of Education. *Atarashii Kyōiku Katei* (New Curriculum). Tokyo, 1958.

——— Ministry of Education. *Bricks Without Straw.* Tokyo, 1950.

——— Ministry of Education. *Education in Japan: A Graphic Presentation.* Tokyo, 1954, 1956, 1957, 1959, 1961, 1964, 1967.

——— Ministry of Education. *Education in (Year): Annual Report of the Ministry of Education.* Tokyo, annually from 1955.

——— Ministry of Education. *Educational Laws and Regulations in Japan: School Education Law,* Series 2. Tokyo, 1955.

——— Ministry of Education. *Gakusei Kujūnen-shi* (Ninety-Year History of the Educational System). Tokyo, 1963.

——— Ministry of Education. *Guide to New Education in Japan.* Tokyo, 1946.

——— Ministry of Education. *Japan's Growth and Education.* Tokyo, 1963.

——— Ministry of Education. Local Affairs Section. *Kyō-shokuin no Soshiki Suru Shokuin Dantai no Gaikyō* (Profile of Employees' Groups Organized by Educational Personnel). Tokyo, annually from 1964 to 1970.

303

Japan. Ministry of Education. Local Affairs Section. *Kyō-shokuin Dantai-ra Kankei Shiryō* (Data Concerning Educational Personnel Organizations). Tokyo, February 1964.

————— Ministry of Education. *National Survey of Educational Expenditures.* Tokyo, 1961.

————— Ministry of Education. *National Survey of Scholastic Achievement.* Tokyo, 1961.

————— Ministry of Education. *Progress of Education in Japan during the School Year 1960-1961.* Tokyo, 1962.

————— Ministry of Education. *Progress of Educational Reform in Japan.* Tokyo, 1950.

————— Ministry of Education. *Revised Curriculum in Japan for Elementary and Lower Secondary Schools.* Tokyo, September 1960.

————— Ministry of Education. *A Survey of Japanese Education with Statistics.* Tokyo, October 1957.

————— Ministry of Education. *Wagakuni no Kyōiku Suijun* (Educational Level of Japan). Tokyo, 1970.

————— Ministry of Labor. *Basic Survey of Trade Unions.* Tokyo, March 1965.

————— Prime Minister's Office. Central Youth Problems Committee. *White Paper on Youth.* Tokyo, March 20, 1964.

————— Prime Minister's Office. National Public Opinion Research Institute. *Kyōiku ni Kansuru Seron Chōsa* (Public Opinion Poll Concerning Education). Tokyo, 1950.

————— Prime Minister's Office. Second Advisory Council. *Report to the Prime Minister.* Tokyo, October 1970.

————— Public Security Investigation Agency. *Nihon Kyōsanto o Chūshitoshita Naigai Dōkō Nempyō* (Chronological Investigation of Movements of the Japan Communist Party and Its Front Organizations). Tokyo, 1954.

Japanese National Commission for UNESCO. *The Development of Modern Education and Teachers Training in Japan.* Tokyo, 1961.

————— *Development of Modern System of Education in Japan.* Tokyo, 1960.

———— *Development of Modern Textbook System in Japan.* Tokyo, 1960.

———— *The Making of Compulsory Education.* Tokyo, 1958.

———— *School Textbooks in Japan: 1953.* Tokyo, 1954.

———— *Youth Work in Japan, 1955.* Tokyo, 1956.

Supreme Commander for the Allied Powers. Civil Information and Education Section. Education Division. *Education in the New Japan.* 2 vols. Tokyo: General Headquarters, 1948.

———— Civil Information and Education Section. Education Division. *A History of Teachers' Unions in Japan.* Tokyo: General Headquarters, 1948.

———— Civil Information and Education Section. Education Division. *Education in the New Japan.* Tokyo: General Headquarters, 1948.

———— Civil Information and Education Section. Education Division. *Political Reorientation of Japan.* Tokyo: General Headquarters, 1948.

———— Civil Information and Education Section. Education Division. *Postwar Development in Japanese Education.* Tokyo: General Headquarters, 1952.

U.S. Department of State. U.S. Education Mission to Japan. *Report of the United States Education Mission to Japan.* Washington, D.C., 1946

———— U.S. Education Mission to Japan. *Report of the Second United States Education Mission to Japan.* Washington, D.C., 1950.

Published and Privately Printed Materials

Adachi, Kenji. "An Interpretation of Article x of The Fundamental Law of Education." *Journal of Social and Political Ideas in Japan,* Vol. 1, No. 3 (December 1963).

———— "Kyōiku Kihonhō Daijūjō no Kaishaku" (An Interpretation of Article X of the Fundamental Law of Education). *Gakkō Keiei,* November 1960.

Adams, Donald. "Rebirth of Moral Education in Japan." *Comparative Education Review*, Vol. 4, No. 1 (June 1960).

────── and Oshiba, Mamoru. "Japanese Education: After the Americans Left." *Peabody Journal of Education*, Vol. 39, No. 1 (July 1961).

Almond, Gabriel A. and Powell, G. Bingham, Jr. *Comparative Politics: A Developmental Approach*. Boston: Little, Brown and Co., 1966.

"The Altered Image of Teachers." *Journal of Social and Political Ideas in Japan*, Vol. 1, No. 3 (December 1963).

Anderson, Ronald S. *Japan: Three Epochs of Modern Education*. Washington, D.C.: U.S. Department of Health, Education, and Welfare, Bulletin Number 11, 1959.

"Answers from the Japan Teachers Union to the Questions Raised by the Committee on Freedom of Association." Mimeographed letter from Kobayashi Takeshi, Chairman of the JTU, and Ohta Kaoru, Chairman of the General Council of Trade Unions, to D. A. Morse, Director-General, Committee on Freedom of Association, ILO, Geneva. February 10, 1962.

Arai, Tsuneyasu. *Nikkyōsō Undō-shi* (History of the Japan Teachers' Union Movement). Tokyo: Nihon Shuppan Kyodo, 1953.

Asahi Nenkan. (Asahi Yearbook) Tokyo: Asahi Shimbunsha, 1955-1970.

Ayusawa, Iwao F. *A History of Labor in Modern Japan*. Honolulu: East-West Center Press, 1966.

Battistini, Lawrence. *The Postwar Student Struggle in Japan*. Tokyo and Rutland, Vermont: Tuttle, 1956.

Bellah, Robert. *Tokugawa Religion*. New York: Free Press, 1957.

Bennett, John W., Passin, Herbert, and McKnight, Robert K. *In Search of Identity*. Minneapolis: University of Minnesota Press, 1958.

Benoit, Edward George. *A Study of Japanese Education as Influenced by the Occupation*. Unpublished doctoral dissertation, Michigan State University, 1958.

Bone, Hugh A. "Political Parties and Pressure Groups." *Pressure Groups and Lobbies. The Annals of the American Academy of Political and Social Science*, Vol. 319, September 1958.

Borton, Hugh. *Japan's Modern Century*. New York: The Ronald Press, 1955.

Brameld, Theodore. *Japan: Culture, Education and Change in Two Communities*. New York: Holt, Rinehart and Winston, 1968.

Brett, Cecil Carter. "Japan's New Educational Laws." *Far Eastern Survey*, November 1954.

Brinkman, Albert R. "Teachers, The Union, and Politics in Japan." *School and Society*, Vol. 92 (August 6, 1955).

Brown, Delmer. *Nationalism in Japan*. Berkeley and Los Angeles: University of California Press, 1955.

Burks, Ardath W. *The Government of Japan*. New York: Thomas Y. Crowell, 1961.

Campbell, Alexander. *The Heart of Japan*. New York: Alfred A. Knopf, 1961.

Coladerie, Arthur P. "The Professional Attitudes of Japanese Teachers." *Journal of Educational Research*, Vol. 52, No. 9, May 1959.

Colbert, Evelyn S. *The Left Wing in Japanese Politics*. New York: Institute of Pacific Relations, 1952.

Cole, Allan B., Totten, George O., and Uyehara, Cecil H. *Socialist Parties in Postwar Japan*. New Haven: Yale University Press, 1966.

Cole, Robert E. "Japanese Workers, Unions, and the Marxist Appeal." *The Japan Interpreter*, Vol. 6, Summer 1970.

"Complaints of the Japan Teachers Union against the Japanese Government." Mimeographed letter from Kobayashi Takeshi, Chairman of the JTU, and Ohta Kaoru, Chairman of the General Council of Trade Unions, to D. A. Morse, Director-General, Committee on Freedom of Association, ILO, Geneva, November 9, 1960.

Cook, Alice H. *Japanese Trade Unionism*. Ithaca: Cornell University Press, 1966.

307

Cook, Alice H. *Public Employee Labor Relations in Japan: Three Aspects.* Ithaca, N.Y.: Cornell University Press, 1971.

Daily Summary of the Japanese Press. Tokyo: American Embassy, Translation Services Branch.

Doi, James Isao. *Educational Reform in Occupied Japan, 1945-1950: A Study of Acceptance of and Resistance to Institutional Change.* Unpublished Ph.D. dissertation, University of Chicago, 1953.

Dore, Ronald P. *City Life in Japan.* London: Routledge and Kegan Paul, 1958.

—————— *Education in Tokugawa Japan.* Berkeley: University of California Press, 1965.

—————— "Education: Japan." *Political Modernization in Japan and Turkey.* Edited by Robert Ward and Dankwart Rustow. Princeton: Princeton University Press, 1964.

—————— "The Legacy of Tokugawa Education." *Changing Japanese Attitudes toward Modernization.* Edited by Marius B. Jansen, Princeton: Princeton University Press, 1965.

—————— "Textbook Censorship in Japan: The Ienaga Case." *Pacific Affairs*, Vol. 43, No. 4 (Winter 1970-1971).

Duke, Ben C. "American Educational Reforms in Japan Twelve Years Later." *Harvard Educational Review*, Fall 1964.

—————— "Education in Japan." *Educational Forum*, January 1962.

—————— "The Irony of Japanese Postwar Education." *Comparative Education Review*, January 1963.

Ebata, Kiyoshi. "Mombudaijin to Tairitsu-shi" (History of the Confrontation with the Minister of Education). *Asahi Jānaru*, Vol. 7, No. 12 (March 21, 1965).

Eells, Walter C. "Curriculum Improvement in Japan." *Educational Administration and Supervision*, Vol. 37 (November 1951).

—————— "Decentralization of Control of Education in Japan." *School and Society,* Vol. 73 (June 23, 1951), pp. 388-91.

―――― *The Literature on Japanese Education, 1945-1954.* Hamden, Connecticut: Shoe String Press, 1955.

Eldersveld, Samuel J. "American Interest Groups: A Survey of Research and Some Implications for Theory and Method." *Interest Groups on Four Continents.* Edited by Henry W. Ehrmann. Pittsburgh: University of Pittsburgh Press, 1958.

Embree, John. *Suye Mura.* Chicago: University of Chicago Press, 1939.

Farley, Miriam S. *Aspects of Japan's Labor Problems.* New York: John Day Co., 1950.

Fearley, Robert A. *The Occupation of Japan: Second Phase, 1948-1950.* New York: Macmillan Co., 1950.

Finn, Dallas. "Reform and Japan's Lower Schools." *Far Eastern Survey,* Vol. 20, No. 19 (November 7, 1951).

Fukutake, Tadashi. *Japanese Rural Society.* Tokyo: Oxford University Press, 1967.

Furayama, Kenju. *Sengo Nihon Kyōiku Ronsō-shi* (A History of Disputes in Postwar Japanese Education). Tokyo: Tōyōkan Shuppansha, Vol. I (1958) and Vol. II (1960).

Gable, Richard W. "Interest Groups as Policy Shapers." *Pressure Groups and Lobbies. The Annals of the American Academy of Political and Social Science,* Vol. 319, September 1958.

Gotō, Kōichi. "Nihon no Atsuryoku Dantai: Nihon Kyōshokuin Kumiai" (Pressure Groups in Japan: The Japan Teachers' Union). *Jiyū,* August 1970.

Hall, Ivan P. "Mori Arinori and the Reshaping of Japanese Education, 1886." Unpublished paper for the Seminar on Japanese Society, Harvard University, 1965.

Hall, John W., and Beardsley, Richard K. *Twelve Doors to Japan.* New York: McGraw-Hill, 1965.

Hall, Robert K. *Education for a New Japan.* New Haven: Yale University Press, 1949.

309

—— *Shūshin: The Ethics of a Defeated Nation*. New York: Teachers College, Columbia University, 1949.

Haruta, Masaharu. "Kyōiku Kenkyū to Kumiai Undō" (Educational Research and Union Activities). *Kyōiku Hyōron*, May 1957, pp. 21-28.

Hayashi, Takeji. "Kindai Kyōiku Kōsō to Mori Arinori" (The Structure of Modern Education and Mori Arinori). *Chūō Kōron*, September 1962.

Hidaka, Daishiro. "The Aftermath of Educational Reform." *Japan Since Recovery of Independence. The Annals of the American Academy of Political and Social Science*, Vol. 308 (November 1956), pp. 140-55.

Hita, Gon-ichi. *The Training of Teachers in Japan: A Historical Survey*. Tokyo: Japanese Education Association, World Conference Committee, 1937.

Igarashi, Akira. "Kyōiku to Rōdō" (Labor and Education). *Minshū Kyōiku-ron* (Democratic Education). Tokyo: Aoki Shoten, 1959.

Ike, Nobutaka. *The Beginnings of Political Democracy in Japan*. Baltimore, Maryland: Johns Hopkins Press, 1950.

—— *Japanese Politics: An Introductory Survey*. New York: Alfred A. Knopf, 1957.

Imamiya, Kohei. *Nikkyōso: Kikō to Sono Seikaku* (The Japan Teachers' Union: Its Organization and Characteristics). Tokyo: Shin Kigensha, 1957.

Inogawa, Kiyoshi, and Kawai, Akira, eds. *Nihon Kyōiku Undō-shi: Meiji-Taishō-ki no Kyōiku Undō* (History of the Japanese Education Movement: The Education Movement during the Meiji and Taishō Periods). Tokyo: San-ichi Shobō, 1960.

International Labor Organization. *Report of the Fact-Finding and Conciliation Commission on Freedom of Association Concerning Persons Employed in the Public Sector in Japan*. Official Bulletin, Special Supplement, Vol. 49, No. 1 (January 1966).

—— Committee on Freedom of Association. *Analysis of the Legislation Governing Freedom of Association and the Exercise of Trade Union Rights in Japan.* Geneva: International Labor Organization, n.d.

Irwin, W. *Letters of a Japanese Schoolboy.* Tokyo: Maruya, 1909.

Ishida, Takeshi. "The Development of Interest Groups and the Pattern of Political Modernization in Japan." *Political Development in Modern Japan.* Edited by Robert E. Ward. Princeton: Princeton University Press, 1968.

————— "Historical Factors behind the Eruption of Pressure Groups in Japan." *The Japan Annual of Law and Politics,* No. 10. Tokyo: Science Council of Japan, 1962.

————— "Pressure Groups in Japan." *Journal of Social and Political Ideas in Japan,* Vol. 2, No. 3 (December 1964).

Ishii, Kazutomo. *Ushinawareta Kyōiku: Nikkyōso Hakusho* (Education Lost: White Paper on the Japan Teachers' Union). Tokyo: Hobunsha, 1954.

Ishikawa, Ken. *Gakkō no Hattatsu* (The Development of the Schools). Tokyo: Iwasaki Shoten, 1951.

Ishiyama, Shuhei. *Kyōshi to Kyōyō* (Teachers and Their Cultural Background). Tokyo: Suakara Shoten, 1954.

————— (ed.). *Kyōshokusha no Rinri* (Ethics of Education). Tokyo: Maki Shoten, 1959.

————— Kinoshita, Kasuo, and Shigematsu, Takayasu, eds. *Gendai Nihon no Kyōshi* (Teachers in Modern Japan). Tokyo: Tōyōkan Shuppansha, 1954.

Ito, Noboru. "The Reform of Japanese Education." *Japan Quarterly,* Vol. 3 (1956), pp. 425-30.

Iwama, Masao. *Kyōin Kumiai Undō-shi* (History of the Teachers' Union Movement). Tokyo: Shūkan Kyōiku Shimbunsha, 1948.

Iwate-ken Kyōin Kumiai (Iwate Prefectural Teachers' Union). *Shin Kumiaiin Kōza Shiryō* (Material to be Studied by New Teachers). Morioka: Iwate-ken Kyōso, 1963.

Jansen, Marius B. "Education, Values and Politics in Japan," *Foreign Affairs,* July 1957.

The Japan Biographical Encyclopedia and Who's Who. Tokyo: The Rengo Press, 1958.

Japan Teachers' Union. *Japan Teachers' Union: Its Organization and Movement.* Tokyo: Japan Teachers' Union, 1966.

———— *Kiyaku Shokitei Saisokushū* (The Constitution and the Statutes). Tokyo: Japan Teachers' Union, 1959.

———— *Kumiaiin Ishiki: Chōsa no Matome* (Consciousness of Teachers' Union Members: Results of a Survey). Tokyo: Japan Teachers' Union, August 20, 1969.

———— *Nikkyōso Jūnen-shi* (Ten-Year History of the Japan Teachers' Union). Tokyo: Japan Teachers' Union, 1958.

———— *Nikkyōso Nijūnen-shi* (Twenty-Year History of the Japan Teachers' Union). Tokyo: Japan Teachers' Union, 1968.

———— Department of Organization. *Nikkyōso: Watakushitachi no Undō to Sono Soshiki* (The Japan Teachers' Union: Our Movement and Organization). Tokyo: Japan Teachers' Union, 1963.

———— Propaganda Section. *Kokumin Kyōiku* (People's Education). Tokyo: Gōdō Shinsho, 1958.

The Japan Who's Who, 1950-1951.

Kaigo, Tokiomi. "American Influence on the Education in Japan." *Journal of Educational Sociology,* Vol. 26, No. 1 (September 1952).

———— "A Short History of Postwar Japanese Education." *Journal of Social and Political Ideas in Japan,* Vol. 1, No. 3 (December 1963).

Karasawa, Tomitarō. "Changes in Japanese Education as Revealed in Textbooks." *Japan Quarterly,* July-September 1955.

———— *Kyōkasho no Rekishi* (History of Textbooks). Tokyo: Sobunsha, 1956.

———— *Kyōshi no Rekishi* (History of Teachers). Tokyo: Sobunsha, 1956.

———— "A New Image for the Teachers of Japan." *Journal*

of Social and Political Ideas in Japan, Vol. 2, No. 2 (August 1964).

————— Nihon Kyōiku-shi (History of Japanese Education). Tokyo: Seibundō Shinkōsha, 1962.

Katsube, Masanaga. "Rinri Kōryō to Kyōshi no Ishiki" (The Code of Ethics and Teachers' Consciousness). Jiyū, January 1966.

Katsuda, Shuichi and Itorio, Teruhisa. "Kokumin Kyōiku ni Okeru Chūritsusei no Mondai" (The Problem of Neutrality in People's Education). Shisō, September 1958, pp. 1-19; March 1959, pp. 92-112.

Kawai, Kazuo. Japan's American Interlude. Chicago: University of Chicago Press, 1960.

Keenleyside, Hugh Llewellyn, and Thomas, A. F. History of Japanese Education and Present Educational System. Tokyo: Hokuseido, 1937.

Kerlinger, Frederick N. "Educational Affairs Board: Precursors of Modern Japanese Boards of Education." History of Education Journal, Vol. 5 (1954).

Key, V. O. Politics, Parties and Pressure Groups. 4th ed. New York: Thomas Y. Crowell Co., 1958.

Kido, Wakao. "Kyōshi no Jikakuto Danketsu" (The Consciousness and Unity of Teachers). Nihon Kyōiku Undō-shi: Meiji-Taishō-ki no Kyōiku Undō (History of the Japanese Education Movement: The Education Movement during the Meiji and Taishō Periods). Edited by Inogawa Kiyoshi and Kawai Akira. Tokyo: San-ichi Shobō, 1960.

Kikuchi, Baron Dairoku. Japanese Education. London: John Murray, 1909.

Kimmu Kyōtei Mondai no Keii (Complexities of the Problems Surrounding the Efficiency Rating System). Tokyo: Todōfuken Kyōikuchō Kyōgikaihen, February 1960.

Kitabayashi, Shuzo, ed. Kimpyō Hakusho (White Paper on the Merit System). Tokyo: Kobundo, 1959.

Kitamura, Fusako. A Study of the Japan Teachers Union and Recommendations for Improvement. Unpublished doctoral dissertation, Teachers College, Columbia University, 1962.

Kobayashi, Takeshi. "Nikkyōso's View of Education." *Kingu*, March 1957, translated in *Summaries of Selected Japanese Magazines*. Tokyo: American Embassy Translation Services Branch, February 18, 1957.

Kojima, Gunzō. *The Philosophical Foundations for Democratic Education in Japan*. Tokyo: Institute of Education Research and Service, International Christian University, 1959.

Kurotaki, Chikara and Itō, Tadahiko, eds. *Nihon Kyōiku Undō-shi*: *Shōwa Shoki no Kyōiku Undō* (History of the the Japanese Education Movement: The Education Movement During the Shōwa Period). Tokyo: San-ichi Shobō, 1960.

Kyōkasho Kentei Soshō Shien Zenkoku Renrakukai (All-Japan Council for Support of Litigation Concerning Textbook Authorization). *Kyōkasho Saiban*, Part I, Vol. 1-2; *Jumbi Shomen-hen* (Collection of Preliminary Documents). Part II, Vol. 1-9: *Hanketsu-hen* (Collection of Judicial Decisions).

Kyōshi no Kai. *Kyōshi to iu Na no Shokugyō* (The Teaching Profession). Tokyo: San-ichi Shinsho, 1965.

Langdon, Frank C. "Organized Interests in Japan and Their Influence on Political Parties." *Pacific Affairs*, Vol. 34, No. 3 (1961), pp. 271-78.

———— *Politics in Japan*. Boston: Little, Brown and Co., 1965.

Letter from Miyanohara Sadamitsu, Chairman of the JTU, to Erik Dreyer, Chairman of the Fact-Finding and Conciliation Commission on Freedom of Association of the ILO, containing an untitled report concerning the limitations of the Personnel Commissions in compensating for the loss of the right to strike. June 25, 1964.

Levine, Solomon B. *Industrial Relations in Postwar Japan*. Urbana: University of Illinois Press, 1958.

Lipset, Seymour Martin, Trow, Martin, and Coleman,

James. *Union Democracy*. Garden City, New York: Doubleday and Co., 1962.

Loomis, A. K. "Compulsory Education in Japan." *Educational Forum*, Vol. 27 (November 1962).

Luhmer, Nicholas. "Revision of the Postwar Educational Reform in Japan." *School and Society*, Vol. 75 (May 1952), pp. 337-40.

Maeda, Tamon. "The Direction of Postwar Education in Japan." *Japan Quarterly*, Vol. 3 (1956).

Maki, John M. *Government and Politics in Japan: The Road to Democracy*. New York: Praeger, 1962.

Maruyama, Masao. *Thought and Behaviour in Modern Japanese Politics*. Translated by Ivan Morris. London: Oxford University Press, 1963.

Matsumoto, Yoshiharu Scott. "Contemporary Japan: The Individual and the Group." *Transactions of the American Philosophical Society*. Philadelphia: The American Philosophical Society, 1960.

Matsuoka, Yoko. *Daughter of the Pacific*. New York, Harper, 1953.

Matsushita, Keiichi. "Rōdō Kumiai no Seiji Katsudō" (Political Activities of Labor Unions). *Seiji Gaku Nempō, 1960: Nihon no Atsuryoku Dantai* (Annuals of the Japanese Political Science Association, 1960: Pressure Groups in Japan). Edited by Nihon Seiji Gakkai (Japanese Political Science Association). Tokyo: Iwanami, 1960.

McNelly, Theodore. *Contemporary Government of Japan*. Boston: Houghton Mifflin Co., 1963.

Mishima, Sumie Seo. *My Narrow Isle*. New York: John Day, 1941.

Miyahara, Seiichi. *Nihon Gendaishi Taikei: Kyōiku-shi* (Outline of Modern Japanese History: History of Education). Tokyo: Tōyō Keizai Shimpōsha, 1963.

——— "The Japan Teachers Union and Its Code of Ethics." *Journal of Social and Political Ideas in Japan*, Vol. 1, No. 3 (December 1963).

———— *Nihon no Kyōshi* (Japanese Teachers). Tokyo: Iwanami Shoten, 1952.

Miyanohara, Sadamitsu. *Watashi no Kyōikuron* (My Theory of Education). Tokyo: San-ichi, 1965.

Miyauchi, D. Y. "Textbooks and the Search for a New National Ethics in Japan." *Social Education*, Vol. 28 (March 1964).

Mochida, Eiichi. "Kyōshi no Kimmu Hyōtei" (The Rating of the Efficiency of Teachers). *Kyōiku Hyōron*, January 1958, pp. 101-109.

———— "The Reform of Boards of Education and Its Aftermath," *Journal of Social and Political Ideas in Japan*, Vol. 1, No. 3 (December 1963).

Montgomery, John D. *Forced to be Free: The Artificial Revolution in Germany and Japan.* Chicago: University of Chicago Press, 1957.

Morito, Tatsuo. "Education Reform and Its Problems in Post-war Japan." *International Review of Education*, Vol. 1 (1955), pp. 338-49.

———— "What Constitutes a Good Teacher?" *Journal of Social and Political Ideas in Japan*, Vol. 1, No. 3 (December 1963).

Moriya, Kiyoshi. "Shinkō Kyōiku Kenkyūsho no Hossoku" (Establishment of the New Education Institute). *Nihon Kyōiku Undō-shi: Shōwa Shoki no Kyōiku Undō* (History of the Japanese Education Movement: The Education Movement during the Shōwa Period). Edited by Kurotaki Chikara and Itō Tadahiko. Tokyo: San-ichi Shobō, 1960.

Muchaku, Seikyō, ed. *Echoes from a Mountain School.* Tokyo: Kenkyūsha, 1953.

Mudai, Risaku. "Minshushugi Kyōiku no Rinen" (The Doctrine of Democratic Education). *Sekai*, June 1961, pp. 137-50.

Munakata, Seiya. "The Fundamental Law of Education." *Journal of Social and Political Ideas in Japan*, Vol. 1, No. 3 (December 1963).

———— *Kyōiku to Kyōiku Seisaku* (Education and Educational Policies). Tokyo: Iwanami Shoten, 1961.

———— "Mombudaijin-ron" (The Question of the Minister of Education). *Sekai*, February 1958, pp. 67-76.

———— "My Declaration on Education." *Journal of Social and Political Ideas in Japan*, Vol. 1, No. 3 (December 1963).

———— *Watakushi no Kyōiku Sengen* (My Declaration on Education). Tokyo: Iwanami Shinshō, 1958.

———— and Kokubu Ichitarō. *Nihon no Kyōiku* (Japanese Education). Tokyo: Iwanami Shinsho, 1962.

Murakami, Shunsuke, and Iwahashi, Bunkishi. "Postwar Reconstruction of Japanese Education and Its Social Aspects." *Journal of Educational Sociology*, Vol. 29 (March 1957), pp. 309-16.

Nagai, Michio. *Kyōshi Kono Genjitsu* (Teachers and Reality). Tokyo: San-itsu Shobō, 1957.

———— *Mombushō to Nikkyōso* (The Ministry of Education and the Japan Teachers' Union). Tokyo: Chūō Kōronsha, 1958.

———— *Shin Kyōikusha* (New Educators). Tokyo: Chūō Kōronsha, 1953.

———— "What Should be Done About Teachers?" *Journal of Social and Political Ideas in Japan*, Vol. 1, No. 3 (December 1963).

Nagai, Yonosuke. "Structural Characteristics of Pressure Politics in Japan." *Journal of Social and Political Ideas in Japan*, Vol. 2, No. 3 (December 1964).

Nagasu, Kazuji. "The Theory of People's Education." *Journal of Social and Political Ideas in Japan*, Vol. 1, No. 3 (December 1963).

Nihon Meishi Nenkan (Japanese Yearbook of Prominent People).

"Nikkyōso no Soshiki Bunretsu no Jōkyō ni Tsuite" (Factors Regarding JTU Splinter Groups). *Kōan Jōhō* (Police Report), No. 126 (March 1964), pp. 29-35.

317

"Nikkyōso Taikai no Jōkyō to Tokuchōten ni Tsuite" (The General Situation and Distinctive Features of the Japan Teachers' Union's Annual Conference). *Kōan Jōhō*, 1966, 1967, 1968, 1969, 1970.

"Observations of the Japanese Government on the Complaints of the Japan Teachers' Union against the Japanese Government." Mimeographed letter from Araki Masuo, Minister of Education, to the ILO Committee on Freedom of Association. January 13, 1961.

"Observations of the Japanese Government on the Complaints of the Japan Teachers' Union against the Japanese Government Relating to the 54th Report of the Committee on Freedom of Association." Mimeographed letter from Araki Masuo, Minister of Education, to the ILO Committee on Freedom of Association. October 10, 1961.

Odate, Shigeo. *Watakushi no Mita Nikkyōso*: *Kyōiku Hōan o Meguru Kokkai Ronsō* (My View of the Japan Teachers' Union: The Debates in the Diet Concerning the Education Laws). Tokyo: Shin Seikisha, 1955.

Ogawa, Tarō. "Reflections on Postwar Education." *Journal of Social Political Ideas in Japan*, Vol. 1, No. 3 (December 1963).

Okatsu, Morihiko. "Shakaika Kyōiku no Jūnen" (Ten Years of Social Studies Education). *Kyōiku Hyōron*, December 1955, pp. 57-69.

Ōkōchi, Kazuo. "Kyōiku Rōdōsha to Kyōin Kumiai" (Educational Laborers and Teachers' Unions). *Shisō*, April 1951, pp. 60-69.

Okuma, Shigenobu. "Culture and Education in Old Japan." *Fifty Years of New Japan*, Vol. 2, Ch. 7. Edited by Okuma Shigenobu. London: Smith, Elder and Co., 1909.

Olson, Lawrence. "The Kyoto Superintendent of Schools." *Dimensions of Japan*. Collected reports of Lawrence Olsen. New York: American Universities Field Staff, 1963.

Orr, Mark T. *Education Reform Policy in Occupied Japan*. Unpublished doctoral dissertation, University of North Carolina, 1954.

318

Osada, Arata. "Problems Involved in Providing Ethical Education." *Journal of Social and Political Ideas in Japan*, Vol. 1, No. 3 (December 1963).

Oshiba, Mamoru. *Four Articles on Japanese Education.* Tokyo: Maruzen, 1963.

Ōshima, Yasumasa. "Japan's Defeat and Ethical Education." *Journal of Social and Political Ideas in Japan*, Vol. 1, No. 3 (December 1963).

Ōta, Takashi. "A Study of Educational Practices in the Postwar Period." *Journal of Social and Political Ideas in Japan*, Vol. 1, No. 3 (December 1963).

Otawa, Koki. "Japan Teachers Union and School Children." *Contemporary Japan*, Vol. 24 (November 1956), pp. 522-25.

Packard, George C., III. *Protest in Tokyo: The Security Treaty Crisis of 1960.* Princeton: Princeton University Press, 1966.

Passin, Herbert. "Education and Political Development in Japan." *Education and Political Development.* Edited by James Coleman. Princeton: Princeton University Press, 1965.

———— *Society and Education in Japan.* New York: Teachers College Press, Columbia University, 1965.

———— "The Sources of Protest in Japan." *American Political Science Review*, June 1962, pp. 391-403.

Potter, Stephen. *Organized Labour in British National Politics.* London: Faber and Faber, 1961.

Pye, Lucian W., and Verba, Sidney, eds. *Political Culture and Political Development.* Princeton: Princeton University Press, 1965.

Quigley, Harold S., and Turner, John E. *The New Japan: Government and Politics.* Minneapolis: University of Minnesota Press, 1956.

Reischauer, Edwin O., Fairbank, John K., and Craig, Albert M. *East Asia: The Modern Transformation.* Boston: Houghton Mifflin Co., 1965.

319

Roberts, Charles Lenz. "The Japan Teachers' Union Under Fire." *School and Society*, May 9, 1959, pp. 218-20.

Rōyama, Masamichi. "Seiji to Kyōiku" (Politics and Education) *Rōyama Masamichi Hyōron Chosakushū* (Collection of Rōyama Masamichi's Critical Essays), Vol. iv. Tokyo: Chūō Kōronsha, 1962.

Saionji, Kimmochi. "National Education in the Meiji Era." *Fifty Years of New Japan*, Vol. 2, Ch. 9. Edited by Shigenobu Okuma. London: Smith, Elder, and Co., 1909.

Sansom, Sir George B. "Education in Japan." *Pacific Affairs*, Vol. 19 (December 1946).

Satomi, Kishio. *Nikkyōso to Kakumei* (The Japan Teachers' Union and Revolution). Tokyo: Hokushinsha, 1954.

Sawada, Fumiaki. *Nikkyōso no Rekishi* (History of the Japan Teachers' Union). Tokyo: Gōdō Shuppan, 1966.

Sayama, Kisaku. "Junior High School Students." *Journal of Social and Political Ideas in Japan*, Vol. 1, No. 3 (December 1963).

Scalapino, Robert A. *Democracy and the Party Movement in Prewar Japan*. Berkeley: University of California Press, 1953.

—— and Masumi, Junnosuke. *Parties and Politics in Contemporary Japan*. Berkeley: University of California Press, 1962.

Schwantes, Robert S. *Japanese and Americans: A Century of Cultural Relations*. New York: Harper, 1955.

Shigematsu, Keiichi. "Ikeda Naikaku Kōitten Araki Masuo" (Strong Man Araki Masuo of the Ikeda Cabinet). *Nippon Zasshi*, April 1965, pp. 116-21.

—— *Oya no Ken-i Kyōshi no Ken-i* (Authority of Parents and Authority of Teachers). Tokyo: Seishin Shobō, 1957.

Shimbori, Michiya. "The Fate of Postwar Educational Reform in Japan." *The School Review*, Vol. 63, No. 2 (Summer 1960).

Shimizu, Ikutarō. "Kyōiku, Kyōshi, Kyōso" (Education, Teachers, and Teachers' Unions). *Sekai*, April 1959, pp. 224-31.

Shimonaka Yasaburō. "Keimeikai Sōritsu Rokushūnen ni Omou" (Thoughts on the Sixth Anniversary of the Keimeikai). *Nihon Kyōiku Undō-shi: Meiji-Taishō-ki no Kyōiku Undō* (History of the Japanese Education Movement: The Education Movement during the Meiji and Taishō Periods). Edited by Inogawa Kiyoshi and Kawai Akira. Tokyo: San-ichi Shobō, 1960.

Shively, Donald H. "Motoda Eifu: Confucian Lecturer to the Meiji Emperor." *Confucianism in Action.* Edited by David S. Nivison and Arthur F. Wright. Stanford: Stanford University Press, 1959.

Singleton, John. *Nichū: A Japanese School.* New York: Holt, Rinehart and Winston, 1967.

Smethurst, Richard J. "The Origins and Policies of the Japan Teachers' Union, 1945-1956." *Studies in Japanese History and Politics.* Edited by Richard K. Beardsley. Ann Arbor: The University of Michigan Press, 1967. Occasional Papers No. 10.

Steiner, Kurt. *Local Government in Japan.* Stanford: Stanford University Press, 1965.

Steslicke, William E. *Doctors in Politics: The Political Life of the Japan Medical Association.* New York: Praeger, 1973.

————— "The Japan Medical Association and the Liberal Democratic Party: A Case Study of Interest Group Politics in Japan." *Studies on Asia,* 1965, pp. 143-61.

Summaries of Selected Japanese Magazines. Tokyo: American Embassy, Translation Services Branch.

Suzuki, Shigenobu. "A Critique on the Nature of the Japan Teachers' Union." *Journal of Social and Political Ideas in Japan,* Vol. 1, No. 3 (December 1963).

————— "Mombushō—Bijon to Iryūjon" (The Ministry of Education—Visions and Illusions). *Jiyū,* January 1963, pp. 54-63.

Swearingen, A. Rodger. *Communist Strategy in Japan, 1945-1960.* Santa Monica: The RAND Corporation, 1965.

Swearingen, A. Rodger, and Langer, Paul. *Red Flag in Japan*. Cambridge: Harvard University Press, 1952.

Tanaka, Kōtarō. *Kyōiku Kihonhō no Riron* (The Theory of the Fundamental Law of Education). Tokyo: Yūhikaku, 1961.

———— "The Theory of the Fundamental Law of Education." *Journal of Social and Political Ideas in Japan*, Vol. 1, No. 3 (December 1963).

Thayer, Nathaniel B. *How the Conservatives Rule Japan*. Princeton: Princeton University Press, 1969.

Thomas, L. G. "Japanese Teachers' Attitudes towards Democracy." *Journal of Educational Sociology*, Vol. 32 (1958).

Tominaga, Ken-ichi. "Semmon Shokugyō no Shakai-teki Chii" (The Social Status of Professionals). *Chūō Kōron*, February 1966.

Totten, George O. "Collective Bargaining and Works Councils as Innovations in Industrial Relations in Japan during the 1920's." *Aspects of Social Change in Modern Japan*. Edited by R. P. Dore. Princeton: Princeton University Press, 1967.

———— *The Social Democratic Movement in Prewar Japan*. New Haven: Yale University Press, 1966.

Truman, David B. *The Governmental Process: Political Interests and Public Opinion*. New York: Alfred A. Knopf, 1964.

Tsuji, Kiyoaki. "Toward Understanding the Teachers' Efficiency Rating System." *Journal of Social and Political Ideas in Japan*, Vol. 1, No. 3 (December 1963).

Tsuji, Kiyoski [Kiyoaki]. "Pressure Groups in Japan," *Interest Groups on Four Continents*. Edited by Henry W. Ehrmann. Pittsburgh: Pittsburgh University Press, 1958.

Tsurumi, Kazuko. *Social Change and the Individual: Japan Before and After Defeat in World War II*. Princeton: Princeton University Press, 1970.

Turner, Henry A. "How Pressure Groups Operate." *Pressure Groups and Lobbies. The Annals of the American*

Academy of Political Science and Social Science, Vol. 319, September 1958.

Uehara, Senroku. "Kokumin Kyōiku ni Tsuite" Concerning People's Education). *Kokumin Kyōiku* (People's Education). Edited by Japan Teachers' Union, Propaganda Section. Tokyo: Gōdō Shinsho, 1958.

———— "Kyōiku no Chūritsusei" (Political Neutrality in Education). *Kaizō,* March 1954, pp. 33-43.

Uno, Hiroshi. "Kōmuin no Sutoraiki ni Taisuru Chōkai Shobun" (Disciplinary Punishment against Strikers in the Public Service). *Jurisuto,* No. 472, February 15, 1971.

Vogel, Ezra F. *Japan's New Middle Class.* Berkeley: University of California Press, 1963.

Walters, Raymond. "Educational Progress in the New Japan." *School and Society,* March 5, 1958.

Ward, Robert E. *Japan's Political System.* Englewood Cliffs, New Jersey: Prentice-Hall, 1967.

———— "Japan: The Continuity of Modernization." *Political Culture and Political Development in Japan.* Edited by Lucian W. Pye and Sidney Verba. Princeton: Princeton University Press, 1965.

———— "Political Modernization and Political Culture in Japan." *World Politics,* Vol. 15 (July 1963).

———— and Rustow, Dankwart A., eds. *Political Modernization in Japan and Turkey.* Princeton: Princeton University Press, 1964.

Webb, R. E. "Education for Democracy in Japan." *Educational Outlook,* Vol. 26 (January 1952).

Willey, Richard. "Pressure Group Politics: The Case of Sohyo," *Western Political Quarterly,* December 1964.

Yagawa, Tokumitsu. *Kokumin Kyōikugaku* (People's Education). Tokyo: Meiji Tosho Shuppan, 1957.

Yanaga, Chitoshi. *Japanese People and Politics.* New York: John Wiley and Sons, 1956.

Yaguchi, Hajime. "Character Building and the Role of Teachers." *Journal of Social and Political Ideas in Japan,* Vol. 2, No. 2 (August 1964).

Zeigler, Harmon. *Interest Groups in American Society.* Englewood Cliffs, New Jersey: Prentice-Hall, 1964.

JOURNALS, PERIODICALS, AND NEWSPAPERS PUBLISHED IN JAPAN

Asahi Evening News
Asahi Jānaru
Asahi Shimbun
Chūō Kōron
Contemporary Japan
Gakkō Keiei
Hōritsu Jihō
Iwate Nippō
Japan Times
Jiji Shimpō
Jiyū
Journal of Social and Political Ideas in Japan
Jurisuto
Kōan Jihō
Kyōiku Hyōron
Kyōiku Nenkan
Kyōiku Rōdō
Mainichi Shimbun
Nikkyōso News
Nippon
Nippon Zasshi
Sekai
Shisō
Shūkan Asahi
Shūkan Kyōiku Shimbun
Sōhyō News
Yomiuri Shimbun

PERSONAL INTERVIEWS

Baba Shirō, Assistant Professor, Faculty of Education, Tokyo University of Education, July 15, 1964.

Beppu Tetsu, Chief, Local Affairs Section, Ministry of Education, November 4, 1970 and January 17, 1971.

Bleha, Thomas, American Vice-Consul, Sapporo, September 9, 1964.

Fujimaki Shimpei, Deputy Director, Secretariat of the Policy Research Board, Japan Socialist Party, June 14, 1963 and March 9, 1964.

Fujisawa Yosaburō, Superintendent of the Board of Education, Tonan Village, Iwate Prefecture, November 28, 1964.

Fukushi Shunro and Ōsawa Toshinari, English teachers at Iwate University Attached Junior High School, October 14, 1964, and March 12, 1971.

Hara Takashi, Specialist on the Japan Teachers' Union, Trade Union Section, Ministry of Labor, December 17, 1970 and January 7, 1971.

Hayashi Takechi, Professor of Education, School of Education, Tōhoku University, April 24, 1963.

Hiragaki Miyoji, former Secretary-General of the Japan Teachers' Union Central Executive Committee, May 3, 1965.

Ichikawa Taishirō, Secretary-General of the Osaka City Teachers' Union, March 2, 1965.

Inaba Takashi, Vice-Chairman, Department of Organization, Japan Teachers' Union, February 12, 1971 and March 12, 1971.

Kobayashi Takeshi, former Chairman of the Japan Teachers' Union and now a member of the House of Councillors, March 8, 1965.

Kumagai Seizaburō, Chief of Administrative Section for Schools, Board of Education, Akita Prefecture, August 27, 1964.

Makieda Motofumi, former Secretary-General of the Japan Teachers' Union, now Chairman of the JTU, February 13, 1965, April 22, 1965, and December 4, 1970.

Miyanohara Sadamitsu, former Chairman of the Japan Teachers' Union, now member of the House of Councillors, February 13, 1965 and April 17, 1965.

Moriyasu Atsutaka, Assistant to the Labor Attaché, American Embassy, Tokyo, December 9, 1970.

Nagai Michio, former consultant to the Japan Teachers' Union and author of a number of books on Japanese education, October 25, 1962 and March 23, 1964.

Nakakōji Kiyō, Chairman of the Department of Organization of the Japan Teachers' Union, February 16, 1965.

Numakunai Shimpei, English teacher, Ueda Lower Secondary School, Morioka, November 13, 1964 and March 12, 1971.

Oda Hajime, Principal of Semboku Lower Secondary School in Morioka City, November 9, 1964.

Ogasawara Rinji, Professor of Linguistics, Iwate University, December 3, 1964.

Ogawa Jun-ichi, former Chairman of the Iwate Teachers' Union, now Vice-Chairman of the JTU, December 16, 1964.

Ōshima Kiyoshi, Assistant Secretary, Akita Teachers' Union, August 27, 1964.

Ōshima, Masao, history teacher, First Senior High School, Morioka, November 30, 1964.

Robinson, Howard T. First Secretary, Labor Attaché, American Embassy, October 8, 1970.

Sawada Michiya, Chief of the Local Affairs Section, Ministry of Education, June 24, 1964; July 7, 1964; February 3, 1965; and April 8, 1965.

Shimizu Hiroyasu and Sakamoto Hironao, Local Affairs Section, Ministry of Education, January 8, 1971.

Shioyama Seinosuke, Vice-Chairman, Iwate Board of Education, Morioka, December 22, 1964.

Shirai Taishirō, staff member of the Japan Institute of Labor, Tokyo, March 25, 1965.

Silverberg, Louis, Labor Attaché, American Embassy, Tokyo, March 26, 1964.

Takahashi Takeshi, Research Officer, ILO Tokyo Branch Office, December 11, 1970.

Tamura Takeo, Professor of Sociology at Aoyama Gakuin, July 21, 1964.

Yakabe Katsumi, standing editorial contributor to the *Nihon Kōgyō Shimbun* (Japan Industrial Newspaper) and specialist on trade unions, January 25, 1971.

Yamagata Kiyoshi, Head of the Research Department of the JTU, February 27, 1965.

Index

329

THE EAST ASIAN INSTITUTE OF
COLUMBIA UNIVERSITY

The East Asian Institute of Columbia University was established in 1949 to prepare graduate students for careers dealing with East Asia, and to aid research and publication on East Asia during the modern period. The faculty of the Institute are grateful to the Ford Foundation and the Rockefeller Foundation for their financial assistance.

The Studies of the East Asian Institute were inaugurated in 1962 to bring to a wider public the results of significant new research on modern and contemporary East Asia.

STUDIES OF THE EAST ASIAN INSTITUTE

The Ladder of Success in Imperial China, by Ping-ti Ho. New York: Columbia University Press, 1962.

The Chinese Inflation, 1937–1949, by Shun-hsin Chou. New York: Columbia University Press, 1963.

Reformer in Modern China: Chang Chien, 1853–1926, by Samuel Chu. New York: Columbia University Press, 1965.

Research in Japanese Sources: A Guide, by Herschel Webb with the assistance of Marleigh Ryan. New York: Columbia University Press, 1965.

Society and Education in Japan, by Herbert Passin. New York: Bureau of Publications, Teachers College, Columbia University, 1965.

Agricultural Production and Economic Development in Japan, 1873–1922, by James I. Nakamura. Princeton: Princeton University Press, 1966.

Japan's First Modern Novel: Ukigumo of Futabatei Shimei, by Marleigh Ryan. New York: Columbia University Press, 1967.

The Korean Communist Movement, 1918–1948, by Dae-Sook Suh. Princeton: Princeton University Press, 1967.

The First Vietnam Crisis, by Melvin Gurtov. New York: Columbia University Press, 1967.

Cadres, Bureaucracy, and Political Power in Communist China, by A. Doak Barnett. New York: Columbia University Press, 1967.

The Japanese Imperial Institution in the Tokugawa Period, by Herschel Webb. New York: Columbia University Press, 1968.

Higher Education and Business Recruitment in Japan, by Koya Azumi. New York: Teachers College Press, Columbia University, 1969.

The Communists and Chinese Peasant Rebellions: A Study in the Rewriting of Chinese History, by James P. Harrison, Jr. New York: Atheneum, 1969.

How the Conservatives Rule Japan, by Nathaniel B. Thayer. Princeton: Princeton University Press, 1969.

Aspects of Chinese Education, edited by C. T. Hu. New York: Teachers College Press, Columbia University, 1970.

Documents of Korean Communism, 1918–1948, by Dae-Sook Suh. Princeton: Princeton University Press, 1970.

Japanese Education: A Bibliography of Materials in the English Language, by Herbert Passin. New York: Teachers College Press, Columbia University, 1970.

Economic Development and the Labor Market in Japan, by Koji Taira. New York: Columbia University Press, 1970.

The Japanese Oligarchy and the Russo-Japanese War, by Shumpei Okamoto. New York: Columbia University Press, 1970.

Imperial Restoration in Medieval Japan, by H. Paul Varley. New York: Columbia University Press, 1971.

Japan's Postwar Defense Policy, 1947–1968, by Martin E. Weinstein. New York: Columbia University Press, 1971.

Election Campaigning Japanese Style, by Gerald L. Curtis. New York: Columbia University Press, 1971.

China and Russia: The "Great Game," by O. Edmund Clubb. New York: Columbia University Press, 1971.

Money and Monetary Policy in Communist China, by Katharine Huang Hsiao. New York: Columbia University Press, 1971.

The District Magistrate in Late Imperial China, by John R. Watt. New York: Columbia University Press, 1972.

Law and Policy in China's Foreign Relations: A Study of Attitudes and Practice, by James C. Hsiung. New York: Columbia University Press, 1972.

Pearl Harbor as History: Japanese-American Relations, 1931–1941, edited by Dorothy Borg and Shumpei Okamoto, with the assistance of Dale K. A. Finlayson. New York: Columbia University Press, 1973.

Japanese Culture: A Short History, by H. Paul Varley. New York: Praeger, 1973.

Doctors in Politics: The Political Life of the Japan Medical Association, by William E. Steslicke. New York: Praeger, 1973.

Japan's Foreign Policy, 1868–1941: A Research Guide, edited by James William Morley. New York: Columbia University Press, 1973.

Teachers and Politics in Japan, by Donald Ray Thurston. Princeton: Princeton University Press, 1973.

Palace and Politics in Prewar Japan, by David Anson Titus. New York: Columbia University Press, 1973.

The Idea of China: Essays in Geographic Myth and Theory, by Andrew March. Devon, England: David and Charles, 1973.